O9-AID-472

Violent No More

"In this updated volume of *Violent No More*, Michael Paymar moves our thinking forward by exploring relationships where men who have battered have not only changed, but stayed with their partners. His exercises for men who have stopped their violence, and are working to transform their relationships, are highly recommended. They are also very useful for the general male reader and for counseling programs alike. This is a valuable and courageous work!"

— Fernando Mederos, Ed.D.,
Co-founder, Common Purpose, Boston

"*Violent No More* challenges men who batter to face and change their behavior. This book is also important for women to help them better understand their abusive partners. Counselors and domestic violence workers would be wise to make *Violent No More* a must read for the men in their groups."

— Catherine Waltz, Ph.D.,
Director, Peace Project, Fort Lauderdale

"A highlight of the book is the many inspiring stories by individual men of their violence and their process of change. This book should convince any man that we can and must stop violence against women."

— Paul Kivel, author of
Men's Work: How to Stop the Violence that Tears Our Lives Apart

DEDICATED TO MY FATHER AND MOTHER

Ordering

Trade bookstores in the U.S. and Canada please contact:

Publishers Group West
1700 Fourth Street, Berkeley CA 94710
Phone: (800) 788-3123
Fax: (510) 528-3444

Hunter House books are available at bulk discounts for textbook course adoptions; to qualifying community, healthcare, and government organizations; and for special promotions and fundraising. For details please contact:

Special Sales Department
Hunter House Inc., PO Box 2914, Alameda CA 94501-0914
Tel. (510) 865-5282   Fax (510) 865-4295
e-mail: ordering@hunterhouse.com

Individuals can order our books from most bookstores or by calling toll-free:

1-800-266-5592

VIOLENT
No More

Helping Men End Domestic Abuse

Michael Paymar

With a Foreword by Anne Ganley, Ph.D.

Hunter House
PUBLISHERS

Copyright © 2000 by Michael Paymar

All rights reserved. No part of this publication may be reproduced or transmitted in any form or by any means, electronic or mechanical, including photocopying and recording, or introduced into any information storage and retrieval system without the written permission of the copyright owner and the publisher of this book. Brief quotations may be used in reviews prepared for inclusion in a magazine, newspaper, or for broadcast. For further information please contact:

> Hunter House Inc., Publishers
> P.O. Box 2914
> Alameda CA 94501-0914

Library of Congress Cataloging-in-Publication Data

Paymar, Michael
    Violent no more : helping men end domestic abuse / Michael Paymar. – 2nd rev. ed.
      p.   cm.
    ISBN 0-89793-268-4 (paper)   ISBN 0-89793-273-0 (cloth)
    1. Abusive men—Rehabilitation. 2. Wife abuse—Prevention. I. Title.
    RC569.5.F3 P38   2000
    616.85'822—dc21   99-059324

Project credits

Cover Design: Brian Dittmar
Book Production: Hunter House
Copy Editor: Lydia Bird
Proofreader: Lee Rappold
Indexer: Kathy Talley-Jones
Production Director: Virginia Fontana
Acquisitions Editor: Jeanne Brondino
Associate Editor: Alex Mummery
Publicity Director: Marisa Spatafore
Special Sales Manager: Sarah Kulin
Customer Service Manager: Christina Sverdrup
Order fulfillment: Joel Irons; A & A Quality Shipping Services
Publisher: Kiran S. Rana

Printed and Bound by Publishers Press, Salt Lake City, Utah
Manufactured in the United States of America

9 8 7 6 5 4 3 2 1   First Edition   00 01 02 03 04

Contents

[Numbers in parentheses in the text refer to endnotes, found on page 268.]

Foreword

You may be picking up this book for the first time, in a bookstore, at someone's home, or in the public library. Perhaps someone gave it to you, or it was assigned reading in a domestic violence intervention program. Or you may be reading it for the second, third, or fourth time. Whatever brings you to this book, welcome to the pages that follow and the journey you are on.

This is a special book. It is here in part because men like you asked for it. In 1978 when I opened a domestic violence intervention program, the first at a Veterans Affairs medical center, no such book was available. It was not until Michael Paymar wrote the first edition of *Violent No More* in 1993, that men had a book of their own to support them on their diverse journeys to becoming abuse free.

In the early years of our batterers' intervention program, men would ask me if there was someone they could talk with outside of their group, someone who knew and understood what they were going through. While they appreciated the program staff and their peers in the group, they just wanted to talk with a guy who had been there and had been successful in stopping his abuse. Or maybe, a few asked, there was something they could read? One by one, I attempted to connect them with another man with whom they could identify, but it was a hard match at times, for each man's experience of being abusive was unique. Some were poor, others wealthy; some highly educated, others had barely completed grade school; some were religious, others not; some were men of color and some not; some were in the military, some not. Their relationships were different as well: some long term, some new; some with children, some without; some had compliant partners, others had challenging partners. Some men had issues other than their abusiveness, such as addictions, health problems, or mental health concerns, others did not. The only thing they had in common was that they all were or had been abusive to someone they loved.

When the first edition of *Violent No More* appeared, I greeted it with relief. Here, finally, was a book that told *many* men's stories, not just one or two. The stories were not only of the abuse but also about the change process. The book was readable, it was practical, and it offered hope. I told everyone who entered the program to buy the book. I wanted each man to have his own copy, to use throughout the yearlong intervention program. And use it they did.

As I listened to the men talk about their experiences of searching for a copy of the book, of having to ask for and then purchase it, I became aware that buying this book, with its challenging title, was sometimes their first experience of confronting their denial of their abusiveness. Then, as they went through the orientation phase, they were assigned the first four chapters, one at a time. They could read ahead if they wanted, and many did, but they had to be prepared to talk about the assigned chapter in the first group meetings. Sometimes there was a non-reader in the program who had another group member as a reading buddy, and as I entered the room early to prepare for the session I might hear one man reading the assigned section softly to the guy sitting next to him.

As the men went through the more intensive phase of the program, we focused on the remaining chapters. Then the book reappeared in the maintenance phase of our program, in which men who had successfully completed the first two stages met once a month to give each other support in staying abuse free. Once again, the men would bring in their books, sometimes using it to look at the positives or to look at the more subtle ways they were being controlling in their families. They talked about how the goals of equality, respect, and teamwork in relationships outlined in the book were attainable or were hard to reach at times.

Over the years I saw the tattered books again and again. I would look over shoulders and see sections highlighted or marked with "me, me, me" in the margins, as a man identified with a particular passage. Sometimes when a group member would bring up an issue or question, he would use a section of the book to make his point, saying, "Remember in the book, where the guy says…?" Group members would argue with each other, jabbing with their fingers at certain paragraphs to emphasize their position. And some would even laugh, saying, "See, I'm doing just what the guy says in the book. I'm just trying to get my way in this discussion."

Yes, the book got used and many of the men genuinely liked it. They said they felt challenged both to act differently and to think differently. They said they never felt talked down to or preached at. And of course they said they liked hearing from a man… and from all the men in the book. They liked that the book was direct and to the point. And yes, the book made my job a little easier. I had a tool that the men liked and that complemented the work they were doing in their programs.

So here you are, reading the foreword to the new, improved edition of *Violent No More*. This edition has follow-up interviews with men and women who appeared in the first edition. They talk about what happened years after they made changes, and about their need for an ongoing, daily commitment to be abuse free. And they say this is true even for couples who choose to stay together following the completion of the intervention programs.

In addition to reading this book yourself, I encourage you to give it to others. You need to develop a team of people who support your new behavior. Many of you have created a circle of folks who collude with your abuse. You have become skilled at explaining away your behavior. You minimize it, deny it, and sometimes lie about it. Or you blame your partner, your children, your family—anyone and anything outside of yourself. You seek out those who will join you in blaming your victim. Oftentimes you convince family, friends, neighbors, your minister, your AA sponsor, your kids, the courts, your probation officer, and even your counselor that "there is no problem...and anyway it's really my partner's fault." If others don't collude with you, you just avoid them. By doing this, though, you have made the task of changing that much more difficult. We cannot change things we don't see we are doing. We cannot see what we are doing and change if others do not hold us responsible for what we have done and for making the necessary change.

There are people in your life right now who want to help. They cannot be supportive, however, if they do not understand your responsibilities and their role in your change. Give this book to the person you abused so that she knows that she has *no* responsibility for changing your behavior. It is not her job to take all—or even part—of the responsibility for your abusiveness. It is not her job to support you or even encourage you as you try to change. It is her job to take care of herself, to help herself and the children heal from your abusive control, and to reclaim her life—with or without you. Whether she loves you or not, she cannot help you with this particular change.

Give this book to your teenage or adult children, not as a plea for support or forgiveness, but so they too can look more honestly at what your abuse has done. Like your partner, their job is not to help you with your job. The book may help free them of the burden of changing you.

Give this book to family and friends, so they can understand that what will help you most is for you to take full responsibility for all that you have done. The book will guide them away from blaming your partner, from making excuses for you, and from ignoring the seriousness of what happened. It will guide them in how to remain supportive of you while challenging you to live abuse free. It will guide them in how to hold you accountable for the changes you must make. To paraphrase another famous saying, "good friends don't let good friends abuse others." But oftentimes friends do not know what to do, and this book can help.

Give this book to your counselor, your doctor, your rabbi, your AA sponsor, your commanding officer, your supervisor...anyone who knows you and knows about the abuse. The book will help them understand you and understand that they can best help you by holding you accountable. Just because they are professionals doesn't mean they know much more than you do about domestic violence. They want to help but do not always know how.

Sharing the book is part of your being more honest with yourself and others. This will make your work easier. There will come a time when you will add your own story to all the stories in this book. And there will come a time when you may give this book to another man to encourage him to start the journey to self-change. When you find it hard to read the book or you feel stalled in your efforts to move forward, remember the men in the book and also the many men who have read the book before you. Each of them struggled to look squarely at what he had done, to take full responsibility for his behavior in order to be free to change and to become who he wanted to be in intimate relationships. And in doing so, many came to a place of self-respect as they lived violent no more.

Anne Ganley
November, 1999

Anne L. Ganley, Ph.D., is a psychologist in private practice and Clinical Associate Professor in the departments of psychology and psychiatry at the University of Washington in Seattle. For twenty years she was the coordinator of domestic violence programs at two Veterans Administration medical centers. Dr. Ganley is a nationally known writer, consultant, and trainer in the field of domestic violence.

Preface

To the men courageous
enough to read this book

Six years ago I wrote *Violent No More: Helping Men End Domestic Abuse* for men who want to stop hurting the ones they love. It holds out a hand to men who have been and are violent in relationships with women, and helps them understand what is behind their abuse, and how to change. It is a practical guide, based on years of working with men who have been violent, and written with the knowledge that most men who have battered are willing and ready to change—once they know how.

In the years since *Violent No More* was first published, I have appreciated and been humbled by the many letters and phone calls I've received from men who have been helped by this book. Many have told me they no longer feel so alone after reading the stories of other men. They liked the emphasis on personal responsibility in the book. They told me they feel hopeful, and believe they have the tools to change. Many of these men have also sought help from domestic abuse programs and counseling in their communities.

I also feel honored that so many practitioners have used *Violent No More* in their groups and as a resource for men and women seeking help to end the violence. I encourage practitioners to continue using the exercises in the book—including the new ones—to help with their work.

Domestic abuse is defined as the use of physical violence in an intimate relationship. The term also includes emotional, psychological, and sexual abuse, as well as any other behavior one person in a relationship uses to control the other. Thousands of women are killed or seriously injured by their partners every year. Violence in the home is lethal—and it is illegal. But even though society is finally saying that domestic abuse is unacceptable, it still occurs in about 25 percent of our homes.

This book is not only for men who have been violent in the past, but also for men who are concerned that their current behavior is hurting the ones they love. If you are violent, you know on some basic level that your behavior is wrong. Fortunately, men who are violent can decide to change. If you are reaching out for help, that is the first and most important step. The next steps will not be easy, because ending violence and abuse requires struggling with long held beliefs and behaviors that will be difficult to give up.

Somehow and somewhere men learn destructive attitudes and behaviors. The relationships of men who abuse their partners are like minefields: nobody knows when things might explode and all hell break loose. Living in this minefield causes terror and hurts the entire family. Inside, the man knows it doesn't have to be like this. All of us have the inherent ability to experience fulfilling relationships that provide meaning and love in our lives.

In this book you will meet several men who have made major changes in their lives. You will read their stories and probably relate to some of them; others may shock you deeply. Yet most of these men did change, and they are living proof that men who have been violent in relationships *can* change.

You will also hear the stories of women who have been battered. Their experiences will help you understand the perspectives and feelings of women who have been beaten by their male partners. If you are not currently in a relationship, think about past relationships as you read these stories and apply what you learn to future partnerships.

I encourage you, in addition to reading this book, to seek help from programs in your community that work to end domestic violence. You will need this support, because it is important to talk to people who have dealt with these issues firsthand. Overcoming violence and abuse in a relationship is hard work and can be lonely and frustrating. Much like the men you will meet in this book, you will go through certain stages in your journey back from violence, a process that may take weeks, months, or years. First, you will begin to understand the big picture: where did I learn this behavior? Second, you will apply the big picture to your own experiences. This stage may be difficult; facing up to personal faults usually brings about resistance, yet it is a necessary step. The third stage is more practical: you will put into practice what you have learned. Whether or not you are currently in a relationship, you will begin to see things differently as you apply some of the suggestions in this book to your life.

In this updated version of *Violent No More* I have included a chapter called "Staying Together," for couples who choose to rebuild their lives after the violence and abuse have ended. While the road is not easy, some couples succeed in working through the obstacles and reestablishing their relationships.

I have also written an appendix specifically for practitioners who work with men who batter. I believe it is important for those of us working in the field to continue to have dialogue about our techniques and principles—we are in the trenches and we can do honorable work. We must ensure that victim safety is a principal theme that guides us.

The central part of the book ends with a chapter on healing. If violence and abusive behavior have forced an end to your relationship, it is important to heal and move on with your life. Hopefully, some of what you learn here, and from counseling, will result in changed beliefs and attitudes so you won't make the same mistakes in future relationships.

If you agree with the direction this book takes you, I hope you will continue the process of change so your life becomes healthier and more fulfilling. Remember, change takes time, but it is your life and it is worth every little bit of effort that you make. I wish you luck and success in your journey.

Important Note

The material in *Violent No More* is intended to provide a guide for men dealing with the issues of domestic abuse. Every effort has been made to provide accurate and dependable information, and the contents of this book have been compiled in consultation with other professionals. However, the reader should be aware that professionals in the field may have differing opinions, and legal policies may differ from state to state and are changing constantly. The publisher, author, and editors cannot be held responsible for any error, omission, professional disagreement, or outdated material.

The ideas, procedures, and suggestions contained in this book are designed to encourage men to work with their personal violence and abusive behavior, but are not intended to replace a professional program. If you have any questions or concerns about applying this information, please consult a domestic abuse intervention program or a licensed therapist. The author and publisher assume no responsibility for any outcome of the use of these materials individually or in consultation with a professional or group.

Acknowledgments

I want to acknowledge and thank the women and men in my life who have helped shape my thinking about relationships, sexism, and men's violence. First, I owe an unpayable debt to battered women who have struggled to change our collective consciousness about the roots of domestic abuse. It is through their continuing struggle and commitment to end violence that someday we may see a more egalitarian and peaceful world.

I also want to acknowledge my dedicated friends from the Duluth Domestic Abuse Intervention Project and the Women's Coalition in Duluth, Minnesota, who have made a difference by working to end violence in our community. Their courage and unceasing dedication have permanently improved the lives of many in Duluth, and their efforts have provided a guiding light to many communities around the world. I owe a special debt of gratitude to the men and women who volunteered to share their life experiences for this book.

I want to thank my friend and colleague Ellen Pence for reviewing my original drafts and for being supportive of me all these years. I also want to acknowledge Anne Ganley, Carol Thompson, Tyran Schroyer, Dick Diver, Amanda McCormick, Ron Templin, and Barry Sky for their help, insight, and ideas. Finally, I want to thank Lydia Bird and Kiran Rana for their thoughtful critiques and editing of my manuscript.

Introduction

- Every fifteen seconds a woman is beaten by her husband or boyfriend in the United States.

- Thirty percent of all female homicide victims are killed by a partner or former partner.

- One out of every four men will use violence against a partner at some time in their relationship.

- Children are present during 80 percent of the assaults against their mothers.

No community is immune to domestic violence. Emergency rooms sew up cuts, fix broken bones, and treat the bruises. Overcrowded shelters provide temporary safety and emotional support to victims. Offenders get arrested and protection orders are issued, but the courts are already overbusy and the jails overcrowded. And the violence continues.

When does it stop? How will it stop? And finally, whose responsibility is it to end this cycle of violence?

Laws alone will not end domestic abuse. Men must stop the excuses and end the silence. Ultimately, men must make personal decisions about how they want to conduct their lives. Men need to understand the origins of their violence against women and commit to ending it in their own lives.

Over the years, I have talked to hundreds of violent men. Most men who hit once usually hit again. Also, most men said that their abusive behavior escalated until they finally got arrested or decided to seek help.

Men who are violent or abusive often project an attitude of not needing or not wanting to change. Deep down, most of them know that something is not right. They start new relationships with high expectations only to see their abusive behavior tear the relationships apart. They medicate themselves with drugs, alcohol, and cynicism about life and relationships. Their friendships with other men are frequently superficial. They see their children acting out in inappropriate ways because of what is happening at home, and they don't know what to do. They see their partners, who once loved them, turn away in anger and in fear. All too often they end up alone, out of touch with their own feelings and cut off from the company and affection of others, pretty much trapped....

If this description sounds familiar, I hope you will continue reading.

There is no single profile of a man who is violent. Abusers are rich, middle class, and poor, blue collar and white collar, old and young. Some grew up with violence in the home and others did not. Some have college degrees and others dropped out of school. Some batter when they are drunk and some when they are sober. They come from all races, religions, and cultures.

Men are not naturally violent, but they learn that violence is an appropriate male response to settling disagreements. Men also learn that violence can bring a feeling of power. However, men can reject the cultural conditioning that spawns this violence. They can reject sexist beliefs that women are less significant than men. We can teach our sons and daughters that men and women are equal, that relationships should be respectful, and that violence is not an acceptable way to resolve conflicts.

Why Write a Book for Men Who Batter?

A book like this can be a catalyst for personal change. By understanding how and why you got where you are, and by recognizing your own potential to change, you can begin a healthier life. Hurting others and yourself will lessen as you commit to this new beginning.

Back in the early 1970s I was very active in political and social causes. The women's movement was just beginning to blossom but, like many other men, at that time I failed to understand the rage and frustration women felt at men's attitudes and the institutional roadblocks they experienced in our society. My attitudes about women were not that different from those of men who battered, who I would eventually work with in jail or in groups. Though I never battered, my sexism was real. I thought on some level that men were better or more competent than women. It was not until female friends confronted me that I began questioning my own beliefs and attitudes. At first, I became defensive. But then I decided to accept the confrontation not as criticism but as a challenge to look deeper. I eventually realized that my sexism was not only wrong but also got in the way of friendships and my ability to be intimate in relationships with women.

At about this time in my life, I decided to get involved with a small group of men who were meeting to discuss issues related to sexism and violence against women. I had recently been elected to the Duluth City Council and chaired a public hearing on sexual violence. Many people testified, and many good ideas were presented. Still, I felt frustrated at our inability to do more about ending violence in our community.

At the same time, in 1980, several women in Duluth began organizing the Domestic Abuse Intervention Project (DAIP), based on the belief that society has an obligation to ensure its citizens aren't victimized, whether in their neighborhoods or in their homes. The year the organizers began their work, a particularly gruesome homicide occurred. After years of brutal beatings, a young woman shot her husband in the stomach with a shotgun. When the paramedics arrived, the man was literally in two parts. This incident and a growing concern about domestic abuse prompted an otherwise resistant justice system to listen to the organizers.

The DAIP sought to change the way the criminal justice system, law enforcement, and human service providers—social workers and counselors—responded to domestic assault cases. The DAIP was instrumental in convincing the Duluth Police Department to reexamine and ultimately change its policies. In the past, police officers had attempted mediation in assault cases, separating the couple and asking one party to leave for the night. Too often, the offender came back and continued or escalated his violence. Under the new policy, police began arresting offenders if they suspected a crime had been committed. The DAIP also secured agreements from the court to prosecute offenders and sentence them if convicted. In lieu of jail, most offenders were placed on probation and given an opportunity to change their behavior by attending counseling or domestic abuse classes. This is where I came in.

When the DAIP began, ten men in Duluth were chosen to counsel men in jail after arrests had taken place. Because I had taken a public stance and expressed interest in confronting violence in the community, the organizers of the DAIP invited me to a meeting, along with nine other men. They asked us if we would be willing to meet with men who had been arrested under the new policy. I now felt I had an opportunity to truly help. After an arrest was made, the battered women's shelter would call me and give me information about the case. The next morning, I would go down to the jail and meet with the man who was detained, listening to his explanation of what happened. Many of the men I met with seemed pleased to have someone to talk to. One of my objectives was to get them to see the impact their violence was having on their families—and its destructiveness. I talked about our counseling program and the help we offered.

Most of the offenders were shocked to be in jail. For many, a secret was finally being exposed. Some were honest with me and said they wanted help. Of course, sitting in the old Duluth City Jail may have influenced their receptiveness to my offer of assistance. (Fortunately, this aging facility is now closed.) Still, I believed they truly felt remorse and were apprehensive about what was going to happen to them.

Other men were angry and defiant, blaming their partners or the police. They would deal with their problems themselves, they said. They made it clear they did not want or need any help from my program or me.

Each of these men had fallen in love with a woman and made a commitment to some kind of relationship. So, what had happened? How did the loving, smiling husbands I saw in the wedding pages of our local newspaper become the angry, hurt faces I was now seeing in the cells of the Duluth jail?

The time I spent talking with these men in jail affected me profoundly, and I started asking questions. Were they so terribly different from me? I reached back into my childhood and began remembering the messages I had received about men and women. "Men should be in charge." "Men settle disagreements in a *manly* way—through fighting." "A man is king in his home, his castle." Was there a connection between these childhood messages and the prevalence of domestic abuse in our society?

The relationship between men's violence and what society tells us is the right way to be "male" became much clearer when I began conducting groups outside the jail for men who battered. In the beginning, the majority of the men were there because they were ordered by the court to attend. I remember feeling nervous as I walked into my first group. Would the men be angry at me because the court had forced them to be there? Would they talk honestly about their abusive behavior? Would they want to change? Would they even listen to me?

My first group was held at an old community center in Duluth. At the start of the meeting, I asked the men to form a circle. They reluctantly carried or dragged their chairs to the middle of the room. Some looked angry, others bored—and we had not even begun. A few looked resigned to the situation and even seemed open to whatever was going to happen.

Most of the men were dressed casually, except for Don and Bradley, who wore suits. Howard, at fifty-five, was the oldest man there. The rest were aged between twenty and forty. Some of the men had been in trouble with the law before, but for most this was a new and embarrassing experience. One man, Paul, had volunteered to attend. He said he did not want to be abusive anymore and felt he was losing his family.

I introduced myself and told the group I realized many of them did not want to be there, but I hoped they would be open to what the program had to offer. I said that sometimes something bad or uncomfortable has to happen before we're ready to make changes in our lives. I said I wanted them to know I believed each of them *could* change—if he wanted.

Then I asked each man to introduce himself and explain why he was there. At first they were quiet, but gradually they started to talk.

As I thought about it afterward, I saw that the men had talked about their violence and relationships with women in three ways:

One group had stated that men and women have separate and distinct roles, and that the man should be the head of the household. Their justification was the belief that "someone has to be in charge." This led to the further belief that if their partners challenged their authority, then some form of abusive behavior could be seen as a justifiable response.

Another group stated that their problems with their partners were mutual and the violence was a result of conflict in the relationship. They admitted that the violence was wrong, but believed their partners had pushed or provoked them.

A third group—a couple of men, including Paul—said clearly that their behavior was wrong. These men seemed truly disturbed by their actions. They were seeing the effects of their violence on their partners, their families, and themselves. They seemed to have hit bottom. Their moral compass was not only indicating that their behavior was wrong, but now was guiding their desire to change.

The initial meetings of the group were challenging because the men had such varied beliefs about their behavior, coupled with a high degree of discomfort about having to attend. By the eighth meeting, however, most of them were talking freely, with much disagreement and debate. That night, I wrote the word SEXISM on the board and asked what it meant to them and whether it had anything to do with domestic abuse. The following discussion took place ("Michael" is the author):

> **Don:** Sexism is when men treat women as unequal. You know, if women are paid less for the same job than men, that's sexism.

> **Paul:** I think it's a belief that men are superior to women. Most boys get taught that at an early age. If we believe that men are superior, then women are obviously inferior in some ways.

I asked how sexism might contribute to hitting a partner.

> **Paul:** Well, for some men, they think of their wives as property and you can do what you want with your own property.

> **Michael:** It's interesting that you speak of wives as property. Until the end of the nineteenth century there were actually laws on the books setting out reasons why a man could beat his wife to discipline her. In fact, the saying "rule of thumb" actually came from a law that said a man could beat his wife with a stick no wider than his thumb.

> **Howard:** Yeah, but don't you think things are changing with all this women's lib stuff? My wife works and she's free to do what she wants.

> **Michael:** You mention women's lib. Why do you think women have organized women's liberation movements?

> **Howard:** I suppose they don't believe that they are equal to men and maybe they're not, in all respects. But I think some of this has gone too far.

Needless to say, we had a lively discussion that night. At the next session, several men told me they had not really thought about the connections between men's violence and women and sexism.

In later groups we talked about domination, and why a woman would resist an unequal relationship with a man. Gradually, some men in the group began to recognize that they resorted to abuse and violence when their partners resisted being controlled. This was an important insight. Other men struggled with the ideas being discussed, while some participated but remained quite unconvinced.

After six months, the first group of men had completed the program. Each said he had learned something from it. All vowed they would not be violent again. Paul talked about how much his relationship with his wife had improved. I told him I thought he had worked hard and I appreciated his honesty. Bradley and his partner had split up, but he was sure that in his next relationship he would not make the same mistakes. We all said our good-byes, and I felt good about the experience.

Three months later I got a call from the women's shelter telling me that two men had been arrested for assault the night before. I got to the jail at 7:00 A.M. and was led down a line of cells to the meeting room. The first man brought in for me to talk to was Paul. He had smashed the headlights of his wife's car with a baseball bat and threatened to kill her.

I was stunned and disappointed. I was so convinced that Paul had turned the corner. Of all the men in my first group, Paul seemed to have truly grasped the issues. He had talked eloquently about men and women needing to respect each other, stating that violence in a relationship was wrong. He had made a commitment to handle conflicts with his wife differently—and now here he was, in jail. I asked him to explain what happened.

Paul said he had not wanted to go to a party the night before, and had not wanted his wife, Robin, to go either.

> I told Robin I was too tired to go and it would be really nice if we just stayed home together. She said she'd been counting on going for several weeks and wanted to go. So I said go ahead, even though I didn't want her to go. I was stewing all night long thinking if she really loved me she wouldn't have gone. And then I started wondering why she wanted to go to the party so badly. It was two in the morning before I heard the car drive up. I was so mad. I went outside with a baseball bat and she ran back into the car. I started screaming for her to get out, and when she didn't I started smashing the car with the bat and threatened to kill her. The neighbor called the police.

This early experience with Paul taught me that understanding the problem of violent and abusive behavior intellectually does not necessarily translate into changed behavior. There's a saying frequently used in chemical dependency treatment: "You've got to walk the walk, not just talk the talk." Knowing what you need to do to change and saying that you ought to change are not enough—you have to put the new behaviors or attitudes into practice as well. I had to keep reminding myself that many of the men in our groups would return to old, familiar territory and, unfortunately, would batter again.

In 1992, Melanie Shepard, a researcher at the University of Minnesota, Duluth, examined the cases of one hundred men who had completed the counseling program at the Domestic Abuse Prevention Project in 1985. She found that after a five-year period 40 percent of these men had either been arrested or had a civil Order for Protection taken out against them for being abusive. They had either abused the same woman they had initially battered, or assaulted new partners.[1]

If 40 percent of the men completing our program were *reported* to law enforcement or the courts, then it would be safe to assume that at least half of the men arrested for domestic assault had reverted to using abusive behavior despite counseling or the threat of jail. However, the more groups I led, the more sure I became that some of the men were making real and significant changes. Sometimes the partners of these men reported marked improvements in their behavior and attitudes. And so I continue to believe in the work we are doing, and to have hope.

I choose to put my energies into this work because I think we as men have a responsibility to end our violence. I believe it is simply inexcusable and a disgrace that women today can still feel unsafe among their friends, partners, colleagues, and lovers. Male violence has been our historical legacy. Our prisons, battlefields, streets, and homes have been marked by our violence. It needs to stop. I believe, to put it a little simplistically, that it is much more "manly" to deal with our own violence: to accept the challenge of struggling with it without violating ourselves or others, and of releasing it so that we are, truly, violent no more.

A Note to the Reader

This book is written for men who are abusive and violent with their female partners. In no way am I claiming that men have not also been victimized by women in intimate relationships. Women do assault men—they use violence in self-defense, they use violence in retaliation, and some women initiate violence. In Duluth, about 10% of the offenders arrested for domestic assault are female—most, but not all were using violence in self-defense or in retaliation. A small percentage could be classified as women who batter. In these incidences, men who are being battered should surely have the same protection and access to resources that battered women have.

It is interesting to note that in Europe, several shelters were opened for men who were being abused by a spouse, but they all closed because men were not using them. This may be attributed to men not needing the services and/or a reluctance on the part of men to admit they have been abused or that they need help,

I do not condone women's violence, but it is clear from my experiences in this field that men and women use violence in very different ways. Most men who have had violence used against them by their female partners are not also experiencing the kind of fear, intimidation, and coercion usually associated with being battered. Most men who have been assaulted by their female partners are not also experiencing sexual violence or the threat of being raped. Most men who have had violence used against them by a female partner will freely claim that they could escape from the immediate abusive situation or end a violent relationship without fear of retribution. We cannot ignore the power differential between women and men. I address these issues and the historical acceptance of men's violence against women later in the book.

Finally, this book doesn't address same-sex battering, which is far more prevalent than originally thought. Men who are victimized by a female or a male in an intimate relationship should seek help from domestic violence programs or human service providers in their community.

This book is written in a style that addresses the violent behavior of men in relationships and marriages with women, since that is the main focus of the author's work. However, most of the ideas, techniques, and processes will also apply to other intimate and familial relationships.

The persons and events described in the interviews in this book are real, but their names—with the exception of Chuck and M'Liss Switzer—have been changed to protect their privacy and their families. The persons and events described in the group sessions are often composites, based on real people and events, but all names have been changed for their protection.

1

A Challenge for Men

Andy's Story—Andy's Story Five Years Later—
The First Step: Owning the Problem—The Next Step:
Getting Help—How to Use This Book

A man cannot be comfortable without his own approval.

MARK TWAIN

Andy's Story

Andy was born in Duluth, Minnesota. He, like some of the other men in this book, grew up with domestic violence in his family. He was arrested in 1982 for domestic assault and was ordered to attend our program. Andy has struggled to understand the roots of his violence. He has been violence free for more than ten years and now works with men who, like himself, have been abusive to women.

I remember coming home from school and my father had my mother by the hair. It was obvious that she'd been crying because her mascara was smeared and her face was all puffy. He had a knife in his hand and he said to me, "Do you want me to kill this bitch? Because I will!" I was crying and begging him not to hurt her.

He battered her frequently and I never saw her fight back. She was always trying to accommodate him. Sometimes her attempts to appease him would work and sometimes they would piss him off more.

My brothers and I frequently got into fights, and my dad thought that was perfectly normal. If we complained or came to him, he would say we had to settle it like men.

I got a lot of my attitudes about girls and women from my father, but mostly I think society provided very negative messages about families in general. For me to get beat by a girl in a sports event was the ultimate in humiliation, and my father always told me you shouldn't hit girls, yet he beat my mother. He died when I was eleven.

I met Debra in 1980 and we started to live together. The worst violence I remember was when Debra said something about me at this party and I got embarrassed. When we got outside, I grabbed her and threw her to the ground and started pounding her head on the sidewalk. She was screaming and there was terror in her eyes. My brother ran over and tried to get me off of her. He said, "Andy, you're going to kill her!" I'm not sure if I would have, but I stopped.

I thought Debra provoked my abuse. She would call me names or criticize my parenting abilities or say something she knew would piss me off, and I felt totally justified in letting her have it.

I usually blamed Debra for the violence. When she would come home late, I felt justified in hitting her. On some level I knew it was wrong to hit her, but I believed she brought it on herself. I always thought if she would just stop resisting me and do as I said, she wouldn't get hit.

After being violent, I would try to get her to see that what I did wasn't that bad. I'd say, "You don't have any marks on you," or, "Other men would have done worse." If I'd slapped her, I'd say later, "Well, I didn't use a closed fist."

One time we got into a fight in the bedroom and I pushed her and she fell over the nightstand by the bed. She ended up with a broken arm and had to have a cast. A couple of weeks later, we were over at our friends' house, sitting around the table, and they asked what had happened to Debra's arm. She made up some story about tripping and falling. I was really uncomfortable and I got angry at her because I was embarrassed in front of our friends.

At the time, I never felt that Debra was afraid of me. If you had come into our house back then and asked me about her being afraid, I would have said, "Hell, no!" I mean, why would she sleep with me if she was afraid or why would she call me a fuckin' asshole if she was afraid? If she was afraid of me why would she say, "You're a sissy; go lay down by your fuckin' bowl by the dog. What are you going to do, hit a woman again?"

Debra was also violent with me. She was tough, and at the time both of us were into the bar scene. Sometimes she would throw things at me, slap me, or try to kick me. Actually, I was glad when she did that, because then I would feel totally justified in beating her up. There were times I would goad her by getting in her face, calling her particular names so she would strike first. When she did, it would give me the green light to knock the hell out of her. After all, she hit me first. I was never afraid of her. Sometimes I would laugh at her after she hit me.

I rarely apologized unless the violence was really bad. When I apologized there was still this hint that it was her fault. I expected her to forgive me, and I would get really angry when she wouldn't. When she didn't accept my apology, I would say, "You fuckin' bitch, you started this stuff, and now look at you!"

I never thought she would leave me, but she did. The police came to our house three times but never arrested me. When they came, I would be real calm and wouldn't show them my anger, and Debra would be real agitated. I would tell the police it was her fault and she started the fight. They would go over to her and tell her not to provoke me.

Finally they did arrest me, because they had told me to leave the house after an incident and I had come back. I was charged with assault. I was really mad at the police, the justice system, and Debra. I felt no one was listening to my side of the story and everyone was blaming me when I thought Debra was just as much to blame. I threatened Debra, telling her if she didn't get the charges dropped I would really hurt her. She went to the city attorney, but they wouldn't drop the charges.

I was ordered into the counseling program and was really resistant at first. I didn't think I belonged there. I would say in group, "What about *her* violence? What am I supposed to do when she slaps me?" The counselors would challenge me to look at my violence and not to focus on her. It finally started to sink in and I realized that Debra didn't have to change for me to change.

After four or five groups something happened for me. It was actually freeing to take responsibility for my own behavior. It was challenging to examine my beliefs. I began to enjoy going to groups and talking about this stuff with other men. Even though I started making changes, it wasn't enough to save my relationship with Debra. I guess too much had happened between us—too much pain and too much of my violence—for us to heal as a couple.

I waited a long time before I decided to get involved in a new relationship. I wanted to be sure I had worked through my issues around wanting to control women. I also wanted to be absolutely sure I would be nonviolent in any future relationship.

I told Beth, my current partner, about my past. It was a risk, but I felt she should know that I had battered Debra. I think it's important to be honest and accountable. Today, I'm constantly challenging my beliefs about men and women. In my current relationship I try to be aware of my body language, because I'm a big guy and I have a loud voice. I need to be careful about how I respond to my partner when I'm angry. I'll always need to monitor myself.

In the past I was frightened at the prospect of being rejected by women, so I tended not to give too much, not to be too vulnerable, for fear I'd get hurt. I think part of it was my upbringing as a male. Men don't share feelings, men don't cry, men are supposed to be strong. It's an unfortunate attribute I see in the men I work with and it's something I need to work on.

When I was battering, it never occurred to me that I didn't need the tough-guy image or that relationships with women could be different. Since I've made these changes in my life, my relationships with women and men have changed. When I'm with men, I'm really aware of sexist comments and attitudes. I don't want superficial relationships with people.

I'm optimistic that men who batter can change. Some of the changes are small and the process is slow, but I believe it can happen. It's been more than ten years since I battered and I've been violence free. Yet I still take an inventory of what I'm doing in my life.

Men who come into our groups in Duluth are so angry, just like I was. They're angry at the police, the courts, and their partners. I know this will sound strange, but the best thing that ever happened to me was getting arrested. I finally had to look at my behavior. I had to stop conning everyone, including myself.

Andy's Story Five Years Later

I sat down with Andy five years after our initial interview. I wanted to find out what had changed in his life, whether he remained nonviolent, and what advice he had for men in similar situations. Andy has been married for six years and continues to work with men who batter. He recently went back to college and earned a degree in psychology.

On his past

An important element in my change process was the way people held me accountable when I got arrested. Equally important was that people believed I could change. When I was ordered into the Domestic Abuse Intervention Project, the group leaders and my probation officer all believed in me—that was important to a twenty-one-year-old who was going down the wrong track. When I began the group, I was kind of scared. I mean, I'd never talked to people about my feelings before, and I'd never been asked the kinds of questions they wanted me to answer. Group process? Bar stools were the closest I ever got to a group. But the process turned out to be comfortable—I wasn't told I was bad, but I did get challenged in a very respectful and helpful way.

On his current marriage

When I told Beth about my past use of violence, I think she was a little nervous about getting into a relationship with me, and for a while I think she was rightly checking me out. We were in love, but our first two years of marriage were definitely rocky.

Our initial problems occurred when I moved into her house. Beth and her kids all had a certain way of doing things and I was thrust into their environment, with their rules. Beth thought that I was avoiding conflict and that I wasn't committed to the relationship because I was working long hours, so in her mind we couldn't work through our problems. We had some very big compatibility issues.

On dealing with conflict

During those first two years of marriage, when Beth and I would argue, I would sometimes get sarcastic, raise my voice, and at other times I would just shut down and withdraw. I would usually apologize when I was acting in an inappropriate manner. This was a painful time for both of us.

It was at about this time that Beth told me there were times she was afraid of me. I couldn't believe it. She would say, "You know, you're a big guy, and when we get into an argument, and if you raise your voice, it makes me afraid sometimes." She would then qualify these statements by saying, "I don't believe you'll physically hurt me, but I still feel afraid." I never sensed she was afraid, because she wouldn't shut down or retreat from any conflicts we were having. When she confronted me about this, it really floored me. I didn't want to own it, I didn't want to entertain it, I didn't want to feel it, and I didn't want to hear it. I so desperately didn't want her to be afraid of me, but she was. Here I was, working with men who batter, and I'm very visible in the community because of my work, and here Beth is telling me that on some occasions she's afraid. It was really depressing. All I had ever wanted was to be a loving husband to Beth and a loving stepparent to the children—I wanted her to love me, approve of me, and think I'm somebody special. So when she told me about being scared, I felt like a monster—I hated it.

She would say things like, "You know you have this history," and I would really resent it, because I was not the same person I was back in 1982. I was angry she would put me in that framework. I felt she was playing the trump card and that was that—everything's over now, I can't do anything and I can't say anything.

On working through problems in his marriage

We were both determined to work things through. We went to marriage counseling and I went to individual counseling. We separated on two different occasions because we recognized we both needed to make some changes, or else we would wind up in divorce. The separation was helpful. We took the time to sort things out and find some better ways of communicating. We're a lot more honest with each other now. I don't walk away from conflicts anymore and we work through our problems. We've actually set up times for dealing with issues.

On his childhood, anger, and healing

I was pretty severely damaged as a child. I experienced and witnessed a lot of abuse and pain, even though my memories of that time are a little hazy. I don't have as much anger inside me today about my family, because I've done a lot of healing these past seven years. At the time Beth and I were having these problems, I decided I wanted to do some "family of origin" counseling and try to get in touch with what my childhood was all about. I interviewed several counselors until I found one I thought would be helpful. I think my separation from Beth was in part a catalyst for me to go back into therapy. It was also at this time that I started thinking about my dad—I finally got to the place where I could forgive him, and I miss him today. I asked my mother about my childhood, but she didn't want to talk about my dad's abusive behavior, so I let it go.

Working on improving yourself is so critical to personal growth. I have a men's group that meets every other week, which is really important to me—we talk about personal growth, relationships, and gender issues and I get strength from them. I've had a lot of healing experiences over the years and consequently a lot of my anger has diminished.

On spirituality

I really think my faith in God has been important to my change process. I draw strength from God when I pray, and there's a lot of wisdom in the scriptures about love, trust, and respect. In my work with men who batter, I really stress the importance of being "plugged in" in some way. Religion, spirituality, whatever—just do something for self-improvement.

On talking to his stepchildren about his past

My three stepchildren know I went to jail and they know I'm an alcoholic. Telling them was a decision that Beth and I made together, and it was relatively easy. They know that, in part, the reason I do this work is because of my past violence. They are very accepting. My relationship with these kids has been just super.

On his life today

Beth and I have a great relationship today. She's my best friend. We have a level of intimacy that's very special. As I said, the first two years were a struggle, but we worked things through. I believe if those kinds of problems surfaced again we would recognize the signs and deal with the issues in a heartbeat. This comes from a deeper level of commitment to our relationship that simply wasn't there those first two years of our marriage. We often talk about our relationship and how far we've come. There have been times that we just hold each other, and we are brought to tears because of how deep our love and intimacy are today. We have created a process to check things out with each other. The love and respect that we have for each other are very powerful.

The First Step: Owning the Problem

Something motivated you to read this book. Perhaps a counselor, minister, rabbi, friend, or family member suggested it. Maybe you are recognizing the pain you are causing your family. Or perhaps you are concerned about behavior that is scaring those around you—and yourself. What you read in the chapters ahead may be hard to accept, and it may cause you to become defensive. That's because taking the first step is never easy. The first step is owning the problem: acknowledging that it exists and taking responsibility for doing something about it.

When I asked Andy what motivated him to change, he responded, "It was a combination of things—getting arrested, spending a night in jail, going to court, having my name in the paper, and being forced into groups. Even more, it was the fact that the secrecy was over. The lies about the black eyes, the cover-up on both our parts was over. Everyone knew—now the secret was exposed."

If there is hidden violence in your relationship, the first step toward change is deciding to end the secrecy. In fact, it's more than likely that people already know about your violence and abuse. It's difficult to keep that kind of secret from children, friends, family members, and neighbors, whether they acknowledge it or not.

Not too long ago, people who had alcohol or drug problems were regarded by many in society as failures. Today, celebrities and sports stars come forward, admit their problems, and publicly go into treatment centers. Much of the time society applauds rather than condemns. While I don't necessarily recommend getting up on a soap box on Main Street and declaring, "I batter my wife and I'm seeking help!" try to realize that society is much more accepting than in the past of people who acknowledge their mistakes honestly and look for solutions to their problems.

The Next Step: Getting Help

I advocate seeking help. I encourage men who abuse their partners to talk to other men, friends, family, clergy, and professionals about what has been happening in their lives. While some people will defend or support your abusive actions because they think that's what you want to hear, those who truly care for you will help you find ways to change and will support your efforts.

Many communities have domestic violence programs. If you have battered or are abusive, you may feel reluctant to go to such a program. You may be embarrassed or uncomfortable talking about such personal issues in a group setting. I urge you to take the risk and join. The other men in the group will have had similar experiences and you will feel less alone.

Men and women should know that services are usually available in their communities. If you are a person of color there may be culturally sensitive programs that you would feel comfortable attending. In Duluth, for example, the Native American community has designed groups for Native American men and women. If you are gay, specific organizations and resources are available for you, too. In different cities across the country groups have sprung up that provide culturally specific assistance and counseling on domestic abuse issues. The Resource section at the end of this book lists many of these organizations; if you have trouble locating the services you need, call a mental health agency, community center, or an information and referral number for help. Don't wait. Do it now.

Counseling programs vary from community to community. In Duluth, the Domestic Abuse Intervention Project works in groups with men who batter. In these groups we discuss the beliefs and attitudes men have about masculinity, women, and marriage. We teach skills so men can remain nonviolent and noncontrolling in their relationships. The program takes the position that battering is intentional behavior. Its purpose is to control another person. The groups focus on ending not only violence, but also other abusive behavior.

Most men in the groups are court ordered to attend. About 10 percent volunteer. I am always saddened by the men who volunteer but then drop out after a short time. From my experience, many volunteer because their partners have told them to get help or get out. Sadly, when things get a little better they quit, thinking they have a handle on their problems. There is no quick fix. When a man drops out of counseling after a few sessions he probably hasn't learned what he needs to learn to change his behavior. Frequently, the relationship worsens and his partner leaves. This can reinforce a sense of failure. Moreover, men who don't get help for themselves often repeat abusive behavior in new relationships.

Some agencies agree to provide individual counseling to men who batter. While this may be helpful, I am a strong advocate of the group process. The group provides an opportunity for men to learn from each other. In Minnesota, many counselors refuse to see men who have battered until after they have been through a group program.

Many men say they would prefer to go to couple or marriage counseling. They insist that the relationship cannot change unless both people get help. Avery, a participant in one of our groups, described his feelings as follows:

> I was so angry at the people at that program. We have a marriage problem, and they wouldn't let us see a marriage counselor. Well, I told them, how the hell are we supposed to work on our problems if we're both going to separate groups? They were adamant. I understand their reasoning today. To be honest, after I got out of jail, I don't think I was ready for marriage counseling and I know Darlene wasn't. We finally did end up going to marriage counseling after I completed the men's groups.

Unfortunately, some professionals in the mental health community provide marriage counseling upon request, even when they know about domestic abuse in the relationship. Unless the violence has stopped and your partner feels safe with you, marriage counseling is inappropriate. Your partner will most likely be reluctant to discuss her true feelings in your presence because she is still afraid of you. I asked Cassie, one of the women I interviewed for this book, about marriage counseling (her story appears in Chapter 3):

> We went to marriage counseling and it was a terrible experience. The counselor said I needed to be more accepting of him. I was angry because he was drinking a lot. The counselor said that on his days off, if he wanted to drink a case of beer in his own house I should accept that.
>
> I was reluctant to bring up the violence and abuse, because I wasn't sure how my partner would react. That was the part of our problem he didn't want known. The one time I did mention the abuse it was basically discounted. When that happened, he felt totally validated. The counselor even said I needed to be more sexually receptive to him and not be so critical of his faults.

The idea of marriage counseling is to sort through problems in the relationship. The goal is to heal and problem solve. However, if a woman can't talk freely in marriage counseling, how can the sessions be successful? Many practitioners believe they can discern if the violence has ceased, or if one party is reluctant to talk. These assumptions are not only naive, but potentially dangerous to battered women. Victims, for survival purposes, must be very good at hiding what is actually happening in their relationships. The cover-up is used with parents, friends, coworkers, and—yes—even therapists. Disclosure may result in further abuse or an escalation of violence. And the battered woman knows her partner will blame her, because she has divulged private matters. Despite the seemingly safe environment of a therapy office and the reassuring statements by the marriage counselor, a victim knows her partner—she knows when it's safe to talk and when it's not.

I believe it is unethical and dangerous for mental health professionals to offer marriage counseling to couples when domestic violence has occurred unless all the following criteria have been met:

1. The man has successfully completed a reputable domestic abuse program that focuses on changing sexist beliefs and attitudes about controlling women.

2. A practitioner is convinced that the battering—violence, coercion, threats, intimidation, and psychological abuse—has ceased.

3. The battered woman has worked with a victims' advocate and has developed a safety plan to get help if her partner becomes abusive.

4. The battered woman feels safe.

5. The practitioner has discussed the risks associated with marriage counseling privately with the woman, and feels relatively sure abusive acts will not take place as the result of these sessions.

Most communities have shelters, safe homes, and advocacy programs for battered women. They provide temporary, safe lodging and may assist a woman in obtaining a protection order from the court. These programs usually provide education and support groups. I strongly encourage women to participate. The groups are a way to help each woman understand what has been going on in her relationship, and to help her realize she is not responsible for the violence. Then she can sort out her options.

A woman's partner may feel threatened when she attends these sessions. He may think the group is anti-male, or that group members plot with his partner to end the relationship. This is not true. The groups are *anti-violence*. Many battered women experience confusion, pain, fear, and rage as a result of being battered. Other women who have had similar experiences offer them support. Men should encourage this as a healing process, and not ask about what their partners or other group members said in the sessions. Respect your partner's need to participate and heal.

How to Use This Book

In the following chapters you will hear stories of men who volunteered or were ordered by the court to participate in our counseling programs. Today, all of them are living violence-free lives and, while they continue to struggle with issues, they are a testimony to the possibility of change. You will also read excerpts from groups I conducted, alone and with others. To protect the privacy of the men and women quoted in this book their names have been changed—with the exception of Chuck and M'Liss Switzer, who have openly shared their stories—but their experiences may sound familiar to you.

You will read examples of things you can do, or do differently, to avoid situations in which you might be abusive. There are also a number of helpful exercises throughout the book. I invite you to complete these exercises. You may be surprised at what you learn about yourself. Use them to analyze yourself, to explore where you have been, and to set goals for the future.

Women who have lived and are living with men who have been violent will also find this book helpful, and certain parts are addressed directly to them. Similarly, counselors who work with men who batter will find the book useful in their work, both in the techniques and processes it describes and as something to share with men they work with.

Buy a notebook or a journal (sold at bookstores or discount stores) for the exercises in the book. No one needs to see it but you. By writing down your thoughts and feelings during this time, you can assess your own change process. And by remembering and writing down in detail your past experiences, you will develop deeper insights into your decision making.

A caution to men and women
It may not be appropriate, at this time, to make use of some of the exercises in *Violent No More*. Most of the exercises are specifically designed to help men monitor and change abusive and controlling behavior. Some are designed for couples working through basic relationship problems such as negotiating, communicating, and arguing fairly. For women, if you are still fearful of your partner's behavior, check with an advocate or a therapist skilled in this area to determine if there is any risk in using the exercises. What seems harmless may be dangerous if your partner is still using violence, threats, and intimidation.

Finally, whether you are a man or a woman, you may disagree with points I make. That's okay. This book will expose you to some new ideas. Your initial reaction might be to slam the cover shut because you dislike what you're reading. Or you might feel what's being said doesn't apply to you. My analysis of the roots of men's violence may make you uncomfortable. *But*—please give it a chance. Read on. If you complete the book I'm confident it will truly guide you toward ending domestic abuse in your life.

2

The Roots of Men's Violence against Women

The Superman Myth — How Our Culture Encourages Violence — The Struggle for Equality — What Men Expect from Relationships

Children have never been very good at listening to their elders, but they have never failed to imitate them. They must, they have no other models.

JAMES BALDWIN

The Superman Myth

These are confusing times for men. Society's expectations of men— and men's expectations of themselves—are varied and in many ways unrealistic and unhealthy. Regardless of certain positive changes that have occurred in society, men still get conflicting messages about what it means to be a man.

Movie star John Wayne was the quintessential tough-guy male. He was big, he swaggered, he fought, and he never let his emotions get in the way. He was a cowboy, a soldier, a real man. The characters John Wayne played expected women to be submissive. In one film, he put a woman over his knee and spanked her like a child. If he showed pain, it was only in private, "like a man."

The modern-day John Wayne types can be found in many of the roles played by Clint Eastwood, Sylvester Stallone, Chuck Norris, and Arnold Schwarznegger. Their characters are tough, fearless, and usually get their way. Their tough exteriors are projected as attractive to the female stars, who they usually save from dangerous situations. These supermen are so courageous that they boldly fight, or kill, scores of bad guys single-handed.

While the media plays up these superheroes regularly, other social institutions perpetuate the superman myth as well. *"We're looking for a few good men."* This advertisement used by the Marines was aimed at young men who were trained to be disciplined and unfeeling, ready to act as killing machines if ordered into combat. In our cities, boys and young men join gangs, wear colors, and are ready to kill each other at younger and younger ages. Gang members are expected to be fearless. Fighting the enemy and being willing to kill proves your loyalty and manhood. Corporations look for audacious, bold leaders to watch the bottom line and defeat the competition. Sports teams demand gutsy participants who will, if necessary, play while injured. Men must win at any cost.

If being a man means strength and toughness, then what are you if you fail to meet these expectations? You are a failure, a sissy, or a coward. I was recently at a playground and listened to young boys as they played and roughhoused. One boy was being picked on for some reason. The others called him a faggot and a woman. Analyzing the put-down was easy. If you aren't a man then you're a homosexual or—worse—a woman.

Boys are taught to purge themselves of anything that society regards as feminine. I remember in junior high school being with a group of my friends at a local hangout. I crossed my legs, but not in the traditional male way of legs apart, one ankle on the other knee. One of the boys ridiculed me, saying I was sitting like a woman. I was humiliated. After that I became very conscious of how I sat, so that I would not be considered feminine by my male peers.

Men are socialized to view so-called "feminine" characteristics— sensitivity and the expression of feelings—with hostility. These qualities are perceived as opposite to what is required to be a *real* man, or a superman. At an early age, boys begin to reject their gentler feelings or any characteristics that may make them seem vulnerable. Failure to live up to the male persona may bring scorn and ridicule by their peers, so boys learn quickly to adapt. By the time they are adults, men have learned to deny sensitive feelings or have lost touch with them altogether. This "real" man now enters into a relationship with a woman, often bringing with him suppressed feelings and unrealistic expectations of how men are supposed to behave. What a recipe for problems and conflict!

Our socialization as boys and the impact it has on us as men is evident in an exchange that group leader Maryann had with one of the men in our groups. Maryann cofacilitated groups with me in the early eighties. She is a formerly battered woman and always brought important insights to our groups. Her interchanges with men in our groups appear throughout the book.

Maryann: Rick, you mentioned an argument you had with your son, and how your wife Sheila was angry with you because of the way you handled it. How did things finally get resolved?

Rick: I'm not sure they did. She thinks I push him too hard in sports. I coach his hockey and baseball team and I can't show favorites. I push the kids, sure. But I think discipline and drive is what it takes to win. I think it's important for boys to learn certain qualities at a young age.

Maryann: Perhaps. Any reactions to what Rick is saying?

Jason: I don't know. I remember my father screaming from the sidelines when I played football in high school. I hated it. It was like winning was so important to him. He was kind of a football star in high school and he talked about his playing days all the time. Even though he thought he was helping me, you know, giving me encouragement, I just felt like a failure. I'll never forget the time I sprained my ankle in practice. I told him I'd told the coach I didn't think I could play in the tournament game. He just looked at me with disgust and said, "You goddamned sissy." I'll never forget that.

From the Bible to literature to modern media, women have been stereotyped as weak and overly sensitive, and male identification with so-called "female" qualities is regarded as something to be shunned. Yet, ironically, on an interpersonal level some men may also perceive women as powerful. They often assert that women get their power through manipulation and really want to dominate men. This translates into hostility toward women, because many men are threatened by women's power. Both in the workplace and in the home, some men try to suppress women's power, whether real or perceived, because it threatens their need for control and challenges their belief that men should be in charge.

Today, many men are finding ways to discard the tough-guy armor and redefine what being a male is all about. This is partly a result of women's frustration with being controlled, and partly men's own recognition of the emotional, spiritual, and physical destructiveness of trying to live up to the superman image. These men are not threatened by equality with women, because they have found benefits they never imagined. They are beginning to enjoy intimacy in their relationships, discover their children, and live healthier lives. These men are joining women in seeking a world where both sexes are equal.

It will be easier to shed our unrealistic expectations of maleness and the negative beliefs men have about women when society as a whole begins to debunk the superman myth. As parents, we can help to dispel our children's false perceptions of masculinity and femininity. We can model and communicate the importance of boys and men living more complete, emotionally varied lives, rather than being trapped in the cold, controlled, one-dimensional tough-guy image that, in reality, is neither real nor healthy—nor tough.

How Our Culture Encourages Violence

How do disagreements get settled in relationships? Who makes the final decision? Who gets the last word? Many men believe the decision should be theirs. They believe there cannot be two bosses, and that someone has to settle conflicts about children, money, social events, and the host of other issues that fill a relationship. In order to justify taking this power, many men fall back on tradition: being the man in the house means getting to call the shots.

John related the following story during a discussion about using money as a controlling tool. Without consulting his wife, Leslie, he had cut up their credit cards and closed their checking account.

John: I told her I was going to do it. Man, she'll be the first to admit she has no self-control when it comes to money. We just can't continue to get in debt the way we do, so I took some action to change things around our spending.

Michael: Don't you think that what you did is controlling? I mean, now she has no access to money without asking you.

John: It might be controlling, but someone had to put a stop to it and I knew it wouldn't be her. When we get caught up, maybe we can change.

Michael: So she gets an allowance from you.

John: I worked out a budget for food, the kids' expenses, and some basic spending money; if you want to call that an allowance, fine.

Michael: And how does Leslie feel about this?

John: She's a little pissed, but she'll get over it.

The group had a lengthy discussion about who gets to decide issues such as handling the family finances. Some men in the group agreed with John, believing the man should take charge. Others saw this as patronizing and controlling. John saw nothing wrong with his actions.

It's difficult to say what lasting impact John's behavior will have on Leslie. She may feel powerless to challenge John and may lose self-esteem, because she's being treated like a child. She may become dependent and fearful. Or she may feel resentful and angry about his controlling behavior, and begin to lose respect for him. All of these will damage their relationship.

If John wants respect, love, and mutual trust in his relationship with Leslie, his behavior is unlikely to help him get it. Yet many men share John's belief that they should make all the decisions, even if they don't come right out and say so. Some feel it is their right; others feel it is their responsibility. In both cases they are responding to traditional forces in our culture.

▓ **EXERCISE:** Calling the Shots

This exercise involves recalling an incident in which you felt you needed to "step up to the plate" and make a decision even though it was contrary to your partner's wishes. You can record your responses in your journal or notebook.

1. Think about an incident in which you imposed a decision on a past or present partner. Describe the incident in detail.

_____

_____

2. How did you justify your decision to impose your position? How did you explain it to her? How did you explain to others?

_____

_____

3. What was the impact on her? What was the impact on you?

_____

_____

4. In retrospect, was there a more fair way of resolving the issue?

Write this down.

As men, it is important that we understand the historical roles and expectations of men and women. With this knowledge we can better understand how, in the past, men's violence in intimate relationships was expected and condoned, which helps us comprehend domestic violence today.

In past generations, the roles of men and women seemed etched in stone. Social expectations were fairly clear: men were the bread-winners, and women took care of the house and family. In most marriage ceremonies, both civil and religious, the words "honor" and "obey" were directed at the woman regarding her new responsibility to her husband. Her obligations included taking care of the majority of the domestic duties: cleaning the house, cooking the meals, bearing and rearing the children, and responding to the emotional and sexual needs of her husband. Clearly, her role was to serve her husband, and this social arrangement was for a long time reflected in law.

In their book *Violence Against Wives,* Rebecca and Russell Dobash note that the first laws relating to marriage were implemented by the Romans. These laws obliged women to conform themselves entirely to the wishes and demands of their husbands. Roman men were allowed to chastise, divorce, or even kill their wives for engaging in behaviors deemed unacceptable.[2]

Throughout medieval times, the Christian church sanctioned the beating and domination of women. The church's marriage manuals advised the Christian world on the importance of the subordination of women and prescribed the use of flogging so that husbands could maintain appropriate moral order at home.

In the United States, the legal standing of a wife vis-à-vis her husband has its roots in European culture and English common law. In the United States, until the end of the nineteenth century, state laws gave husbands the legal right to beat their wives for various indiscretions. Even after the laws were repealed, domestic abuse was widely accepted as a private matter between husband and wife. Not until the late 1970s did states give law enforcement greater authority to intervene and make arrests when they had grounds to believe a crime had been committed.

Although wife-beating is illegal in most countries, in practice women are continually beaten by their husbands. To understand this tolerance, it is instructive to examine the status of women around the world. In many countries and cultures the position of women seems to have altered little since the Middle Ages. In some Islamic countries, women must cover their faces with the traditional veil, or risk punishment for not complying with religious customs. In some Orthodox Jewish communities, a wife cannot get a divorce without the agreement of her husband. In India, although illegal, women are still burned for not bringing big enough dowries to their new families. In Afghanistan, the Taliban forbids women to work outside the home, attend school, or leave the house unless accompanied by a male relative. An Afghan woman must wear a *burqha*, a garment that literally covers her entire body, leaving only a small opening for her to breathe and see. Throughout Latin America, men are excused for having a mistress, while women are ostracized for similar behavior. Also, if a man kills a woman in a jealous rage, he can successfully use his emotional state as a defense in court. In Japan, thousands of predominantly Southeastern Asian women are virtually enslaved in a sex industry to serve Japanese men. In many European countries the police won't intervene in a domestic assault case unless the injuries are severe. In many countries, reporting domestic abuse brings shame to the family, so most women just accept the violence as part of being married.

You might be thinking the role of women is very different in the United States, and in fact this country has made impressive strides toward equality. Still, American women earn half or less what men are paid in the workplace. While the glass ceiling is shattering for some, there are still very few women in the upper echelons of government and business, and 50 to 85 percent of working women will experience some form of sexual harassment during their academic or working life. When it comes to violence against women, Western countries share the same dreadful statistics as other countries around the world. In the United States, 1,500 women are killed every year by their husbands and boyfriends, and according to the Department of Justice a woman is raped every five minutes by a stranger, acquaintance, or husband. We still have far to go![3]

Some men in our groups use examples of other cultures to argue that male domination of women is perfectly acceptable, and to justify their own behavior. But, if you peel back the rationalizations, most men, regardless of culture, know that devaluing and hurting women and girls is not right. Using violence to dominate another is morally and ethically wrong. We need to rethink outdated beliefs that dehumanize women and—though in a different way—men as well.

In our groups we often talk about sexism as a contributing factor in domestic violence. Sexism is an arbitrary stereotyping of male and female roles based on gender. Sexist beliefs and attitudes lead men to use violence and abusive behavior as a means to control women in intimate relationships. You may not see yourself as sexist, or as someone who believes in male dominance, but the male gender in all its institutions has discriminated against, or sought to control, women. An individual man may not perceive himself as being advantaged. He may have a low-paying job, a dead-end job, or no job at all, and question this notion of male dominance. But as men we can't deny the historical facts, even though individual men may be at the bottom of the economic ladder. Even in our changing society, job opportunities and higher pay are usually biased toward men, despite the fact that many men don't realize these advantages.

On some level, all men benefit from male violence, whether we wish to or not. Even though I try not to participate in acts of sexism, my experiences are shaped by a sexist culture. For instance, when the sun goes down, my mother, sister, and female friends cannot walk downtown or even in their own neighborhoods because they are afraid of being attacked by men. I do not experience that fear, and consequently have more mobility in the world than women.

One night, a female friend called and asked if I would walk her to the store. She was afraid because a number of sexual attacks had occurred in her neighborhood. I remember feeling somewhat powerful and even a little chivalrous in my traditional protective role. She had chosen me to protect her from all those other men. What was I, as a man, gaining from this situation? A feeling of personal power in relation to her and her dependence—however momentary— on me. The situation boosted my sense of traditional male power.

Violence against women will begin to diminish when men renounce the thinking and practice of sexism. We can do this on an individual basis at home, at work, and in our community. When we begin to speak up, other men will listen and the seeds of change will be planted. Men should take the initiative and work with other men to confront sexism and violence, not to get approval from women, but because it is the right thing to do for women, men, and our children.

If you have a daughter, I am sure you want her to have every opportunity to succeed. You want her to be able to work without fear of harassment, and to be safe from sexual assault. If she marries, you want her husband to treat her with respect. If you thought she was being battered, you would be outraged. Yet your daughter, like all women, faces real danger at the hands of men. Throughout her life, because of sexism, she will face obstacles to achieving what she can in the world. There are many reasons for men to change; these are just a few.

Every day, throughout this country, women are dying as a result of domestic abuse. From our farms to our towns and cities, people are asking: what can be done? First, we can try to understand how our attitudes and beliefs about women, men, and relationships ultimately influence how we treat each other. Once we understand this, we can make lasting changes.

History teaches us that societies and cultures change through awareness and struggle. We once thought the world was flat and bloodletting cured disease. These beliefs seem foolish today. By breaking through the walls of ignorance and prejudice we *can* change long-standing beliefs. Hopefully, the belief that one gender, race, or religion is superior to another will one day seem as ridiculous as sacrificing humans to please the gods.

The Struggle for Equality

Working toward an equal relationship—and dealing with the changes it brings—raises profound issues for men and women. We are sometimes unsure how to relate to each other in a world of changing norms and expectations. For many individuals, personal experiences with marriage and relationships have been confusing. Only a generation ago, few questioned the traditional arrangement of male and female roles. But in these changing times, men and women often give and get conflicting signals and messages about who they should be and how they should act and interact with each other.

Women are demanding equality in the workplace, the family, and all institutions of society. Men can support this effort, yet many do not. Some resist the prospects of equality because they think there are certain "natural" reasons for men to be dominant. Even those who profess to support women's liberation sometimes experience confusion, fear, and distrust in their relationships with women. Where does this come from? What do men fear about equality with women? Why are we so resistant?

The following discussion occurred in one of our groups:

Michael: Terry, you say you believe in equality between a man and a woman, but that the man gets to make the decision when the two together can't.

Terry: Yes. The Bible's clear about this. It basically says the man should treat the wife with respect, but the wife should submit to the judgment of the husband.

Michael: I'd appreciate it if we could leave the Bible out of this discussion.

Terry: Fine. But it's not just the Bible. Men think on a rational basis, and women react on a more emotional basis, and that's just a plain fact. So it makes sense that in certain situations the man should make the final decision.

In the group, about half the men agreed with Terry.

Michael: Well, I don't know about your relationship, Terry. From my experience, unless someone wants to be in a submissive position, there will always be conflict. You will be imposing your will on your partner, based on your belief that you have the right to have power over her because of her gender.

Terry: I'm not imposing my will, because she also believes it's her role in the family.

Variations on Terry's beliefs are numerous. In order to justify having power over someone, on some level you must assume there's a rational or "natural" reason for that power. Consider the following analogy:

European settlers and explorers came to the Americas about five hundred years ago. They sought to exploit natural resources and claim the land for their use; however, they encountered indigenous people who had been on the continent for thousands of years. The church at that time believed all non-Christians were savages and heathens. Consequently, the explorers believed they had God on their side as they sought to take over the new land by dispossessing the indigenous people.

In order to oppress, the oppressor needs to dehumanize the person or persons he is oppressing, which is precisely what the invading Europeans did. They saw the indigenous people as defective because they did not embrace European culture and religion. So, persecution was easily justified.

Paulo Freire, a Brazilian writer and activist, wrote extensively on the effects of oppression. In his book *Pedagogy of the Oppressed*, he explains, "The more oppressors control the oppressed (indigenous people), the more they change them into inanimate things. When the oppressed resist subjugation, they are perceived by oppressors as savages and subversives who are violent and barbaric when they react to the violence of the oppressors."[4]

Notice the parallels between the European view of indigenous people and the beliefs some men have about women. Men who batter often call their partner vile names prior to an assault—calling her "bitch" or "cunt" makes her less than human.

People who are oppressed usually resist their oppressors. No one likes being hurt or treated unfairly. No one likes being silenced. However, this is what a man who batters does. He robs his partner of autonomy and equality in the relationship and he imposes his will by violence and other abusive behaviors.

This does not mean that all women are oppressed. Most women experience discrimination and sexism in their lives, but are not necessarily individually oppressed. In *Ain't I A Woman*, bell hooks discusses how it has been inappropriate for white women in the women's movement to compare their experiences with those of people of color. She calls attention to the fact that in the hierarchy of American society white men are at the top and white women are second.[5]

Additionally, not all women are oppressed in their relationships with men. In many relationships there is an equal distribution of power. In some relationships women may exert more control than men in the household. And, clearly, women of economic means have many more options open to them than some poor men. While all women live within the framework of a sexist society, their experiences and reality are not all the same.

Regardless of class, race, and religion, however, when violence is introduced by an individual or group of people, it changes everything. Violence is the weapon of those seeking and attempting to maintain power—it works and it is effective. When a man who batters uses violence, he may get what he wants initially—he ends an argument and prevails in a power struggle with his wife or girlfriend. But at what cost? A man who batters may get to call the shots, but his partner is most likely alienated and resentful, and the relationship for both is unsatisfying.

When people are confronted with new ideas, they often resist. You may already be resisting the views in this book. You may feel the ideas discussed so far attack men or portray women as helpless victims. That is not the intent. I want men who batter to understand the roots of male violence. With this clarity, men who want to change have the ability to maintain healthy and loving relationships with women, free of violence. I hope you read on.

What Men Expect from Relationships

When men and women date or get married, they bring certain expectations to the relationship. Although these expectations are changing, many men and certainly some women adhere to what we might define as a traditional relationship.

In traditional relationships, the woman takes on the role and responsibilities of a "traditional wife." She is responsible for the majority of household and child care responsibilities and agrees to some form of subordinate relationship with her husband.

Some women say they still find satisfaction with this arrangement. However, society increasingly undervalues the traditional stay-at-home mother, perceiving a woman's work in the home, including child rearing, as less important and far less prestigious than her husband's work outside the home. It is no wonder that in the last few decades women have questioned and resisted their traditional role, demanding something different.

To this was added the economic reality that a one-person income was no longer enough to support a large majority of American families. Beginning in the 1960s, women entered the work force in huge numbers, finding a different kind of meaning in their lives, something that gave them economic independence and social freedom. These changes have not been easy for women or their families. Although attitudes are changing, many men would still prefer the traditional nuclear family in which Dad works outside the house and Mom stays home with the children.

The following discussion about the roles of men and women took place in one of our groups:

Maryann: We've been discussing what it means to be in a traditional relationship these past couple of weeks. Many of us grew up in that setting. Do you see any problems with this kind of relationship?

Carl: I don't think today that it's possible. It's pretty rare that your wife can stay at home and do the traditional wifely things, purely because of economics.

Bill: Yet, I feel that even though the "Father Knows Best" family isn't very commonplace, if I had the opportunity, that's what I would want.

Maryann: What do you mean by that?

Bill: If I had the money, I would want my wife to stay home, rather than work. Sometimes I feel like I've failed as a husband and a father because I can't make that happen.

Maryann: You would want your wife not to work and stay home with the children?

Bill: You bet. I don't think it's a good situation for kids to be in day care. I know this sounds old-fashioned, but I think a woman should be in the home, at least until the kids have grown.

While some men in the group did not share Bill's beliefs, others expressed confusion about what women, other men, and society expects of them. For many men, the inability to make enough money on their own creates a sense of failure. This was particularly true for men who had traditional and often rigid expectations of the roles of men and women.

I have heard men say they would not mind staying home during the day, sheltered from the demands of the workplace with no worries about making money. After further discussion, however, most men admit they would feel isolated and in many ways powerless if they had to rely solely on their partners for money; they would not feel equal or comfortable in the traditional wife's role.

At one of my training sessions, we had a heated discussion on the roles of men and women in marriage. Some people in the audience argued that a traditional relationship is fine provided both parties are in agreement and the man handles his dominant position in a benevolent manner. Others countered that anytime you have a relationship in which one person has economic control over the other, you have a power imbalance despite the good intentions of the person who is in the dominant role. We discussed whether any of us would be happy if our well-being and perhaps even our life depended on the "benevolence" of another. Not many wanted to be in that position.

For a long-term relationship to function in a healthy way, in fact to function at all, inequality must be abandoned. This doesn't mean a man and a woman can't construct their own roles in their relationship or marriage. I know couples who take turns working so that one person can spend more time with their children, go back to school, or become involved in community or social change activities. They make financial agreements and don't place a higher value on the person who is providing most of the income. For many couples, economic realities make this difficult, but some do manage, and they don't have a conflict with the arrangement—in fact, it releases them to do other things they believe are valuable in their lives.

While many people don't embrace the traditional relationship today, I recognize that some couples will mutually agree to all or parts of this arrangement. They make this choice usually on the basis of strong religious convictions. This traditional relationship fortified by religious beliefs becomes controversial when the woman submits to the subordinate role out of obligation or coercion. Domestic violence in this kind of traditional relationship is viewed as a marital problem caused by the woman not fulfilling her wifely obligations.

You will meet Chuck and M'Liss in a later chapter. Their experience with the church is important to our discussion on traditional relationships. M'Liss explained her belief at the time:

> I believed Chuck had the authority in the household based on our religious orientation. It was in the Scriptures, or at least the way they were interpreted. We went to church three days a week for eleven years. When members of the congregation would see me battered they would say, "What did you do to make him so mad that he would beat you like that?" We finally quit the church after Chuck was ordered into counseling for battering me.

Chuck explained:

> I beat M'Liss up once and her face was all swollen, her arms were bruised, and her glasses were broken, yet we still went to church. The word got to the pastor that I had beat her up. The preacher called me to his back room and asked me if I'd beaten her. I said, "Yes, I

did." And he said, "If that's what it takes to keep her in line, well—" and he pointed to the door and I left. Nothing else was said. Our church would not tell the congregation that domestic abuse was wrong.

Men who subscribe to rigid sex roles are inclined to justify their use of violence against a partner who is struggling for equality. When men say things like "You've got to keep her in her place," or "She's just an uppity woman," or "There can't be two people in charge," they are echoing the traditional male expectations of the roles of women, men, and marriage. These beliefs and attitudes are at the heart of sexism and perpetuate men's use of violence.

Historically, whenever major change has occurred in society a period of uncertainty and resistance follows. After the American Revolution, unstable economic times and foreign policy blunders caused many to question the viability of the new Republic. When the Supreme Court in the case of *Brown v. Board of Education of Topeka* interpreted the Fourteenth Amendment to outlaw racial discrimination in public schools, a backlash by white supremacists and increased Klan activity occurred. Similarly, after the growth of feminism over the last twenty-five years, a backlash against women's rights has been occurring. Many men and some women openly talk with disdain about feminism as the ruin of the American family. Right-wing talk-show hosts like Rush Limbaugh use the term "feminazi" to the delight of the neoconservative listener. Right-wing politicians like Pat Buchanan speak of the culture war and the perceived attack on traditional family values. While disturbing, this backlash is to be expected, but hopefully not accepted, by the reader.

For most men reading this book, understanding the roots of your violence will bring you face-to-face with striking contradictions in your thinking. Despite the propaganda you might hear or even believe about feminism, you have experienced firsthand the conflict that occurs when you have tried to force your will upon your partner. When she wouldn't shut up, you hit her. When she wouldn't do what you wanted, you hit her. And now you are searching for answers.

The roots of male violence are embedded in a belief of entitlement and control based on gender. A relationship or marriage doesn't have to be that way. Men don't have to be threatened by equality—a partnership can be yours. It is truly your choice.

A note to the Christian reader

If this chapter causes conflict based on your interpretation of Scriptures, I would strongly encourage you to read *Keeping the Faith,* by Marie Fortune. Marie is an ordained minister in the United Church of Christ and has written this easy-to-read book for Christian families touched by abuse.[6]

3

The Origins of Abuse and Sexual Violence

Cassie's Story — Bernice's Story — Women and Violence —
The Violence We Learn at Home — The Violence We Learn from
Society — Why We Use Violence — Sexual Violence — The
Impact of Violence on Sexual Relationships

Although the world is full of suffering,
it is full also of the overcoming of it.

HELEN KELLER

I interviewed Cassie and Bernice about living with abusive men.
Their accounts of what they experienced offers a perspective that
men often do not hear. In this section and throughout this book
you will hear their stories.

Cassie's Story

My ex-husband and I lived together for eleven years. We were both
in the armed services when we met. When we got out of the service,
we moved to the Virgin Islands. The physical abuse started almost
immediately. I was taught that you stay in a relationship no matter
what, so I was determined to make things work.

I left him one year because of the continued abuse and went to
live with my family in Michigan. He came up there and we started to
work on our issues. I moved in with him again. He wasn't violent
during that year but when we'd argue he would throw stuff close
to me. He'd throw an ashtray a few inches from my head, then he'd
say, "I didn't hit you." At the time I thought, well, that's true, he
didn't hit me.

We moved back to the Virgin Islands and the violence started
again. After he hit me, he would say if I just hadn't done this or said
that, he wouldn't have hit me. So I stopped doing or saying things

that apparently were setting him off. He told me not to yell, so I stopped yelling. He told me he wouldn't hit me if I got a job, so I got a job. He told me he wouldn't hit me if I didn't drink, so I quit drinking. But the violence didn't stop. He always had a reason. I kept trying to change my life so I wouldn't get hit.

I think the worst time was when he punched me so hard in the face that it split my head open. On another occasion he kicked me in the stomach and broke three of my ribs.

I got a restraining order against him and he left the island. I have limited contact with him today except for visitation with the children. I think he could have changed if he had gotten some education or been confronted with his behavior early on. We didn't really know what to do or where to go. We went to counseling once but the counselor didn't want to address the abuse that was going on.

I know that he knew what he was doing wasn't right. Once he introduced me to a female friend of his who was being battered. He was outraged and concerned and wanted to find ways of helping her. Ironically, he couldn't make the connection between what he was doing to me and what was happening to this woman. That's why I think if there had been some direct intervention by a counselor or someone he might have been forced to look at his own behavior.

Healing for me is a long process. I thought when I left him everything would be okay, but it wasn't. It wasn't until I started going to women's groups and sorting through everything that had happened that I started to heal. I never thought I was a battered woman. But I'm gaining self-confidence. I don't know if I'll ever marry again. It's strange that after all that happened, I still have feelings for my ex-husband. I mean, we spent eleven years together and had children together. Yet I don't think I could ever go back. My trust level with men is pretty low and I'm not sure I would want to take the chance of another relationship.

Bernice's Story

I lived with my partner for three and a half years. When we first started dating, I liked the fact that he had claimed me. It made me feel good that he found me attractive and wanted me. At that time, he was very supportive and bought me a lot of presents.

He was an up-and-coming public official and looks were important to him. He wanted me to dress a certain way so we looked good together. I went along with that, but he became more and more controlling. I had mixed feelings about his controlling nature, but I grew up believing that men were supposed to have the power in the house-hold, that the man was master in his home. I believed a woman's role was to maintain a neat home, be well-organized, and make good meals. I thought these domestic things were a reflection on me as a person, as a woman.

He insisted that I make the bed right after we got up in the morn-ing. After dinner, especially if we had company over, I had to clean the dishes immediately after we ate. He would give me a certain amount of money each week, and if it wasn't enough he made me show him the receipts. At the time none of this seemed unreason-able. Of course, today I recognize how controlling he was. I know his expectation that a woman should be subservient was wrong.

The first time he hit me was after we got home from a political event. Some of the men were talking and putting women down. They were saying things like the only way women get ahead is by sleeping their way to the top. I got into an argument with them and my partner pulled me away and said, "Who the fuck do you think you are? Don't you ever talk that way in front of my friends again." He was upset with me because he believed what these guys were saying and he didn't want me speaking my mind and embarrassing him. All the way home he berated me, telling me I was stupid and worthless. When we got home, he slammed me up against the wall and punched me several times. And though he apologized later, he told me he wouldn't tolerate his woman asserting herself.

The violence continued and I finally told him if it didn't stop I was leaving. He said the only way I would leave would be in a body bag. I stayed because I was afraid of him, but I finally made the move. We were arguing about my leaving and he hit me in the face with a pop bottle and knocked out most of my teeth. He waited five or six hours before he brought me to the hospital. There I was, dazed, with my teeth hanging out and my face completely swollen, listening to him apologize. I left after that happened.

I'm not sure this man is capable of change. I'm sure he's battering another woman today. His whole existence revolved around having power over women. And in a strange way I think he got off on the violence.

I'll never forget how he treated me. Because of him, I see all men as a threat to me. Sadly, even my male sons are a threat because of their size and the way boys and men are socialized. As long as men have power over women, I'll be resentful. I'd like to be in a relationship at some time but it's something I can't visualize because of those experiences.

Women and Violence

Now that you've heard the stories, you can visualize what violence is all about: hitting, slapping, punching, yelling; knocked-out teeth, split-open heads, broken ribs; angry stares, death threats, flying ashtrays; domination and control.

Both Bernice and Cassie were devastated by the violence they experienced. Both changed to meet their partners' demands. They adapted to survive, yet the violence continued. Finally, both women made the decision to get out.

These women were battered severely. Your violence may not have escalated to the levels described in their stories. You may even be inclined to measure your behavior against the actions of Cassie's and Bernice's ex-partners, and think that what you've done isn't as bad. It is vitally important to remember that in both cases *the first incident was not severe*. Apologies and promises followed. But in both cases the violence escalated and both men became criminally abusive.

In an attempt to understand the reality of a woman living in an abusive relationship, researchers Rebecca and Russell Dobash interviewed 109 women who had been battered. They found that the women's experiences and responses to the violence were fairly similar.[7]

The Dobashes found that when the first assault occurs most women think the act is an aberration; in other words, they think that the behavior is not normal. The man usually apologizes and the woman accepts his promise that he will never be violent with her again. When the second assault occurs, the level of violence increases and most women leave. They go to a parent's or a friend's home or a shelter. But the Dobashes found that when a woman leaves at this stage, her motivation is to teach her partner a lesson, not to end the relationship. If the woman believes that her partner has learned a lesson, she returns.

After the third assault, the violence escalates further and the woman usually leaves again. This time she returns because she does not have the financial resources to live on her own, or she fears she will lose the children, or she fears for her safety, not because she thinks her partner will change.

If she stays in the relationship it is because she has to, not because she wants to. She may begin abusing alcohol or drugs to anesthetize herself against an unbearable situation. She may become

physically or emotionally sick. Some women try to adapt. They pla-
cate their partners to lessen the chances of being hit and try their
best to live with the situation. Like Cassie and Bernice, they abandon any hope of salvaging the relationship. The love they once felt
evaporates and they prepare to leave.

I advise women to leave an abusive relationship after the first
assault. That may sound harsh, but my experience working with
men who batter is that the violence simply continues unless there is
intervention.

As the Dobashes concluded in their research, women often go
back initially because they want to believe the relationship can be
saved. I ask women who go back to their partners to talk to women's
advocates from their local shelter. Battered women need to understand the dynamics of an abusive relationship and to be aware that if
their partners do not get help, they will usually batter again.

Any woman who has been battered should develop a safety plan
so that when she needs to get out, she can do so with relative safety.
A safety plan includes emergency phone numbers, people the woman
can call for assistance, and places to stay if she senses her partner
becoming abusive again. She should also insist that her partner get
help, which does not mean just a couple of counseling sessions. If
he is truly motivated to change, he will make a commitment to counseling or a domestic violence program. If he is willing to get help and
be accountable for his behavior, the relationship can heal. Only when
a woman is relatively certain that her partner will not use violence
again can the couple work on their problems together.

For men who are currently in a relationship and have been violent, your partner may be at the stage where she is willing to give
you another chance. Make use of the opportunity: get help. However,
she may be at the stage where she wants to end the relationship. This
is a familiar consequence of domestic abuse. If that is the case, you
cannot undo what has occurred but you can begin to make changes
for yourself. You will probably enter into a new relationship at some
point and you should get help now to avoid becoming abusive with a
new partner.

The Violence We Learn at Home

Boys who witness domestic assaults when growing up are more likely
to use violence as adults. Researchers estimate that 50 to 70 percent

of men who batter either witnessed battering at home or were themselves abused by a parent.[8]

Many researchers conclude that men learn to use violence as children. They see their fathers use violence with no negative repercussions for their actions, and they get the message that this kind of behavior works and is an acceptable response to conflict.[9]

Another message the child gets is that the father is boss. He has the right to discipline not only his children, but also his wife. He seems omnipotent. Sometimes the child may sense there is something wrong with the behavior; at other times he may conclude that his father has a rational reason for becoming so angry and abusive.

Either way, the messages etched in the minds of children who observe violence are indelible. Men in our groups have said they vowed not to repeat the domestic abuse they saw as children. However, for most of them, when conflicts arose with their partners and they felt they could not win or control the situation, a light from the past would signal: hit her. With a hit or a punch they could change the situation, just like their fathers did. And if there are no consequences for the violence—such as getting arrested or losing the relationship—the behavior becomes reinforced.

Many men have had unhappy childhood experiences. Some were abused or mistreated by parents; others watched their fathers abuse their mothers. Some did not experience physical violence but were verbally abused or received little emotional support at home.

Even if you had a terrible childhood, it is important that you not blame your past for your actions today. For one thing, holding onto painful childhood and adult experiences only aggravates an unhealed wound. Second, regardless of how and where you learned about violence, you must address your *current* way of reacting to women in relationships because that is something you can change. Remember: men make a *personal* choice to become violent regardless of what they have been exposed to during their childhood.

Barbara Hart, an attorney who has written extensively on domestic violence, states, "Perhaps growing up in a culture of violence and in a family marked by violence desensitizes people to violence or makes it harder for them to choose lives free of violence. But what has been learned can be unlearned and relearned."[10]

■ **EXERCISE:** Learning about Violence

In order to understand some of the reasons for violence in your life, walk through your personal history and examine your past experiences. Some of those experiences still affect you today, and reliving them may make you feel uncomfortable. In the following exercises you can either write down your responses in a journal or notebook, or remember your responses as you go through each step.

Step One: Find a comfortable chair, relax, and close your eyes. Think back to the first time you witnessed someone being physically hurt by another person. This scene doesn't necessarily have to be one that took place in your childhood. Some examples might be one parent assaulting another parent, a parent beating your sister or brother, a bully abusing a friend or schoolmate.

Try to recall the incident in detail. What was your reaction to the violence? How did you feel? Did you talk to anyone about what you saw or how you felt?

_____

_____

Maryann had the following discussion in one of our groups about the impact of witnessing violence. She asked Reggie about how he felt when he saw his father beating his brother for stealing a car.

Reggie: I was horrified. I'd never seen anyone get punched like that close up except on TV. I remember my brother covering up his head to shield himself from the blows. I felt totally powerless to do anything. I realized he probably deserved to be punished for stealing the car but even at my young age I could tell the beating was severe.

Maryann: Were you surprised by the fury of your father's anger?

Reggie: I was definitely surprised by his anger and his actions. I'm not sure what the lasting impact was on me, except maybe the experience made me conscious about never getting so angry at my children that I could resort to violence like my father did that night.

Step Two: Think of a time you were the victim of abuse or violence as a child or adult. If you have never been a victim of abuse or violence, describe a situation in which someone was abusive or violent in a manner that felt intimidating.

What was your reaction to being the victim? How did you feel after the incident? Did you talk to anyone about what happened?

In one of our groups, Maryann had the following discussion with Roland about being a victim of violence:

Maryann: You said you felt powerless during the mugging. Do you really think you had any other option?

Roland: I think most men fantasize that they could do something heroic. My fantasy is that I had a black belt in karate. I can visualize my hits and kicks as I take these two guys down. Just like in the movies.

Maryann: So because you couldn't be like Clint Eastwood you saw yourself as a failure?

Roland: In part because my wife was there, I felt like less of a man.

Maryann: How did your wife react to you after the incident?

Roland: Well, both she and the police kept emphasizing that we had no other options, but I *still* wish I'd done something. It's amazing how men are socialized about violence. I think most of us are horrified when we're confronted with it, but feel that somehow we should be able to stand up to any challenge.

Maryann: Does that experience affect you today?

Roland: Sure. I think about it and my inaction a lot. I'm nervous walking in certain parts of town. If I see more than one man coming toward me, I start to prepare. I'm much more sensitive to the psychological impact of violent crime on victims.

Step Three: Recall a time when you used violence against someone. Think of an adult experience that really had an impact on you. If you have not used violence, think of a time you used intimidation against a past or present partner or your children. If neither applies, think about a childhood experience when you used violence or intimidation.

What was your reaction to your own violent act? Did anyone confront you about your behavior? If yes, how did you respond to their questioning? Did you make excuses, blame the other person, or admit what you had done?

In one of my groups, we discussed the use of violence:

T.J.: I remember slapping my daughter Elisha hard. I couldn't believe I did it. She was in shock and the look she gave me was one of total disbelief, almost betrayal. She ran from the room screaming.

Michael: How did she respond to you afterward?

T.J.: She was actually concerned about how upset I was. I apologized and promised her I would never allow my anger to get to that point again.

Michael: Do you think that slap changed things?

T.J.: Well, I think some of the innocence of our father-daughter relationship changed. I also became very aware of my temper and my ability to be violent. We've had many arguments since, but I'm very conscious of what I'm capable of because of that incident.

Step Four: Review step three, when you recalled being violent to someone. Imagine the same situation occurring today. How would you respond now? Would you handle the situation differently? What are the alternatives to using violence or intimidation in that situation?[11]

The purpose of this and other exercises in this book is to learn from our past experiences and our mistakes. Much has happened in our lives to shape who we are, yet each of us has the strength and capacity to change. We can live our lives differently by learning from the past.

The Violence We Learn from Society

Many men who choose to use violence did not grow up in households in which their fathers hit their mothers. In a society in which negative attitudes and violence toward women are commonplace, boys and men may experiment with behaviors that conflict with the values they learned in the home.

Our attitudes about women, men, and relationships can be traced to many childhood experiences. Our characters are developed by what we learn and observe in school, church, neighborhoods, and our families of origin. Our experiences become a blueprint for living, a foundation for how we respond to situations throughout our lives.

Boys learn a great deal of violence from the culture in which they live. They play imaginary games of war, compete in violent sports, read violent comic books, watch violent movies, play violent video games, and are exposed to violent pornography. Boys are taught at an early age that violence is an acceptable way to handle conflict. If they refrain from using violence, they may be ridiculed by other boys. When this occurs, they feel they do not measure up as men.

In Chapter 6 you will meet Mark. He explained that when he was growing up his father treated his mother with respect. He rarely heard an argument and saw no violence between them. In school, though, his male friends had a strong influence on him and he began putting girls down to become accepted within a certain group. Like his friends, he wanted to be in charge when dating. And like his friends, he learned that slapping a girl was something a boy was entitled to do if his girlfriend flirted with another boy, ignored him, or talked back. Using violence against women was not something Mark learned at home. He developed these attitudes among his peers, and got reinforcement for his behavior from his male friends.

The following discussion in one of my groups focused on what influenced our beliefs about violence and women:

Lewis: You know, it's strange. Seeing my father kick the hell out of my mother all those years, and the way he treated us kids, I promised myself that when I became an adult I would never be that way to my wife or kids. And here I am in this damn group.

Phil: I guess it's something we just learn.

Michael: Are you saying that if you see and experience this stuff as children, then you automatically become abusive?

Phil: No, but this is what I apparently learned from my childhood. I used to think my dad hitting my mom was somewhat justified, because I could tell what would set him off and I couldn't understand why she couldn't.

Randy: My father was never violent with my mother. In fact, all I saw was the two of them being very affectionate.

Michael: So, Randy, you didn't observe violence in the home, yet you battered your wife. Phil just said he thought he learned violence from watching his dad. Why do you think you started to be violent with women? Where do you think you got your messages about women and relationships?

Randy: I suppose just living. Some of my friends in high school would talk about slapping their girlfriends if they got out of line and everyone would laugh. My friends meant a lot to me and they had a lot of influence over decisions I made. When I played on the football team, I started developing this tough-guy image because I thought it would impress people. Getting into fights and slapping up your girlfriend was all just part of it.

Why We Use Violence

Violence produces immediate results. It works. Except in cases of real self-defense, I never met a man who battered who would dispute the fact that his motive was to stop his partner from saying or doing something he disapproved of, or to punish her for doing something he didn't like.

To see if this description fits for you, do the following exercise. It is a variation on an exercise I designed together with Ellen Pence of the Duluth Domestic Abuse Intervention Project.[12]

▓ EXERCISE: Why We Use Violence

You can do this exercise by yourself or in a group. It involves recalling an incident in which you used violence toward a partner. You might want to record your thoughts and feelings in your notebook or journal. If you have not been violent, think of a time when your behavior was intimidating, for instance, when you screamed, pounded your fist on a table, hit a wall, glared, or threw something at or close to someone.

1. Violent incident: Think about the most recent episode in which you used violence, threats, or intimidation against a past or present partner. Choose an incident that stands out in your mind. Describe what happened and what you did.

_____

_____

2. Purpose: Describe why you were violent at that time. What did you want to have happen?

_____

_____

3. Impact: What were the short-term and long-term impacts of the violence on your partner, yourself, and the relationship?

Short-term impact:

_____

_____

Long-term impact:

_____

_____

Reread your answer in the purpose section. Your purpose probably was to gain something very specific, like stopping an argument or getting your way.

Now look at the impact sections. You will probably notice two things. First, in the short term you most likely got what you wanted, at least initially. Your partner may have stopped arguing, not gone out, or otherwise altered her behavior.

In the long term, however, what probably happened is the exact opposite of what you wanted. Your partner may have become distant, and intimacy between you may have been diminished. She probably became furious with you for your behavior and may have contemplated leaving the relationship.

Does this coincide with your experience?

To complete this exercise, close your eyes and relax. Review the incident you just described above. Imagine a way you could have handled the situation differently, without being violent. You may have been justifiably angry or hurt by something your partner did but, after reflection, can you think of a way you could have responded to the conflict without being violent?

Participating in a counseling group can help some men understand how growing up male in this culture has influenced their beliefs about women and relationships. Others, especially those who grew up in violent households, may need to see a counselor or a therapist to unravel some of the past and finally say good-bye to it. Regardless of how you got where you are, you alone are responsible for what you do next. It is helpful—sometimes even necessary—to understand your past, but it is completely up to you to take charge of your future.

Sexual Violence

Strangers and family members have molested and raped girls and women for centuries. In times of war, invading soldiers rape defenseless women as part of their conquest. Few countries and cultures have been immune to these crimes. As Iris Chang stated in her landmark book, *The Rape of Nanking,* "Chinese women were raped in all locations and at all hours. An estimated one-third of all rapes occurred during the day. Survivors even remember solders prying open the legs of victims to rape them in broad daylight, in the middle of the street, and in front of crowds of witnesses. No place was too sacred for rape. The Japanese attacked women in nunneries, churches, and Bible training schools. Seventeen solders raped one woman in succession in a seminary compound."[13] The systematic rapes in most wars tell us much about male thinking about women and violence—rape is the ultimate form of dominance and humiliation.

In some countries, if a woman reports a rape her husband and family may stone or ostracize her. She conceals the sexual assault because she would be considered unclean and unacceptable for marriage. Many girls and women do not report rape because they fear they will not be believed or will suffer the anguish of a public trial and media exposure.

The effects of being sexually abused are varied. Most sexual assault victims feel violated and are often full of rage. Some experience guilt because they were not able to stop the assault. Some victims have difficulty trusting others or develop sexual problems. Some heal quickly; for others the psychological effects of the trauma last for a long time.

Males are also the victims of sexual abuse but in far lesser numbers than females. Boys have been sexually abused by women and some men are considered rape victims of women. However, most male victims of sexual assault are abused by men and other boys. There are 1.5 million people in our federal and state prisons and county workhouses, and most are boys and men. In many of these institutions, men and boys are raped or coerced into sexual acts. For some perpetrators the acts are for sexual gratification, but often the rape and sexual coercion is used for punishment and as a tool to ensure the domination of the powerful. As James Gilligan states in his provocative book, *Violence: Our Deadly Epidemic and Its Causes,* "The rape of males is one of the most widespread—indeed, virtually universal—features of the penal system as I have observed it, and as many others have confirmed." Gilligan claims that prison authorities simply look the other way as the practice of rape occurs, with few inmates daring to report the offenses.[14] The short- and long-term effects on males who have been sexually violated are generally parallel to the effects on females.

Whether women or men are the victims of sexual violence, the statistical facts don't lie—men are the primary perpetrators. Since rape is undeniably an act of violence, it is only fitting that men challenge the culture that supports this act. Men need to speak out—we can and must teach our sons a different way. Men can't just assume that this is a woman's problem, because it is very much *our* problem. We must confront the tacit "boys will be boys" tolerance of rape that pervades so much of our culture.

What is the intent of sexual abuse? While sexual desire is a part of the act of rape, the principal factors are violence and domination, which make the perpetrator feel powerful. He has *conquered* this girl or woman. Boys are socialized to believe they should initiate or pursue sex aggressively. Often they learn about sex by being exposed to pornography, which features women as objects or bodies, not as persons with feelings. All this results in convoluted messages about what girls and women want and what boys and men are supposed to do.

Aggressive and even abusive male sexual behavior is sometimes excused as an inherent, uncontrollable biological urge. In this view men supposedly have a sexual appetite that is dictated by testosterone, so their need for sex "must" be satisfied. This argument, however, is simply another excuse for objectification and dominance.

The language many men use reflects these common, exploitative sexual attitudes toward women. "Hitting" on women, "scoring," and "getting laid" are terms that have little to do with love, intimacy, or even acknowledging another person, and much more with sexual conquest. With this language men are reducing women to objects to be obtained and used.

According to the Duluth Domestic Abuse Intervention Project, 50 percent of women who have been physically assaulted also experienced sexual abuse at the hands of their partners. Many men believe that sexual access is their contractual right after marriage, and those who force or coerce their partners into having sex view their behavior as normal. Many women do not define forced acts of intercourse in a marriage or long-term relationship as rape because of confusion about perceived marital or relationship obligations.

It is a rare human being who has not been affected by societal messages about sex. Human sexuality gets categorized into right and wrong, proper or dirty. We grow up with guilt, confusion, and anxiety about sex and have few outlets to talk frankly and ask questions about our feelings and experiences. As adults, we often do not—and cannot—communicate about sex with our partners. Also, for better or for worse, both sexes engage in certain sexual "games." These games can result in unacceptable and sometimes criminal behavior.

In one of my groups, I described the following scenario: A man takes a female friend out to dinner. He pays for the dinner and then they go dancing and have several drinks. She invites him into her apartment. When he attempts to have sex with her she refuses and resists. He pursues her and forcibly has intercourse with her. When I asked the group members whether they thought the man had raped the woman, many said no.

Several men in the group believed there is an expectation that men are entitled to sex, given certain conditions. If a man buys something for his date, if she dresses a certain way, if they've been drinking, or if she is demonstrative, some men believe they have permission to pursue. If she resists or says no, he may not believe her or may not care.

I then described another scenario in which a man pressures his wife to have sex. He tells her it is her duty and that if she doesn't have sex with him, he'll "get it" elsewhere. She submits. Again, many of the men in the group did not see any problem with this kind of pressure.

Sexual abuse is not limited to coerced sex. One woman told me how her husband would consistently make derogatory comments about her body, particularly about the size of her breasts. Sometimes he would make these statements in public or in front of their children, despite the humiliation it caused her.

Another woman related how her husband would bring home hard-core pornographic videos. He would make her watch the films and copy what they viewed. Many of the sexual acts were violent or painful, yet she felt she had to submit.

As men, we can untangle the negative cultural messages that all males have been exposed to about sexuality. We can speak up when media, friends, and coworkers trivialize sexual abuse through comments and jokes. When Indiana basketball coach Bobby Knight made the comment that if a woman is raped she might as well lie back and enjoy it, a firestorm of criticism followed. Women reacted in outrage, but men were relatively silent. They either saw it as a harmless joke or were afraid they would be seen as unmanly if they criticized the remark.

Martin Luther King Jr. said, "A time comes when silence is betrayal." Men betray their wives, sisters, mothers, and humanity by their silence when words and actions contribute to violence against women.

It does not have to be this way. Men can refuse to participate in the sexual objectification of women. We can teach our sons not to use women, and to understand the importance of sexual respect in relationships. In your current or future relationship, your sexuality can be based on mutuality and respect for each other's needs.

The Impact of Violence on Sexual Relationships

My discussions with men who have battered and women who have been battered show that the sexual relationship usually changes after violence occurs. Intercourse after a violent episode is common. A man often believes that if he is sexual after being violent, his partner will see how sorry he is or how much he really loves her, and will forgive him for the violence. He may believe that the tenderness he expresses makes amends for his abuse. For some men, the violence also provides an erotic charge.

For many women, having sex after an assault can be a way of calming down a partner, and women will often submit out of fear of further violence. The experience, however, is often degrading and devoid of tender or intimate feelings. Other women are confused by sexual expression following a violent episode. They hope for the relationship to be made right. They want to be intimate and feel loved.

As Bernice explains, her sexual relationship with her partner was a mixture of violence and confusion:

> To me, it's the ultimate in control when a man has sex with you after he's beaten you. I think my partner had this strange way of equating sex with negative attitudes about women; basically, a woman's function was for the sexual pleasure of men. It was all very confusing for me. Here this man beats me and then he's making love to me.

My partner raped me many times, although I'm not sure he saw it that way. Sometimes when he had friends over he would make derogatory sexual comments about me. I felt humiliated and violated. When we were making love and I responded in a certain way to a position we were in, he would become abusive and beat the hell out of me. He would accuse me of sleeping around and practicing these positions, because of the way I responded. This was especially traumatic—to get beaten right after making love.

Since I left my partner, I haven't been sexual. I was dating this one guy and the issue of sex came up and these old memories came up and I got frightened. That part of me has really been damaged.

Cassie also experienced sexual abuse throughout her marriage, especially after a violent episode:

I learned very early that I had no option. Sometimes he would force himself on me. I told him I wasn't going to respond sexually but he didn't seem to care. That really reinforced this whole thing that he didn't care how he was getting sex. It didn't matter to him if I participated or not. It was the ultimate in objectification.

I either had sex or I got beaten up. I never saw it as sexual abuse at the time. Whenever we had a fight, it was never completely over until we had sex. Even when I was feeling rotten I had to submit, and for him everything was supposedly okay.

For both Bernice and Cassie the sexual abuse they experienced has stayed with them years after their relationships ended. They have been robbed of something precious: the ability to trust another human being in intimate, loving contact.

If you are still with someone you have abused, it is important that you listen to your partner's concerns and respect what she needs. She may feel distant or may not feel like engaging in sex because of what has gone on in the past. If she needs time, honor her request *without* making her feel guilty or pressuring her in any way. These can be confusing times for her and wounds can take a long time to heal. Guilt or pressure will only reinforce her pain and distrust.

▓ **EXERCISE:** Analyzing Healthy and Negative Sexual Behavior

The following exercise is *only* for those men who *want* a healthier sexual relationship without using coercive or abusive behaviors. Think carefully about each step of the exercise and write your responses in your journal or notebook. If you don't feel comfortable writing this exercise down, you can think about your responses instead.

1. List several incidents when you were sexually abusive or sexually inappropriate.

Examples of violent or coercive acts:

Expected sex even though she didn't want it. Pressured her to do things she didn't feel comfortable with. Made her watch pornography. Inserted objects into her against her will. Made her have sex with someone else. Used violence during sex. Forced her to have sex while she was sleeping. Wanted to have sex in front of the children or others.

Examples of demeaning sexual behavior:

Compared her body to other women and to pictures in magazines. Made her feel bad about her body and her sexual abilities. Made degrading sexual statements. Made her pose for pictures when she didn't feel comfortable. Accused her of having affairs when she did something different sexually. Called her sexually demeaning names.

Examples of using sex:

Told her I'd get it elsewhere if she didn't submit. Used sex as a reward. Blamed her when I wasn't satisfied, but didn't care if she was satisfied. Disclosed intimate information about her in public. Wanted sex after I'd been violent and expected her to forgive me.

2. Pick an incident from your list that most stands out in your mind. Describe this incident in detail.

---

3. What was the purpose of your behavior? Describe what you were feeling and thinking.

---

4. What were the short-term and long-term impacts of your behavior?

Short-term impact:

_____

_____

Long-term impact:

_____

_____

5. Looking back at the incident and knowing how your actions hurt your partner, how will you ensure that you won't repeat the behavior with your present or future partner? If you are in a group, ask the group members or the counselor for ideas.

_____

_____

Practitioners who work in this field unfortunately underestimate the degree to which sexual violence occurs in relationships. Women as well as men are often reticent to discuss sexual abuse when describing what has transpired in their relationships. They may also have trouble identifying certain behavior as sexual abuse.

For instance, a woman may describe an incident during which she submitted to sex when she wasn't interested. She may not see her partner's pressure as coercion, and may not present it as such. A practitioner who fails to understand abusive patterns of behavior may misinterpret the level of sexual abuse in a relationship. A man may report viewing a lot of pornographic material, and may claim it has no effect on his partner or on the relationship. The practitioner should be skeptical of these assertions and seek further information on the impact of pornography on the relationship.

In summary, not all men who batter are sexually abusive, but they are more likely to be than nonbatterers. We need to address this issue squarely. Men cannot assume that marriage provides a license to sexual access. Acknowledging sexual abuse in counseling or with a partner may produce shame or guilt, but, like all the aspects of accountability discussed in this book, it is a part of taking full responsibility for your violence. It is a necessary step on your road toward making real changes in your life.

4

It's More Than Just Physical Violence

Jim's Story — Using Intimidation to Control — Using Threats — Blocking Her Freedom to Decide — Using the Children to Get to Her — The Pain of Emotional Abuse — Understanding and Stopping Battering

When elephants fight, it is the grass that suffers.

AFRICAN PROVERB

The word *battering* refers to the systematic use of abusive behaviors, including physical violence, to establish and maintain control over another person. Ending your use of physical violence is the first step in your process of change. But you must also commit to ending other abusive behaviors.

Jim's Story

Jim grew up in a middle-class neighborhood in a small community in California and moved to Minnesota in his twenties. He was arrested for domestic assault and was ordered to attend our program. He was thirty-four at the time of this interview and had been married three times. In his story, Jim describes the very brutal violence he used in his relationships. He also discusses how he used other abusive behaviors to intimidate and control his partners.

I came from a very violent home. One night, my dad was really drunk and he was trying to force himself into the house. I knew he would either do something to my mother or she would do something to him. The next thing I knew they were fighting outside the doorway of our apartment. He was beating on her and she grabbed a knife and stabbed him in the side and pushed him down the stairs. My father survived but the relationship didn't.

There were many times when I hid under a table to avoid the violence around me. I was always afraid, because I was constantly witnessing my father and mother hurting each other. It's strange—as a kid it all seemed kind of normal to me. I thought all families were like mine. When I started assaulting women, I never correlated my action to my upbringing, but I think now that it must have had an impact.

My stepfather also battered my mother. He punched her in the mouth, pulled her down, and kicked her when she was on the floor. I would try to stop him, but I would get thrown aside. Sometimes when I would intervene it would slow the fight down, so every time they got into a fight I'd try and stop it. I remember many times I would be upstairs and I would be listening to their fights for hours. I would take the pillow and cover my head and cry for the longest time. I really was afraid they would kill each other.

My stepfather would discipline us kids with a belt that had studs on it. I remember actually feeling the welts on my rear end. Many times, my parents would go to a bar and leave us in the car while they went in to drink. In the winter we would be freezing. My brother would go into the bar and tell our parents we were cold and then they would finally come out. If we said anything in the car my stepfather hit us.

My mother was also abusive to us. When I was a teenager, I had come home late and as I rode my motorcycle into the driveway my mother hit me on the back with a broom handle. I fell off the bike and she began hitting me on the head and on the back with this broom handle. At the time I didn't see this as abusive, because all the violence in our home seemed normal.

All through my childhood, I was very rough. I would beat up on my younger brother and my older brother would beat up on me. One time in the seventh grade I got into a fight with a kid at school. I remember being scared of him because he was kind of a bully, but I couldn't back down. When we fought I smashed his face into the brick wall of the school. I remember feeling very powerful, especially with all the kids around me saying how great I was. Also, to have beaten up this kid who I perceived to be so tough felt good.

I was violent with girls from the time I started dating. My first steady girlfriend was Terri. Once we were at a party and everyone was drinking. I wanted her to drink and have fun, but she didn't want to. We got into an argument in the car and I grabbed her by the throat and pushed her up against the door and told her she was going to do what I wanted her to do. When I let go of her, she slapped me. I slapped her back especially hard and got into a total rage. I punched the window and broke it and left her crying in the car.

The messages that I got growing up were that women should be submissive to men. The man had total say. I believed that if women crossed the line, you had to put them in their place. I grew up believing that women were to be used and so that's what I did.

I was nineteen when I met Cathy. She was seventeen. I had just entered the armed services. I didn't hit her until after we got married. After I had that marriage license, things changed. I felt like I owned her. After we were divorced, she told me that when we were living together I treated her like a queen, but as soon as we got married, I changed. I guess I felt, prior to marriage, that I could lose her, but once I had that piece of paper, she was mine.

Of all the women I physically abused, Cathy got the worst of it. I can remember having parties and getting extremely intoxicated. I would get into an argument with her, throw her around, and punch her in the face. She cooked, cleaned, and took care of the children. When I wanted sex, we had it and there was to be no flak about it. In some ways I'm surprised she stayed as long as she did.

One time when she was three months pregnant with my daughter she went to a high-school football game. She wasn't home when I thought she would be. I was in a total red rage and went looking for her. I came home and she was there. She was scared when she saw how mad I was and tried to leave. She screamed, "I'm not going to get beat up by you again!" I grabbed her and threw her fifteen feet; she landed on the couch. I went over to the couch and put my left hand on her throat and began backhanding her with my other hand numerous times. She lay on the couch crying and bleeding. Even though I felt bad for what I'd done to her, I thought she'd brought it on herself. I was convinced she was out looking for another guy. The way I saw it, she shouldn't have been gone so long and she should have been home with me, case closed. I really believed she asked for it.

Some years later I was up for a promotion at my job. Cathy had prepared a big meal that night with candles and everything because she knew we would find out about the promotion that day. She was all positive and in a really good mood. Well, I didn't get the promotion and was in a terrible mood when I got home. I took it out on her. I was mad because she had this meal all fixed up. I started yelling and screaming and then I threw the dinner off the table.

When I beat her, I'd feel very powerful. When I would see the terror in her eyes, I knew I had won. Sometimes, though, I would feel guilty. I would tell her how ashamed I was for what I was doing, that I would get help for my drinking. I would apologize. I would usually want to have sex after my violence, and she would agree. I thought it was because she loved me, but I think now she agreed to sex to pacify me.

Our neighbors out in California used to call me the green-eyed

monster, because I was always exploding in a jealous rage. Cathy is a
very pretty woman and I felt she got a kick out of men eyeing the way
she walked. I thought she flaunted her beauty and her body. I felt
since she hurt me by making me jealous, I would hurt her by being
violent. We were having a party one night and I became jealous of a
male friend of ours who was talking with Cathy. I'd been drinking a
lot and was doing a lot of PCP. I started to slap her up. I made a big
scene and told everyone to leave. That night, I destroyed the apartment. She left me after that incident.

Eight years after Cathy left me I was still hanging onto the relationship. I would call her, write her, and go to the town where she was living
and try to see her. I would beg her to take me back. One time, I got
very high on PCP, put a gun to my head, and told her I would kill myself
unless she took me back. I would tell Cathy that our daughter needed a
father in her life. I tried everything but she was through with me.

I married Gretchen two years later, after a very short courtship.
We moved to Duluth and remained married for seven years. My violence toward her was mostly grabbing her by the arms and pushing
her down. I think I only hit her once. I really didn't have to be very
violent with her, because she was submissive and I could make her
afraid by just yelling at her. I would give her a certain look and she
knew I was upset. In that marriage, I was the ultimate ruler. I don't
believe I was ever in love with her, but I stayed with her because it
was convenient.

One time, I came home really drunk and demanded she make me
a steak. I went into the kitchen and there were all these dirty dishes in
the sink and I flew into a rage. I started throwing the dishes at her
and then I hit her in the face with the back of my hand. I started
breaking everything in the house. It was Christmastime and I smashed
all the presents. The kids were watching this. I threw the Christmas
tree through the window. Our neighbor called the sheriff and they
brought me to the detox center for drunks.

Toward the end of this relationship, Gretchen and I got into an
argument about who was getting custody of our child. I punched her
several times in the face. She tried to leave but I was determined not
to let her take our daughter. Gretchen called the police. I attacked
the police officers and was charged with assault. The court ordered
me into outpatient treatment for my alcoholism and the Domestic
Abuse Intervention Project in Duluth for my violence.

While in treatment, I continued to drink. When I went into the
Domestic Abuse Intervention Project I was in total denial. I didn't feel
I needed any help and was very angry the court had ordered me into

counseling. But after several weeks, something touched me in the group and I realized I had a problem. The program was helpful for me because I heard the other men's stories and realized I wasn't alone. I started to see that the abuse was really wrong and that it was my responsibility to change. After completing the program and probation, I stayed on as a volunteer.

In my current relationship with Toni things are dramatically different. When there are problems, we sit down and talk about things and I explain how I feel. When we have conflicts today, I'm able to express my feelings and, perhaps more important, I listen to Toni rather than just flying off the handle. I still take time-outs. When I have visitation with my children from my past marriages, they don't see the anger and the abuse that they used to. I know they see the difference.

When I think back, I know I was dependent on women, emotionally, financially, and sexually. I felt I needed a female partner in my life to make me whole. I had very low self-esteem and a lack of love for myself. I'm not jealous with Toni like I was in past relationships. I'm more secure with myself.

I'm proud of where I'm at today, because I made the changes to stop drinking and stop the violence. I hope that in my family the abuse stops here. My parents never recognized the abuse. I got the help I needed because I got arrested and because I went through the programs. I'm dedicating myself to being a positive role model for my children and for other men.

I call myself a recovering abuser. I do something similar to the twelve-step program for alcoholics. I try to do positive things in my life, analyzing myself when I need to and associating with positive people. You have to get to know yourself and love yourself and then you can love others.

Using Intimidation to Control

Many men use physical violence infrequently but abuse women by resorting to other overt and covert behaviors, including intimidation. They learn how to intimidate women, other men, and their children. Some use body language. They glare, tower over their partners, or block their physical space. Some men slam down their fists, punch walls or doors, or throw things. Intimidating behavior is frightening; the person being intimidated is never sure if physical violence will follow.

Andy, who told his story in Chapter 1, said, "If we were at a party and my partner was talking to another man, I would just look at her and she would be at my side. No one knew what was going on. It was just a look or a crooked smile and she knew."

As Bernice explains, intimidation brings immediate fear:

> When my partner was angry at me, he would walk around me while he was talking or yelling so I never knew what to expect. I'd try to maintain eye contact with him because he had hit me in the back of the head before. He wouldn't necessarily have to be talking angrily but the fact that I had to turn around and watch him was very intimidating. He knew exactly what he was doing.

Getting what you want through intimidation or simply venting your anger in the house may be temporarily satisfying for you. You may get what you want at the time. However, if people you say you love are afraid of you, how can intimacy, trust, and caring exist? Because you have behaved like this for a long time you may be oblivious to your family's fear, but I assure you, your partner and your children are afraid.

In one of my groups, George was coming to terms with his past intimidating behavior. He did not want his family to be afraid of him. He acknowledged that his abuse affected his family, and he wanted to change.

George: Ever since I started coming to this group, I'm really becoming aware of how much fear I instilled in Holly and the kids. It doesn't feel very good to know they're still afraid of me.

Michael: That fear may be there for a while and you're going to have to be patient. You can't expect them just to forget what happened.

George: I know. But it bothers me. I can tell when I walk in the door that things change. I don't want them to be afraid of me anymore.

Michael: George, what are you like when you come home? Are you smiling and cheerful or angry and tense?

George: Well, I'm usually pretty tired. I have a stressful job and it takes a while for me to unwind. I wouldn't say I'm overly cheerful but I'm not always angry, either.

Michael: Well, when you're feeling a certain way, sometimes your body language projects that emotion. So if you're tense, your body language may project a message like "Stay *away* from me!" What do you think?

George: Well, it's certainly possible.

Michael: Are you willing to try something?

George: Sure.

Michael: For the next week, I want you to practice the following exercise. When you get home, take a forty-five-minute walk before you go into the house. As you walk, think positively about yourself and your life. Put the day out of your mind. Every time something from work enters your mind, push it out, and focus on something pleasant and enjoyable. Take deep breaths when you walk and try to relax. When you enter the house, be positive.

The next week, George reported to the group that he noticed a change. People in the house seemed less anxious. George was really surprised that after only one week of doing things like taking a walk, using positive self-talk, and making an effort to change his demeanor he achieved so many positive results.

Men who use intimidation, whether deliberately or not, need to become aware of how they respond to conflicts and problems that arise in the home. Self-monitoring and feedback from others may be necessary. If you are upset or in a bad mood, let your partner and children know that your mood has nothing to do with them. For example, you can calmly say, "I'm in a bad mood, it has nothing to do with you, and I need some time to be alone."

Sometimes men are not aware, or *choose* not to be aware, of how scary and intimidating they can be when they are angry. In a relationship in which there has been no abuse, anger is not so frightening. But partners and children who have been abused have vivid memories of violence, and anger will elicit fear in them even if violence does not follow.

Sometimes men in our groups will say that punching a wall or door is better than hitting their partners. This is true. But punching an inanimate object in your partner's presence can produce the same results as hitting her, which is why intimidating behavior may be considered domestic assault in a court of law. A punched wall or a thrown object may give your partner the impression that she is next.

Men who batter can use their voices to terrify and control. A common way that men intimidate is by shouting. Some get right into their partners' faces and yell. The purpose is obvious: most people are unnerved by it. As Lila told me, her husband's yelling was particularly frightening:

His foremost weapon was his voice. He had an extremely loud and deep voice. I remember one time when he was yelling at me, I could actually feel the sound waves hitting my body. It was extremely intimidating—like I was being slapped in the face with his voice. It was always hard to hear after he had one of those tirades.

If you are serious about changing, this kind of intimidation must stop. Monitor yourself by making a commitment not to shout, and to lower your voice during times of conflict.

If you are angry or upset, find another outlet to deal with your emotions. Talk with a friend, walk away from the situation that is upsetting you (see Chapter 6 on time-outs), and practice restraint. All of the men I interviewed for this book said they continue to take time-outs when they are angry. They also said they consistently need to monitor themselves. They have learned the importance of responding to conflict in a nonintimidating manner and they do what it takes to be nonviolent.

▨ **EXERCISE:** Stopping Intimidating Behavior

The following exercise is for those men who *want* to stop intimating family members. Think carefully about each step of the exercise and write your responses in your journal or notebook.

1. List several incidents when you used intimidation with a past or current partner.

_____

_____

Examples of physical intimidation:

Punched walls and doors, slammed tables, threw things. Destroyed property. Displayed weapons. Crowded her space. Hurt a pet.

Examples of intimidating body language:

Glared, stared, gave her angry looks, pointed, made a fist.

Examples of intimidating language:

Raised my voice, screamed. Gave her the silent treatment. Left a threatening note. Talked in a way I knew scared her.

2. Pick an incident from your list that most stands out in your mind.

Describe this incident in detail.

_____

_____

3. What was the purpose of your behavior? Describe what you were feeling and thinking.

_____

_____

4. What were the short-term and long-term impacts of your behavior?

Short-term impact:

_____

_____

Long-term impact:

_____

_____

5. Looking back at the incident, what could you have done differently in the same situation to avoid being intimidating, even if you were upset? If you are in a group, ask the group members or the counselor for ideas.

_____

_____

6. Practicing: If you are currently in a relationship, design a life-change plan to keep yourself from being intimidating with your partner or your children in the future. (A life-change plan is a simple but honest commitment to change something—a behavior, an attitude, your life.) If you are not in a relationship, identify other situations in which you become intimidating and make a similar life-change plan to change this behavior. If you are in a group, ask other group members or the counselor for ideas.

_____

_____

Examples:

Stay aware of my voice and talk in a nonthreatening manner. Stay aware of my body language. Leave if I sense anger and tenseness building. Allow her to express herself; don't get agitated or controlling. Do some stress-reduction exercises (walking, deep breathing, meditating, working out) before going home. Practice interacting without using gestures, glares, or raising my voice.

7. After several weeks of following your plan, write down the results of your actions in your journal or notebook.

The following is an example from Bill in one of my groups:

1. List several incidents when you used intimidation with a past or current partner.

Threw things, pounded on the table, screamed at my wife and kids.

2. Pick an incident from your list that most stands out in your mind. Describe this incident in detail.

Sometimes I get really angry if the house is in disarray, especially on the weekends when I'm home and I want to relax a little. I don't believe I should have to remind the kids to do things, and if I say anything to my wife Kathy, we end up arguing. One time the house was a mess—dirty dishes in the sink and stuff laying around, so I started pounding my fist on the kitchen table and went from room to room screaming at the kids. When Kathy tried to intervene, I came at her like I was going to hit her. I just stood there screaming and swearing at her for not getting on the kids.

3. What was the purpose of your behavior? Describe what you were feeling and thinking.

I wanted the house to be clean and orderly. I thought the kids were being disrespectful by not keeping the place clean. I also thought Kathy was enabling the kids' behavior by not doing more to enforce the rules. I felt disrespected and angry.

4. What were the short-term and long-term impacts of your behavior?

Short-term impact:

When I pounded on the table and started screaming, everyone was scared. The kids started picking things up and doing what I was demanding. Kathy tried to calm me down, but when I screamed at her, I'm sure she was afraid, because I've hit her for stupid things when I was upset.

Long-term impact:

We had planned on having a family dinner that night, but the whole day was ruined because of my outburst. Kathy wouldn't talk to me and the kids avoided me the rest of the day and that evening. On the weekends, I've noticed that the kids will try to make plans so they don't have to be at home, because of me.

5. Looking back at the incident, what could you have done differently in the same situation to avoid being intimidating, even if you were upset? If you are in a group, ask the group members or the counselor for ideas.

I could have waited for a time when I wasn't upset, talked with Kathy about how I was feeling, and then worked out a plan with her. After we agreed on a plan, we could have both talked to the kids. I could have taken a time-out when I was feeling agitated.

6. Practicing: If you are currently in a relationship, design a life-change plan to keep yourself from being intimidating with your partner or your children in the future.

Kathy and I did agree on some basic rules about keeping the house clean and how we would ensure that the kids did their fair share. We had a family meeting and the kids reluctantly went along with the plan. I've also tried to be aware of my agitation level, because even though the family agreed to things, I still think the kids should do more. I've taken time-outs and gone down to the neighborhood Y when I've gotten agitated. I haven't gotten upset with Kathy or the kids for several weeks, but they still seem nervous around me, especially on the weekends.

Bill did ask for help from the group. The group members thought Bill should have talked over his feelings and expectations about the house with Kathy when he wasn't upset. They thought that Bill and Kathy could have come up with an acceptable and workable plan, had a family meeting, and outlined some basic ground rules for the house.

The group also discussed that it was possible that Bill was over-reacting and that his expectations might be too high. Bill wasn't certain about this, but he said he was willing to think about it. Several group members gave similar examples of letting things build up and then "going off" on someone. The group thought Bill should have taken a time-out when he started getting agitated.

When Bill asked the group for suggestions, he was quite sincere in wanting to change an aspect of his life he found troubling. I remember him saying to the group that he truly didn't want his family to be afraid of him anymore. He also thought Kathy shouldn't be fearful anymore because he was going to his groups.

Change takes time. Each family member's perception of whether you have actually changed will vary. You must give people time to observe your behavior—it's only when your family begins to feel safe that trust can be restored. The fact that Bill stopped pounding the table and screaming about the house being in disarray will not erase his family's memories of those intimidating times. He needs to be patient.

This example is just one idea for designing a life-change plan. If you have battered, you probably have many ways of intimidating. Some men have said they like having the power and "respect" in their households, and that intimidation is a means to that end. But at what cost? Do you really want your partner and children to be fearful of you? Do you want your family to walk on eggshells whenever you're home?

Using Threats

Sometimes men who batter threaten further violence. Women who have been beaten in the past obviously take these threats seriously. Several men in our groups have said that their partners know they wouldn't actually do what they threatened to do. But how can their partners be sure? And if the men have been violent in the past, why wouldn't their partners think the threats were real? Why did the men make threats in the first place?

Threats are used to elicit a response or to get your way. Whether you intend to carry out the threat or not, your partner has a reason to be afraid. Threats are a form of violence.

Some men threaten to take away or gain custody of the children. They know women feel particularly vulnerable in this area, and they choose to exploit this vulnerability. Other men threaten to harm themselves. In one of our groups, Al discussed his threat to commit suicide.

Al: I don't know why Beverly put that stuff about me wanting to commit suicide in the court affidavit. She knows I would never do something like that.

Michael: How would she know that for sure?

Al: She knows.

Michael: In the statement, it said you took the gun from the basement, went upstairs, and told her that you were going to kill yourself, and then you left. Why would you make those threats?

Al: Well, she had been real cold to me after I hit her. You know, real unforgiving. I thought maybe the threat of losing me would shake her up a little and things would change. It was a stupid thing to do, but she knew I'd never really kill myself.

Many men threaten suicide, usually when they think they are losing their relationships. A man threatening suicide may believe his partner will rethink her decision and stay with him. But destructive relationships are rarely saved by threats, and his intimidation may only prolong and intensify the breakup.

▧ **EXERCISE:** Stopping Threatening Behavior

The following exercise is for those men who *want* to stop threatening their partners. Think carefully about each step of the exercise and write your responses in your journal or notebook.

1. List several incidents when you used threatening behavior with a past or current partner.

_____

_____

Examples of threats:

Threatened to leave. Told her I'd hurt her, family members, the children, her friends, pets. Browbeat her when she talked of leaving the relationship. Threatened to take all the money. Threatened to expose something personal to family, friends, or her coworkers.

Examples of pressure:

Forced her to drop charges. Didn't show up at the hearing. Pressured her to give up friendships. Pressured her to do illegal things.

Examples of warnings:

Told her I'd kill myself if she left. Threatened to take the children. Threatened to report her to welfare or child protection services. Threatened to call her probation officer.

2. Pick an incident from your list that most stands out in your mind. Describe this incident in detail.

_____

_____

3. What was the purpose of your behavior? Describe what you were feeling and thinking.

_____

_____

4. What were the short-term and long-term impacts of your behavior?

Short-term impact:

_____

_____

Long-term impact:

_____

_____

5. Looking back at the incident, what could you have done differently in the same situation to avoid being threatening, even if you were upset? If you are in a group, ask the group members or the counselor for ideas.

_____

_____

6. Practicing: If you are currently in a relationship, design a life-change plan to keep yourself from being threatening with your partner.

_____

_____

Examples:

Be aware of threatening comments. Accept the legal consequences for my violent behavior, with the knowledge that good things will ultimately happen. If I'm feeling suicidal, I'll get help—I can work through these problems. Recognize that threats will be met by resistance and in the long run won't work. Talk to group members about feelings and issues. Commit to not pressuring her in any way.

A note to women

You *should* take all threats seriously. If your partner is threatening you in any way, get advice from a battered women's program in your area. You may need to use the legal system or find a shelter to protect yourself. A man who is threatening violence or suicide or threatening to take the children is dangerous and his behavior is illegal.

Blocking Her Freedom to Decide

In battering relationships, men often attempt to isolate their partners. Either through sabotage, manipulation, or demand, men curtail women's relationships with particular friends or family members. Typically, a man who batters either demands an end to relationships he finds threatening or puts up obstacles that make it difficult for his partner to associate with people he doesn't like. If she resists his demands, his behavior often escalates into violence. In Bernice's case, her partner cut off her relationships with friends for a specific reason:

> When we first started dating, I had a lot of friends and my partner seemed okay with that. But things changed, especially when the physical violence intensified. He started to devalue my friends. If a friend of mine gave me clothing as a Christmas present, he would use it as a rag to wash the car. He'd say, "I don't know why you want to hang around her, she ain't no good."
>
> He wanted the power to make me feel bad and to make me feel good. So my having friendships was a threat. He feared them because they could make me feel better and he wanted that exclusively.

For Cassie, her partner wanted her to better herself, but only up to a point:

> My partner encouraged me to go back to school and I did. But as I got close to graduating from college he made things very difficult. I don't think he ever thought I'd get to that point, so when I did he

said I was neglecting the house and the kids. It was literally a fight for me to get out the door to attend my classes.

After I graduated, he encouraged me to get a job. He'd say, "You're a smart woman, you've got a degree, and you can get a good job." So I got a job, but I had to start at the bottom. Everything was okay and he was supportive until I started to work my way up the ladder. He got real threatened by the people I worked with. And I think he felt inadequate because I was making more money than him. That's when the beatings started getting real bad. I think he felt less of a man.

Why does a man who batters try to inhibit his partner's relationships with others? Here are three reasons:

First, he may be afraid his partner's friends or family members will give her information or support that will help her get out of the abusive relationship. He is usually aware of the pain he is causing and knows the abuse will make her think about leaving. He identifies her friends as a bad influence because he suspects them of plotting with his partner to help her leave.

Second, he may be, and often is, very jealous of others—especially other men. If his partner goes out with friends, he fears she is seeking the company of another man. He is insecure, and because of his past treatment of her, his insecurity about the relationship increases. He asks himself, "Why would she want to stay with me after the way I've treated her?" He is also particularly suspicious of divorced or single women because they are independent and he fears they will give his partner ideas about leaving.

Third, he may believe his partner does not need friends and needs only limited contact with her family. "Anything she needs emotionally or intellectually she can get from me," he thinks. He wants her world to revolve around him, and by keeping her isolated he encourages her dependence on him.

In one of our groups, we discussed isolating behavior and some of the beliefs and expectations men have when they enter a relationship:

Michael: Allen, you were talking last week about how you told Stephanie not to associate with a certain friend she'd known since childhood. Do you believe men have the right to decide who their partners are friends with?

Allen: I didn't decide anything. We've been having this argument for a long time and I think she knows I'm right. Kate, this friend of hers, is in the bars constantly, and she has a reputation. I think as her husband I have some say in this. After we talked, she agreed with me so it wasn't like I forced her.

Michael: What do the rest of you think? Should Allen have a say in who his partner can be friends with?

Bob: I think both people in a relationship have a right. My wife criticizes my friends all the time.

Toby: Yeah, if his wife's friend is loose it reflects badly on him.

Michael: So when you marry you have the right to give the thumbs-up or thumbs-down to your partner's friends if you think it reflects badly on you? The marriage contract gives you that authority?

Bob: There has to be compromise and give-and-take in the relationship. And I think if your partner makes a bad decision, you have an obligation to protect her.

Toby: I think it's more an act out of mutual consideration than an authority or control thing.

Michael: It seems very controlling to me. I wouldn't like my partner to have that power over my friendship decisions and I don't believe I have the right to interfere in hers.

We spent the entire session discussing this issue, with no resolution. Most but not all of the men believed it was perfectly acceptable to tell their partners not to associate with certain people. They were either protecting their partners or protecting their reputations. Most believed this was a marital responsibility. The next week we took up the theme again, and I asked Allen to participate in a role play with me. I would play him and he would play his wife, Stephanie. He reluctantly agreed.

Stephanie [Allen]: Allen, I really don't think you're being fair about Kate. Yes, she's divorced, and yes, she dates men, but so what?

Allen [Michael]: She's a bad influence. I don't trust her.

Stephanie: It sounds like you don't trust me.

Allen: I know what it's like when you're with those women. How do I know you won't get tempted being with her, listening to the things she's saying to you and getting worked up? And I know she thinks I'm an asshole.

Stephanie: We just have a drink and talk.

Allen: I told you: I don't trust her and I don't want you to see her anymore! No more discussion!

I ended the role play and asked for feedback from the group.

Bob: Well, if it happened that way, I wouldn't think it would be fair.

Michael: Why?

Bob: She seemed like she was telling the truth.

Others nodded in agreement.

Michael: But earlier you guys said he had the right to decide what friends she could have if he thought they were a bad influence. Allen, how did it feel being in that position?

Allen: Not good. I didn't mind it so much until you ended it the way you did.

Michael: What did that feel like?

Allen: I felt kinda like a kid.

Accepting your partner's autonomy and independence requires more than just trust. How can you trust your partner if you assume a position in the relationship that gives you the power to decide fundamental issues in her life?

If you have battered and are still in your relationship, remember that healing takes time—and sometimes never happens. Back off. Let her have her own life and allow her the time to sort things out. Trying to isolate her or continuing to isolate her may give you desired results in the short-term, but ultimately you will drive her away.

Many of the men I interviewed for this book said that understanding why they had isolated their partners in the past was important for their future relationships. They needed to let go and stop controlling their partners' lives. They had to trust. Perhaps what is more important, they needed to get to a place in which they were truly supportive of their partners' aspirations. Today they encourage their partners to have friendships. They support their partners' desires to go back to school, change jobs or get a job, take a class, or pursue other activities that make their lives more whole. As their partners' lives become more satisfying, their relationships improve.

From time to time these men probably feel quite threatened.

Change can be scary. But as they practice what they have learned, they begin to respond differently. Men who make thorough changes in their relationships know that attempts to control are self-defeating. People *want* to have their own lives. People *need* space to grow independently of each other. Then they can support each other's goals and aspirations, because their union is based on love, concern for each other's happiness, and trust in the relationship.

▨ **EXERCISE:** Stopping Isolating Behavior

The following exercise is for those men who *want* to stop using isolating behavior. Think carefully about each step of the exercise and write your responses in your journal or notebook.

1. List several incidents when you used isolating behavior with a past or current partner.

Examples of checking up on her:

Made her tell me what she did and who she talked to. Listened to her phone conversations and read her mail. Accused her of doing things behind my back. Called her workplace, friends, and family to monitor her activities. Questioned her when she came home. Demanded to know where she'd been when she was late.

Examples of trying to stop her from doing something:

Discouraged her from going to school. Tried to persuade her not to change jobs. Got jealous when she worked late or spent time with work friends. Sabotaged her involvement in community groups, counseling, and women's groups. Went to her workplace when I wasn't expected.

Examples of interfering with her social life:

Made it difficult for her to have friends I didn't approve of. Wouldn't let her have male friends. Wouldn't let her go to parties or functions without me. Acted jealous in public and in private. Accused her of having affairs or flirting. Undermined family social activities. Got into fights before a social activity so she'd be too upset to go. Wasn't available to take care of the children, so she couldn't leave. Disabled the car. Didn't have a telephone; didn't share the car. Purposely moved to an isolated area.

2. Pick an incident from your list that most stands out in your mind. Describe this incident in detail.

_____

_____

3. What was the purpose of your behavior? Describe what you were feeling and thinking.

_____

_____

4. What were the short-term and long-term impacts of your behavior?

Short-term impact:

_____

_____

Long-term impact:

_____

_____

5. Looking back at the incident, what could you have done differently in the same situation to avoid controlling or isolating your partner, even though you might have been jealous or feeling insecure? If you are in a group, ask the group members or the counselor for ideas.

_____

_____

6. Practicing: If you are currently in a relationship, design a life-change plan to change the isolating behavior.

_____

_____

Examples (you should list specifics):

Support her goals; respect her right to chose her own friends; avoid sabotaging her plans; keep negative thoughts about her choices to myself; talk with group members or a counselor about feelings of jealousy; avoid undermining social events, checking up on her, or trying to control her life.

Using the Children to Get to Her

Unfortunately, many men resort to using their children as weapons against their current or ex-partners. A man may belittle and undermine his partner in front of the children. He may threaten to take the children away or gain custody by claiming his partner is an unfit mother. Sometimes he threatens the children's lives; sometimes he carries out the threats.

Not all men who have battered use their children as weapons, and many men are loving and devoted fathers. Yet all too often, because of the bitterness of the failed relationship or as a tactic to get what they want, men make custody threats. Some do it under the guise of love for their children, and others base it on their rights as fathers.

For most women, the thought of losing their children is extremely distressing. Men who batter have told me they exploited these fears in order to get their partners to drop assault charges or restraining orders. Many women have told me they stayed in abusive relationships rather than risk losing their children.

As Bernice explains, the threat of losing her children was powerful and made her stay—but the effect on her children was not positive:

> I think my children lost confidence in me because I stayed in an abusive relationship. I think they felt they couldn't trust me to protect them since I couldn't protect myself.
>
> The worst thing was that when I threatened to leave him, he said he would kill one of my kids if I left and I believed him. I stayed longer than I should have because of those threats.

Cassie knows that what her children saw at an early age has long-term implications.

> My kids saw the violence from the very beginning. I was breast-feeding one of my kids and my partner and I got into an argument. He punched me in the nose and blood was flowing all over and my child was screaming.
>
> I see the impact of the violence on my children all the time. When they get into arguments with each other they get violent. They had to learn that stuff somewhere. My oldest boy never takes responsibility for any of his actions. I know his exposure to his father's constant denial and blame has affected him.

If you have battered, consider the effect your violence has had on your children. The impact of children experiencing family violence in the home is well documented. Exposure to domestic violence increases the risks in children of developing attitudes of acceptance of aggression as a norm, especially in boys.[15] While you may not be directly abusive to your children, their exposure to your violence has a profound effect. Children witnessing domestic assault usually develop some behavioral and health problems, depending on the level of violence they observe. They may have difficulty concentrating in school, become disruptive, or get into fights. Other children from abusive situations have a difficult time trusting people and establishing relationships. Some children blame their mothers for "letting" the violence occur, while others assume responsibility for the violence themselves. They become confused and feel guilty.[16]

As Jim stated at the start of this chapter, the violence he witnessed seemed normal. He tried intervening to stop it, failed, and then learned to adapt. Unfortunately, he then modeled to his children the very behavior he had witnessed.

Children are influenced not only by the violence they observe, but also by the breakup of the family. Their stress level increases as they observe the continued hostility between their parents. And they are often put squarely in the middle as their parents struggle, often in court, over custody and visitation.

If your relationship has ended or is ending, try to be as fair and reasonable as possible with your ex-partner. If you are thinking of asking for custody of your children, think also about your motives. Are you seeking custody as revenge on your partner or as a way of maintaining some control over her life? Do you want the responsibility of raising your children? Can you fulfill it? Would it be in *the children's* best interests to live with you—or with their mother?

The following discussion about custody took place in one of our groups:

Grant: Angela let me know that she's filing for divorce. I told her fine, but I'm going for custody.

Maryann: Are you going to seek joint custody or full custody?

Grant: Full custody, man.

Maryann: You're working full-time, right?

Grant: Yeah, but she's working too. I'll find a way to manage. I think a man can be just as good a parent as a woman.

Maryann: I think men can be wonderful parents. I'm curious, though, do you know where Angela is going to live?

Grant: Well, her plans are to live with her mother for a while. I guess her mother will take care of the kids while she's working.

Maryann: I'm asking these questions because I wonder whether you've been thinking about what would be best for the children. Your children have been through a lot. I'm just wondering if you've considered what would be the most supportive environment for the kids.

Grant: Well, in some ways it would be better for them to be at their grandmother's house. She really loves them and it would be better than day care. But if Angela gets custody, pretty soon they won't even know they have a father. She'll meet some guy and then he'll be in their lives.

Maryann: Not having full custody doesn't mean you give up being their father. You have to decide what kind of father you want to be, how you want to spend your time with your children and, ultimately, what is best for the kids.

Even if you have no custodial relationship, a thousand and one other things can make you a loving and responsible parent. You can take your children to a sporting event, museum, or stage play. You can provide encouragement and participate in their activities such as music, scouting, or softball. You can take them to special places: a park in the city, or perhaps camping in the country. You can be supportive of your children and help them resolve problems in their lives. Get involved in their schools. Show your love, and be the kind of caring father who makes a difference in his children's lives.

Whether you or your ex-partner has custody, don't make the children suffer for the problems in your relationship. You may be angry or hurt but you don't have to poison your children. Custody and visitation are often difficult issues, but you and your partner can make decisions that are in the best interests of your children.

In one of our groups, John and I had the following interchange about using the children in a manipulative way during visitation:

Michael: John, you said last week that your ex-wife was angry with you because of things you said to the kids when you had visitation. Do you understand why she was angry?

John: I know that last week I was defending my questioning of the children. I know that puts them in the middle. But I still don't want my children exposed to an unhealthy environment. I mean, I think any of the men here would be pissed if their kid's mother was having men overnight. What kind of example is that for the kids?

Michael: It sounds like you're still defending what you did.

John: I know I shouldn't have used the kids that way, but I still believe I have the right to be concerned. I'm not the only guilty one here. The kids tell me the rotten things she says about me.

John's ex-wife Claudia called me about these incidents. She said John repeatedly asked the kids questions about her, and they felt they were being interrogated every time he had visitation. She said he implied to them that she was immoral because she had a boyfriend, and that it was her fault the relationship ended. She also said her oldest boy was always hostile toward her after spending time with his father.

Obviously, John and Claudia's children are emotionally affected by this behavior. It's true that you can't keep things from your kids. You can't hide what is happening in your relationship. However, you should not attempt to use them as allies against their other parent. When John questions his children, they feel guilty if they give too much information and fear what their father will say about their mother. They may try not to take sides or internalize the negative comments that are made, but this is a terribly unfair position in which to put children. The scene gets played out in various ways in far too many divorced families.

■ EXERCISE: The Children in Your Life

The following exercise is for those men who *want* to stop using the children as a way to get back at their partners or former partners. It will also help men commit to being better dads. Think carefully about each step of the exercise and write your responses in your journal or notebook. Skip this exercise if you don't have children.

1. List several incidents when you used the children to get back at a past or current partner. Or list incidents when you were abusive to your partner while the children were present.

_____

_____

Examples of making your partner feel guilty:

Told her she was a bad, unfit, and incompetent mother. Threatened to report her to child protection services. Compared her to other women who I think have better parenting skills.

Examples of using the children:

Told the children that their mother is bad, amoral, and the cause of the relationship ending. Used the children to relay messages to their mother. Tried to obtain information from the children about their mother's activities, especially when she was dating. Told the children they couldn't do something they wanted to do because of their mother.

Examples of making threats:

Threatened to get custody. Threatened to take the children and leave the state. Threatened to harm the children.

Examples of abuse in front of the children:

Was violent, threatening, and intimidating while the children were present. Called her names and put her down while the children were in the house. Criticized her parenting skills in front of the children.

2. Pick an incident from your list that most stands out in your mind. Describe this incident in detail.

_____

_____

3. What was the purpose of your behavior? Describe what you were feeling and thinking.

_____

_____

4. What were the short-term and long-term impacts of your behavior?

Short-term impact:

_____

_____

Long-term impact:

_____

_____

5. Looking back at the incident, what could you have done differently in the same situation to avoid involving the children, even if you were angry with your partner or former partner? If you are in a group, ask the group members or the counselor for ideas.

---

6. Practicing: If you are currently in a relationship, design a life-change plan to keep yourself from using the children against your partner or former partner in the future, and develop a personal commitment to become a better dad.

Examples:

I'll avoid arguing when the children are present, telling the children negative things about their mother, and harassing their mother when I'm picking up or dropping off the children from visitation. I'll be a positive role model, do more things and spend quality time with the children, and share parental responsibilities.

Regardless of the anger and resentment you may feel toward your ex-partner, think about the effect your actions and words could have on your children. Be honest with them, but don't abuse their trust. Your children are also victims of the situation. Yet, they are resilient and will heal if you make a commitment to put more care and effort into your relationship with them. Be a good *father*. Keep your issues with your ex-partner separate—and away—from your children.

The Pain of Emotional Abuse

In order to thoroughly control, you have to tame the spirit.

BELL HOOKS

I'm sure you can remember a time from childhood when a parent, teacher, or sibling put you down in some way. If you remember that incident, you can probably still feel the hurt. If someone said you were stupid, you may have questioned your abilities. If someone said you were no good, perhaps your self-esteem was diminished. We are all sensitive to the opinions others have of us.

Both men and women can be emotionally abusive. Even in the healthiest relationships, people occasionally reach down into their personal bags of known remembrances, past disagreements, and unresolved issues, and fling hurtful comments at their partners. Usually when we do this we're reacting defensively to feeling hurt ourselves; one partner may inadvertently say something hurtful and the other responds in kind. However, in healthy relationships, partners usually don't make hurtful or shaming comments on purpose, and if it does happen, the person who made the comment often acknowledges that the put-down or remark was wrong. There's usually some accountability, honest explanation, and apology for what was said. The confrontation may have been painful, but probably not destructive.

Emotional abuse within the context of battering takes on an entirely different dimension. In the arsenal of battering, emotional abuse is a powerful psychological weapon designed to cause pain, depersonalize the victim, and increase power for the batterer. Men who batter almost always make dehumanizing comments before assaulting their partners. It is easier to rationalize your behavior when you are negatively labeling the person you are hurting. When you call a woman a bitch or a slut you have reduced her standing as a human being entitled to consideration and respect.

As Bernice explains, emotional abuse usually accompanies physical violence:

> I hated being called a bitch. I'd tell him, "I'm not a bitch; a bitch is a female dog." One time during a bad assault he made me get down on all fours. He said, "See, you *are* a bitch." He never totally broke my spirit despite the things he said and did, although, if I'd stayed with him, he probably would have.

In Cassie's relationship, she started believing the things her partner was saying:

> I believed the things he told me. He told me I was ignorant and incompetent. When I first got my job, I thought these people who hired me must not realize I'm incompetent. And when he would tell me that no judge would give me custody of the children because I was a bad mother, I believed him.
>
> When we were intimate, I would tell him personal things. But I always regretted sharing them because he would use them against me. It was almost like he was recording those conversations and waiting for the appropriate time to use them. His name-calling was always hurtful and made me feel less than a person.

Language is a prime tool of emotional abuse. What happens when people are called "niggers," "dirty Jews," "savages," or "cunts"? What does it do to our psyche? Not only do we feel direct, incalculable emotional pain, we also internalize the abuse—the victim begins to believe what is being said.

Paulo Freire wrote: "Self-depreciation is a characteristic of the oppressed, which derives from the internalization of the opinions the oppressors hold of them."[17] In other words, oppressed people feel they are worthless or undeserving because they accept the hostile opinions of their oppressors as true statements. How does this relate to the impact of emotional abuse on women who are battered? I would like to try to illustrate what I think Freire meant by giving you an example from my life.

I grew up in a community that had its share of anti-Semitism. As a young Jewish boy in a primarily Christian neighborhood, I heard the taunts of other children as they called me "kike," "Christ killer," and "dirty Jew." These children did not make up those words; they heard them at home and in church. Whoever said "Sticks and stones may break my bones but names will never hurt me" was wrong. Those derogatory names made me feel that I was a bad person, that I did not belong in "their" neighborhood, and that there was something wrong with being Jewish.

My mother encouraged us to watch films about the Holocaust. These films show the ghastly details of the extermination camps in Europe. She wanted us to know and be aware of this history. The humiliation, destruction, and confiscation of property, the yellow star, the beatings, cattle cars, gas chambers, and ovens all became images etched in my mind. Why were these people—my people—so despised that something like this could have happened? At my young age, I couldn't comprehend.

During the Christmas season, I felt utterly isolated. Every year our school put on the traditional Christmas program. The school choirs sang religious songs. In junior high, the entire student body attended the program—except for a few Jewish students who were forced to sit in the principal's office because our parents would not permit us to go. The office was enclosed in glass, and as other students walked by on their way to the auditorium they all could see us, the outcasts, sitting in the office. Their taunts and my embarrassment made me resent being different and, of course, resent my Jewishness.

As I got older, I refused to acknowledge that I was Jewish. If someone made an anti-Semitic remark, I pretended I hadn't heard it. I hated being a Jew.

I learned that Jews were hated because of their refusal to accept Christianity. But they were also hated because, throughout history, when no quotas restricted Jews from certain occupations, they held powerful positions in the sciences, medicine, education, law, and government. During times of economic or political upheaval they were often targets for abuse from the few people in power as well as the many out of power. Politically, people on the left and the right assumed Jews were either international bankers or Communist conspirators or a combination of the two.

My hatred of myself as a Jew began to consume me. I left the United States in 1973 and, ironically, moved to Germany, where I lived for almost a year. I remember driving down the *autobahn* (German freeway) and seeing a sign that read "Dachau—Next Right." I never stopped at the concentration camp where hundreds of thousands of my people perished in the ovens and gas chambers. Why? Because, as Freire said, I had internalized the opinions that anti-Semites had of me. I did not want to be associated with "those people." This form of self-hatred, based on what I had experienced in my youth, stayed with me for a long time.

I began to change when I came back to the United States. I read books and reflected on this subject and realized other Jews shared similar experiences. When I started working in the domestic violence field, I found some interesting parallels between my denial and lack of self-esteem and the feelings of women who had been emotionally abused.

As Maria explained in our women's group, emotional abuse can have a lasting effect:

> My partner would have this look on his face and say things like, "You're nothing but an ugly cunt—no one would ever want you." If I screwed up, he'd say things like, "You stupid bitch, you can't do anything right." At first, I was shocked when he'd say these things. I would cry and usually he would feel bad and apologize. But living with that constant emotional abuse destroyed my self-esteem.

In the domestic violence programs I have been involved with, we attempt to contact the partners of men in our groups. In almost all the interviews we have with these women, I hear repeatedly how the victim's self-image has been damaged, not only by the physical abuse but also by the continued emotional abuse.

Most of the men in our groups admitted that, when angry, they would make the one comment or put-down they knew would hurt their partners the most. Frank explained that the emotional abuse he used was cruel, but at the time he felt justified:

> I was always into my jealousy stuff with Leila. Whenever she came home I would really give her the third degree about where she'd been and who she was with. If I didn't like the response or didn't believe her, I'd grab her by the hair and say, "You fuckin' slut, you goddamn whore!" I'd call her sexual names because I knew that hurt her. I was so jealous at that time. I thought, if she hurts me then I'll hurt her back.

Name-calling and put-downs are designed to hurt. They eventually chisel away the spirit and erode self-concept. Much like my experience of self-hatred at being Jewish, many women who are battered begin to believe, or internalize, their abusive partners' opinions of them. Many women indicated that they started believing, or at least doubting themselves because of the terrible things their partners were saying about them. "Why would he say these things if they weren't true?" some of them thought. They began to believe they were bad mothers or inadequate wives. They questioned their physical appearance. They questioned their abilities and competence.

The combination of name-calling and violence is very powerful. For a man who batters, name-calling and put-downs are often designed to destroy the independence and spirit of the person he was once attracted to, because those qualities are now threatening. They are threatening because he needs his partner to be dependent on him. If he can make her feel ugly, stupid, or incompetent, she begins to have doubts about herself and her worthiness. With low self-esteem, she may cease to resist the abusive attacks. Resigning herself to the control of an abusive partner becomes her reality.

For some, the kind of disparaging name-calling or put-downs described here do not, or did not, occur in their relationships. Yet, I think it is a rare person who has not said something in anger that he or she wished had not been said.

Throughout this book, I talk about the long healing process many women must go through after being abused and why, if you are still with the partner you have abused, you need to be patient. I hope an increased understanding of the impact of emotional abuse will not only increase your empathy, but act as a reminder of how painful words can be. That old saying, "You can't take the words back," is true.

■ **EXERCISE:** Stopping Emotionally Abusive Behavior

The following exercise is for those men who *want* to stop using emotional abuse. Think carefully about each step of the exercise and write your responses in your journal or notebook.

1. List several incidents when you were emotionally abusive with a past or current partner.

_____

_____

Examples of name-calling:

Called her derogatory names with sexual connotations (slut, cunt...) Called her names that made her feel bad about her body (ugly, fat...).

Examples of put-downs:

Told her she was stupid, incompetent, lazy, a bad mother, a bad lover, and that no one else would ever want her. Said, "I must have been crazy to marry you," and "Can't you do anything right?" Said negative things; humiliated her in front of the children, friends, coworkers, family.

Examples of making her feel guilty and degrading her:

Blamed her when the kids did something wrong, and for financial problems and arguments. When sex wasn't good made accusations and disparaging comments about her body and lovemaking ability. Threw food at her; made her clean up a mess. Played mind games; insinuated that she's mentally ill.

2. Pick an incident from your list that most stands out in your mind. Describe this incident in detail.

_____

_____

3. What was the purpose of your behavior? Describe what you were feeling and thinking.

_____

_____

4. What were the short-term and long-term impacts of your behavior?

Short-term impact:

_____

_____

Long-term impact:

_____

_____

5. Looking back at the incident, what could you have done differently in the same situation to avoid being emotionally abusive, even if you were angry, defensive, hurt, or felt rejected in some way? If you are in a group, ask the group members or the counselor for ideas.

_____

_____

6. Practicing: If you are currently in a relationship, design a life-change plan to keep yourself from being emotionally abusive in the future. If you are in a group, ask the group members or counselor for ideas.

_____

_____

Examples:

If I'm angry at her, I won't call her names or use put-downs. I will listen to her in a nonjudgmental manner. I won't blame or criticize her if things go wrong, or if she makes a mistake. I will use positive self-talk and take time-outs when I'm agitated or angry. I will talk to my group members and counselor about my plan to eliminate emotional abuse in my relationship.

Understanding and Stopping Battering

You have learned in this chapter that domestic abuse is more than physical and sexual violence. The Duluth Domestic Abuse Intervention Project created the Power and Control Wheel (page 89) to illustrate the abusive behaviors used by batterers to silence, scare, manipulate, confuse, and control their partners. If you have difficulty reading the wheel, see the text reproduced in the Appendix.

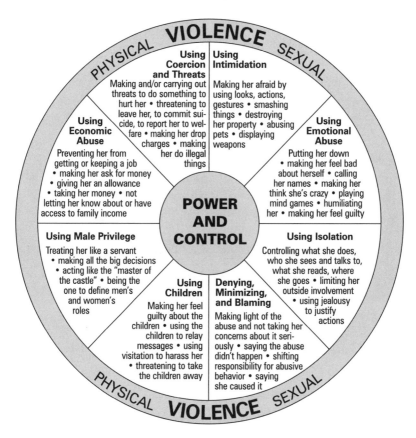

You might be asking, "Is everything I do in my life considered abusive?" Of course not. But like a basketball player trying new moves and plays to get to the basket, a man who batters purposely and reflexively shifts his behaviors to control or influence his partner. The more you know about what and why you do what you do, the easier it will become to catch yourself before you say or do something abusive.

Men who batter frequently try to minimize their conduct with comments such as, "I only hit her once." That may be true. But whether you hit your partner one time or fifty times, once violence has been introduced into your relationship, everything changes. The other behaviors on the Power and Control Wheel take on added significance because your partner never knows when violence may be used again, despite your assurances. Many men fail to recognize the power and impact that the abusive acts identified on the Power and Control Wheel have on their partners; in our program we emphasize that you are still battering unless you stop using *all* these behaviors.

■ EXERCISE: Weekly Inventory

If you are currently in a relationship, take an honest inventory on a weekly basis to monitor how you may still be using abusive behavior. Refer to the Power and Control Wheel as well as the lists you have generated from already completed exercises. You can write your responses in your journal or simply think about them.

1. List any abusive behavior you used in the past week.

_____

_____

2. What was the purpose of your behavior?

_____

_____

3. How could you have handled the situation differently?

_____

_____

If you are in a relationship now or are contemplating getting involved with someone, pay attention to your reactions to your partner, especially when you are having conflicts. Catch and stop yourself every time you start using abusive behavior to hurt, control, or punish your partner. Seek constructive alternatives. Self-control and making personal decisions about how you will act are your responsibility and yours alone.

5

Getting Past Denial

Sid's Story — Taking Responsibility — Minimizing Violence —
Self-Defense or Retaliation? — Letting Go of Blame —
Alcohol, Drugs, and Violence — Anger

Self-pity in its early stages is as snug as a feather mattress.
Only when it hardens does it become uncomfortable.

MAYA ANGELOU

In this chapter you will read about how men avoid taking responsibility for their abusive behaviors. You will read how hard it is for some men to see the difference between self-defense and retaliation, and how they minimize their violence. You will also read why some men blame their partners or alcohol for their violence and why all men should dispel the myth that anger is a causal factor in domestic abuse.

In the following story, Sid talks about how he justified his violent behavior. He also talks about the steps he took to change his perceptions of domestic abuse and how he currently lives his life.

Sid's Story

Sid, aged forty-two, is a musician and is just completing his law degree. He grew up in Owatonna, a small town in southern Minnesota, and now lives in Minneapolis. He has been public about his past because he wants other men to change. He talked about his battering on the *Phil Donahue Show* and currently conducts groups for abusive men in the Minneapolis/St. Paul area.

I grew up in a middle-class environment in a small town. My father was a plumber and my mother was a homemaker. I was overweight as a youth and consequently my experience with girls was limited. I had an abusive experience with my first girlfriend. She wanted to break up with me and I was really angry. I called her up and started swearing at her and her dad was listening on the other line. She ended up getting grounded.

Later that month, my buddies and I went to a dance. I heard through the grapevine that my ex-girlfriend was pissed at me because I had gotten her grounded and that she was going to tell me off and slap me at this dance. I remember talking to my friends about how I was going to hit her back, and, of course, they encouraged me not to take any shit from no girl! Well, sure enough she confronted me and slapped me. I punched her so hard that she went flying and her glasses went flying. I felt really exhilarated. My buddies came up and slapped me on the back. I got total reinforcement.

Even though I felt powerful and good when I hit my girlfriend, I also felt ambivalent about what I had done. I didn't really want to hurt her, but felt an incredible amount of pressure to protect my honor. I just couldn't let a girl hit me without hitting back.

It was the early 1970s when I married Sharon. We had a child the first year of our marriage. My violence started with me breaking things, smashing chairs, putting my fist through walls, and screaming. I could get her to stop arguing by screaming at her. She would shut up immediately.

This was the "peace and love" era of the sixties and seventies and I didn't feel I had to be accountable to anyone. You know, you do your thing and I'll do mine. Even though we had a child together, I didn't feel very responsible.

I came home one night and Sharon confronted me about not letting her know where I was. I told her I'd been out with my friends and she said I was stupid. I told her not to call me stupid and she called me stupid again. She kept calling me stupid and I told her if she said it again she was going to get it. She was lying on the bed on her stomach and repeated that I was stupid and I punched her in the middle of her back with all my might. She doubled up and screamed with this incredible pain. I remember her picking up the baby and sitting in a chair, sobbing uncontrollably.

We were married for seven years, and one day she came home with a police officer and took her stuff. We divorced shortly afterward.

I met Rhonda and we started dating. We lived in a small town close to Minneapolis. The violence began right away. She said something that embarrassed me at a party. When we were driving home, I told her I didn't like what she said. She said I was overreacting and I backhanded her across the face. She was crying all the way home. We got to my apartment and by then she had assumed total responsibility for what happened. She was apologizing and I wasn't budging. I wouldn't accept her apologies, and even though I wasn't angry anymore, I was getting off on her groveling and the pure power of the situation.

The violence would happen every couple of months. On one occasion, I came to her apartment and she was typing something for her college class. I wanted to talk but she told me she needed to finish her work. I started belittling her for going to school and demanded that she talk to me. When she got mad and told me to leave, I became enraged at the rejection. I pushed her over a chair and threw her around the kitchen, slapping and punching her and throwing things. A guy from the downstairs apartment came up to see what was going on and he and I started fighting. I finally left.

The violence got more intense when she wanted to get out of the relationship. One night, we were at a local bar and she talked about breaking up with me. In the middle of the argument, I grabbed her, threw her down on the floor, and started choking her. I didn't stop until people in the bar dragged me off. After that incident, Rhonda slept with a baseball bat under her bed because of her fear of me.

Rhonda and I were in an on-again, off-again relationship for fourteen years. Despite my violence, the relationship didn't seem unhealthy to me at the time and I'm sure Rhonda didn't think so either. Our relationship and our issues seemed dramatic, but I certainly didn't see myself as a batterer. Outwardly, I was intellectual. I believed in equality and feminism, and was immersed in the art culture. In retrospect I can see I had this outside posture, but at the time I really felt that women were to be used, primarily to meet my sexual and emotional needs.

I always thought the abusive stuff was sort of a glitch in the relationship. In other words, the relationship would be going along fine and then we'd have an episode. I felt justified when I was abusive, because *her* behavior and actions made me angry. I'd minimize what I did, and when she would confront me I'd say, "You're crazy."

I'd punch out windows, slam doors, drive fast in the car to scare her, and pound my fist on the table. The exhilaration of the outbursts gave me a sense of power. I'd get this rush when I was abusive. The abuse seemed to underscore my importance. My behavior seemed like an appropriate response to the situation.

Rhonda was a gregarious person and I was extremely jealous. I would do what I could to isolate her and keep her from having contact with other men. I'd do this big guilt and pity thing and say things like, "You don't give a shit about me."

You really get a lot of support from other men when you're abusive. I remember one time I put my fist through a window and had my hand all bandaged up. I went down to the bar and my friends asked me what happened and I said I'd been fighting with Rhonda again. No one ever confronted my behavior as being wrong. Instead they said, "Yeah, those fuckin' women," and "Why do you put up with her?"

In the early eighties, I started getting confronted by some of my women friends about my battering. I had to look at myself, and what I saw wasn't very pretty. But that confrontation led to a personal decision and commitment to change. I didn't want to batter again and I didn't want a woman I loved to be afraid of me.

I hooked up with some other men who wanted to address men's violence. We met regularly and discussed the origins of our violence. It wasn't easy to admit some of my behavior to the other men. The more we met and talked, the more I learned about myself and the more determined I was to change. I started speaking out publicly about my violence. I think to be public is a real motivator for change, whether it's getting confronted by people or getting arrested. There's something very humbling about it.

Even after I committed to not being violent with Rhonda, she was still afraid of me. If I got angry or depressed, I knew she was not sure what might come next. I had to learn to communicate my anger in different ways. I was responsible for her fear because of my past violence, so I felt obliged to alter my interactions with her. If we got into a disagreement, I told her I wasn't going to be violent. I reassured her and tried to create a safe space.

I'm convinced that my battering was a key reason why my relationship with Rhonda ended. Even though I was committed to being nonviolent, there was a certain level of trust that we could never restore, and we lost a level of emotional spontaneity because of the past.

The *Phil Donahue Show* was doing a program on domestic abuse. I was asked to be on the show because Rhonda and I had told our stories publicly in Minnesota. When I explained that my violence was an attempt to control and punish Rhonda, people in the audience asked, "What did she do to provoke you?" The whole thing about provocation can be seductive. But my violence was a personal choice.

Today, in my current relationship, I have more of an internal dialogue going on. I'm aware of what I'm doing and what I'm saying; it's kind of a self-monitoring process. I listen more. I talk honestly about what's going on in my life. I realize now that when I was abusive I was getting my way but I was also losing out. My partners didn't trust me. They had to be concerned about my moods. They were fearful when I got angry. It's difficult to be intimate when someone is afraid of you.

Men don't understand what kind of fear many women live with— the fear of rape and battering and of being afraid of men. It seems to me that we men have to take responsibility and confront our violence.

It has been important to me to disclose to my present partner,

Linda, the fact that I battered. I think she has a right to know who she's dealing with. All of this is part of being accountable for my past and my present.

I like working with men and sharing my experiences with them. I guess I think that as men we are kindred in many ways and accept that we each make individual choices. I feel rewarded when men talk straight about these issues and really make some commitments to change. It gives me hope that if men keep talking to men we can begin to change the attitudes that lead to violence against women. I like being part of the process and this work forces me to continue to examine my own stuff.

Taking Responsibility

Somehow, it just seems like human nature to make excuses for ourselves when we screw up. We do it all the time. If we make a mistake at work, we blame others or the nature of the job. If we respond inappropriately to something at home, we blame our children or our partners. If we're in a bad mood, we blame the world.

It isn't easy owning up to our mistakes. We know that "to err is human," yet it's rare to meet someone who has an easy time admitting to being wrong. What a difference it would make if parents, teachers, politicians, professionals, bosses, coworkers, friends, and family members stopped blaming others and took responsibility for their own actions. And that is exactly what men who batter need to do: own up, and take responsibility for their violent behaviors.

Outwardly, society takes a dim view of men beating women. Most boys are taught never to hit girls. Men who are arrested or in some other way publicly confronted with their violence find it difficult to face their friends, family, and society. Many men feel ashamed of their actions, while others feel bad that they were caught. Still others feel self-righteous and justified.

Some men cannot get beyond the excuse that the violence would not have happened if their partners had acted differently. They see their violence as the logical result of a certain situation, and find it difficult to see any alternative. They are full of rationalizations—if she had stopped bitching, not come home late, understood what I was feeling, not put me down, been a better mother, not drunk so much—all blaming statements that provide an excuse for the violence. In one of our groups, Rod explained an episode that led to his arrest.

Rod's wife, Nicole, had come home late from an office Christmas party. She had tried calling home, but couldn't get through. Rod was supposed to be at his pool league. He couldn't get a baby-sitter, so he had to wait for Nicole to get home before he could leave, and he was furious.

When she got home, Rod began insulting Nicole, calling her a goddamned bitch, threatening to beat her up. She responded by telling him to grow up, which further enraged him. He pushed her down the hallway, screaming at her all the way. She attempted to stop his pushing by kicking him. He punched her twice in the head and was subsequently arrested.

Maryann asked Rod to describe his behavior in more detail.

Maryann: Rod, you've just explained the incident to us. You outlined how you felt, how angry you were, and why. Looking back at the way you handled things, can you envision yourself doing things differently in light of everything that has happened?

Rod: Well, not really. I mean, the kids were home, she had been drinking, and she knew I was supposed to be at the pool league.

Maryann: So pushing and punching her resolved that dilemma?

Rod: I wouldn't have punched her if she hadn't tried to kick me in the nuts. The way I look at it, it was self-defense.

Maryann: I'm concerned about how you chose to react to her. Are you saying that you had no other option?

Rod: Well, I suppose I could have not gone to my league or blown it off. But pool is important to me and she should have been home.

Maryann: What about not pushing her down the hallway and not hitting her?

Rod: I hit her on the side of the head, not in the face, and believe me, it wasn't that hard or she would've been out. The cops had no reason to arrest me.

Rod had difficulty seeing other options. He could have left the house and cooled down when Nicole returned. He didn't have to call her names or push her. And when she tried to kick him, he could have tried to deflect her. He certainly didn't need to respond by punching her. Instead of taking any responsibility he blamed Nicole, and downplayed his violence by claiming that he didn't hit her that hard.

Often, men seem to have a more difficult time acknowledging personal faults than women, perhaps because of the ways in which they are socialized. Men are brought up to be strong, in control, and "right." Men often think they'll be seen as failures if they admit to being wrong or to having problems. As a result, they lie, minimize, or blame others. In Rod's case, if he was honest, he would have to be accountable to Nicole for what he did. He does not want to be accountable, so he rigidly holds on to the lie that his violence was justified.

Honesty *is* valuable. If you are honest, even if you have done wrong, people judge you far less harshly than you think. You are less alone and people tend to trust you and respond honestly in return. Rather than seeing you as a failure, people respect the fact that you are taking responsibility for your actions and are doing something concrete to make personal changes.

If you are—or have been—violent in a relationship, taking responsibility for your behavior is critical if you're serious about changing. Being accountable is a sincere acknowledgment and acceptance of responsibility. It isn't easy, and it is often humbling, but it must be done.

Minimizing Violence

When explaining your violence to others or to your partner, you may have heard yourself making comments like these:

- "It wasn't that bad."
- "I only hit her once."
- "I only slapped her."
- "I would never punch her with a closed fist."
- "She bruises easily."
- "I didn't hit her that hard."
- "I was drunk."
- "This is the first time I've ever done something like this."
- "I just lost it."

These statements may make you feel slightly better, but they minimize the seriousness of your violent and abusive acts against your partner.

Men often downplay an incident to get those who are con-

fronting the violence—police officers, counselors, friends, or a partner—to believe the abuse was not that bad. The more you downplay
what you did, the more difficult it will be to come to terms with your
behavior. You will also miss precious opportunities to change.

Morris described the following incident in one of our groups:

> I came home after having a few drinks after work. I'd had a really bad
> day and I was upset. Paula hadn't made supper and I told her I was
> hungry. She said she wasn't going to make me dinner because I came
> home late and because she was watching TV. I started screaming at
> her. I kicked the TV off the table, grabbed her by the hair, and told
> her that I should beat the shit out of her. I slapped her and she
> started screaming because I think she really believed I was going to
> beat her up.
>
> I felt that she cared more about that stupid TV show than me. I
> guess I wanted to let her know I was hurt. I did feel kind of guilty
> about slapping her later. The next day I apologized and told her I'd
> been upset about things at work. I also told her I'd been drinking on
> an empty stomach and that when I felt rejected by her, I just lost it. I
> mean, I would never really hurt her.

Note how Morris started his explanation by saying he'd had a hard
day. When he apologized to Paula, he said he'd been drinking on an
empty stomach. Then he said he "lost it" when it was quite clear he
was angry because Paula was not doing what he wanted her to do.
Morris made a *choice* to become abusive.

Saying "I lost it" or "I lost control" are common ways of describing a violent episode so it appears it wasn't really you doing the hitting. The message is that when you get angry something unavoid-
able happens to you—and you become violent.

If that's the case, why don't you lose it at work and hit your boss
when he's being a jerk? One reason is you'd probably lose your job. If
you're upset, depressed, or mad at the world, why don't you lose it
on the subway, on the bus, or in a store? You'd probably get arrested.
Bosses, friends, and strangers are usually not the targets of our violence, in part because of the potential consequences.

Claiming that the violence was not that bad also minimizes it,
and negates the reality of the person being hurt and abused. Denying
or downplaying the incident or blaming your partner for the violence
only puts off your accepting full and total responsibility for your use
of violence.

Seeing the truth requires not only an honest appraisal of what happened, but also a willingness to be accountable for your actions. If you want to check whether you've been minimizing your abusive behavior, try a simple test. Ask yourself whether you would want what you did to your partner to happen to you. Would you still say, "It wasn't that bad"?

Self-Defense or Retaliation?

A common theme heard in our groups is that the man's use of violence was an act of self-defense. There are many variations of this explanation, but in most cases the story is similar to Eric's excuse for beating up his wife, Kristen:

Michael: Eric, will you explain your situation again? I'm having trouble hearing you take any responsibility for your actions.

Eric: Well, like I said before, I was trying to leave the house. I guess I was trying to teach her a lesson about not bringing in her share of the money. Anyway, she stands in the hallway and tells me I'm not going anywhere.

Michael: She's blocking the doorway?

Eric: Yeah, more or less. So I get my coat and tell her to get the fuck out of the way.

Michael: Did you say anything else to her?

Eric: I probably called her a bitch. You know, like, "Get the fuck out of the way, bitch!"

Michael: Then what happened?

Eric: She slapped me, so I nailed her. I mean I told her, you ever hit me, you're going to get it. You know, it's this double standard, like women can hit men and we're not supposed to hit back. Well, I think that's bullshit. She hits hard. As far as I'm concerned, a man or a woman hits me, I hit 'em back.

Michael: Do the rest of you agree with Eric? If a woman hits you does that give you permission to hit her back?

Many in the group agreed, nodding cautiously, though Tim was not quite convinced.

Tim: Well, I guess it would depend on what you did. I mean, men

are a lot stronger and more used to fighting than most women I know.
I suppose if you slapped her back that would be okay.

Michael: What did you do, Eric?

Eric: I already told you: I nailed her!

Michael: You punched her? Kicked her?

Eric: I punched her.

Tim: How many times?

Eric: This is bullshit. I don't know. A couple of times. And I only hit her
once on the side of the head. I mean there were no black eyes or
broken bones. She told the cops I kicked her in the stomach and they
believed her and now I'm here. Look, I warned her.

Many men feel the way Eric does. He defends his actions by emphasizing that his partner hit him first and then by saying the lack of
bruises or broken bones means he used reasonable force given the
situation. He repeatedly uses her slap and his past warnings to justify
his violence. In order for Eric to change, he will have to ask himself
some hard questions: "Was my use of violence really justified?" "How
much physical force do I really need to defend myself?" "Was this
really self-defense?" "Did I have alternatives?"

I use the legal definition of self-defense to describe what is and is
not acceptable. According to law, self-defense is the use of force rea-
sonably necessary to prevent imminent injury. Self-defense does *not*
authorize a person to seek revenge or punish another. And self-
defense does *not* include retaliation. In other words, if your partner
throws something at you or slaps you, that does not give you the
right to punch her.

Women do use violence in self-defense, and some women initiate
violence. At the Domestic Abuse Intervention Project in Duluth,
about 10 percent of the offenders mandated to our program are
women, which is consistent with most national research. However,
in most cases when a woman initiates violence the male retaliates
far more severely. Some men have told me they were glad when their
partner hit them, because it gave them permission to beat their partner and feel justified. After all, they think, she hit me first.

As Cassie explains, there is a distinct difference between her violence and her partner's:

Not that my violence was right, but the impact was totally different.

One time, I was furious with my partner. I broke every window in the house with an iron pan—and I mean every window, upstairs and downstairs. I know he must have been scared at the rage he was seeing because he just stood there. That was wrong and violent.

But on one occasion when we were intimate, I told him I loved water. I loved rivers and the feel of water on my body. It was my solace. I never thought he would use that against me, but he did. When he was angry with me, he would wait until I got in the shower and then he would come into the bathroom and beat me. One time he hit me so hard, he split my head open. There I was when the police came, naked and bleeding in the bathroom.

After all these years, I am still terrified when I take a shower. I give explicit instructions to the children not to enter the bathroom. I have a clear shower curtain so I can see the door. And to this day, I'm still afraid. When *he* hears glass break, though, do you think he shudders because of that evening when I broke the windows? You can't tell me my rage and fear are the same as what he experiences.

In my groups, while never condoning violence, I try to differentiate between women's and men's acts of violence and battering. Some of the men in the groups claim that women are just as violent as men. I ask these men to answer the following questions with a Yes or No:

1. Do you ever wait on pins and needles when you hear your partner coming home, wondering what kind of mood she will be in?

2. Does your partner ever strike you for absolutely no reason that you know of?

3. Do you ever fear you will be asked to have sex with your partner after she has beaten you?

4. Do you flinch when your partner is angry and makes intimidating gestures? Do you fear that her actions are a sign that you will be hit?

5. If you decide to separate from your partner, are you afraid she will break into the house and beat you? Or try to kill you?

6. Are you afraid of your partner?

Men usually answer *No* to all of these questions. Some men in our groups even chuckle when I ask them. A woman's use of violence usually differs from a man's because there is an imbalance of power.

In addition to a man's physical size, his violence is often accompanied by other battering behavior, which increases his power. He may threaten to kill his partner. He may kill a pet or display weapons in a threatening manner.

Guidelines for Remaining Nonviolent

Most men who claim they acted in self-defense will later admit there were alternatives to using violence. In order to remain nonviolent, many formerly abusive men have committed to the following principles:

1. Violence is not okay unless I am truly in fear of being hurt, and then I should use only as much force as I need to defend myself.

2. In the future, I will be aware of flash points—issues or situations where I become agitated or very angry—that in the past have prompted violence by me or my partner.

3. I will leave situations—take a time-out—rather than use violence. (For more about time-outs, see Chapter 6.)

4. I will accept the fact that my use of violence is based on my desire to control a situation. I do not always need to be in control, to be proven right, or to win.

5. I will strive toward respectful resolutions of conflicts without being abusive.

Do you believe there are conditions to making these commitments? Exceptions? Do you feel a resistance to accepting them? Committing to these principles is not just an intellectual exercise. These five principles are the foundation for your efforts to remain nonviolent and nonabusive. If you can agree to them only with strings attached, then you have more work to do.

Some women do use violence as a way to punish or hurt their partners. And in some cases men are legitimately fearful of their partners' rage and violence. If you have never used violence or have stopped using it and your partner is engaging in physical abuse, take appropriate steps. Retaliatory violence does not have to be one of them. You can leave, call the police, obtain an Order for Protection, or seek help from domestic violence programs in your community.

Reacting to provocation or violence with violence makes it seem as if there are no alternatives.

A note to women

If you are a woman who uses violence against a partner you should be clear about whether you are responding to your partner's violence, defending yourself, or initiating the violence. Talk with friends who will help you decide which it is. Don't take the blame if the violence is your partner's; say no to it and get away from it. If you find that you are clearly initiating the violence, get help. Programs or counseling are available in most communities, and the resource section at the end of this book lists several organizations that may be helpful.

Letting Go of Blame

It may be difficult to stop blaming your partner for your violence. The following group discussion shows how one group member found it hard to take responsibility for his actions:

> **Michael:** Why do you think it's so hard for us to get beyond blaming our partners for our violence?
>
> **Julio:** Well, for me, it's just recently that I've seen I could have acted differently. I mean, I still want to hold on to all the things that Anna did or said.
>
> **Michael:** So you still believe she shared responsibility for the violence?
>
> **Julio:** In my head I know I'm responsible. But when I think about the times I was violent, it's hard to let go of her part in this. I mean, there were times when I thought she was egging me on so I would hit her. Our fights were totally outrageous. I had told her not to push me and she knew I would hit her if she kept going. So when she kept on pushing, I kind of thought she knew what the consequences were going to be. It doesn't justify what I did, but that's the way I saw it.
>
> **Michael:** Are you saying you think Anna wanted to get hit?
>
> **Julio:** No. But I couldn't understand why she wouldn't just shut up when I warned her to stop. She would say shit that got me so pissed off I would just lose it.
>
> **Michael:** So if someone says something I don't want to hear or says something that hurts or offends me, then it's their fault if I hit them?

Julio: When you say it like that, I would say no. But there are two people in an argument. Are you saying she didn't have any responsibility in this? I mean, I'll own up to my use of violence, but she needs to recognize when she's pushing my buttons.

Michael: I'm not saying Anna hasn't done or said things that might be inappropriate or hurtful. What I am saying is that regardless of what she says or does, your violence is yours and yours alone. I think it's really important to stop blaming her. You say you've acknowledged your violence, but all your comments have this qualifying statement that says she shares responsibility. Until you come to terms with that, I'm afraid you'll remain stuck.

Julio: I hear you. I don't know why I'm having such a hard time letting go of that.

Julio's comment about Anna pushing his buttons makes him sound like a robot whose buttons are being pushed on and off. The whole notion that words can provoke us into using violence is an argument that we must set aside. If our response to the words is violent, it is a *choice* we make.

Similarly, a man who batters frequently believes his partner should be a mind reader, knowing when to approach him and when to leave him alone. Failure to approach him in the "correct" way results in him getting angry and rejecting his partner or hurting her feelings. This can lead to an argument, which may escalate to violence.

As Cassie states, men who batter often have twisted perceptions of what provokes violence:

There were times when I would start arguments that resulted in fights. I mean, we had a lot of issues that caused problems, from money to the children. And I know there were times when I said hurtful or mean things. But when I would bring up a problem we were having, he would say I was provoking him. But I wasn't starting a fight so I could get beat up. Nothing I said gave him the right to do that. He would take any form of communication that made him feel uncomfortable and he would become abusive. Later, he would blame me and say I had provoked him.

The idea that one's partner provokes the violence is a difficult one to relinquish. Men who batter often believe their partners are pushing them into conflict. But the conflict usually has more to do with their own anger and resentment over their partner's wanting something or having a different opinion. When their partners assert themselves or disagree, men who batter see their partners' need for autonomy as a hostile provocation.

Andy described his resistance to seeing the truth and accepting responsibility for his behavior:

> I'd hang on really rigidly to my position and try to convince other people that my partner brought the violence on. I'd say, "I'm not to blame here. Yeah, I did some stuff, but it's a two-way street. There are two people in this relationship." I hung onto that. I hung onto that for dear life. I finally started to change when I let go of that and realized she didn't have to change for me to change. And she wasn't to blame for my behavior, and I alone was responsible for my violence.

Alcohol, Drugs, and Violence

Being under the influence of alcohol or drugs is a common explanation for violent behavior from men who have assaulted their partners. Fifty percent of men who enter the Domestic Abuse Intervention Project in Duluth were drinking or using drugs when they used violence against their partners. While research indicates that men under the influence are likely to batter more severely, it is dangerous and wrong to use alcohol or drug abuse as an excuse for violence.

Russ, a former police officer from Chicago, met with me to enroll in one of our groups. He was upset as he told his story.

Russ: Last night I punched my wife, Lynn, and began to choke her. I was totally drunk and just lost it. I've never done anything like that before.

Michael: Is she okay?

Russ: Yes. I mean, I think so. She's at the women's shelter. I've been trying to get in touch with her.

Michael: Tell me more about what happened.

Russ: Well, I was really drunk and I just flipped out when she got home. I don't remember everything, but I was on top of her and I was choking her. And then she lost consciousness and I let go. When she came to, I tried to apologize. I mean I would never, never do something like that if I was sober. I'm not that kind of a person. I must have been in a blackout or something, because I was totally out of control. Anyway, she was crying and upset and wanted to go but I wouldn't let her. I must have passed out, because when I woke up, she was gone.

Michael: You say you were totally out of control. Why do you think you didn't kill her? I mean, you stopped choking her. As drunk as you say you were, as out of control as you say you were, you stopped choking her.

Russ: I don't know. Something snapped, I guess. I'm very confused.

For Russ, alcohol functions as an excuse. The use of alcohol is a way for him to cope with, and try to explain away, his violence. There are two problems, however, with using drug or alcohol abuse as an excuse for violence. First, some men deliberately drink to excess to give themselves permission to become abusive. Many times the purpose is to bring up certain situations or issues that are hurtful or unresolved. Getting drunk or high with the intent of entering into a confrontation with a partner is a setup for abuse. After the violence, the man can chalk the situation up to being drunk or stoned, and say to himself, "It wouldn't have happened if I'd been sober."

The second problem with accepting alcohol and drug abuse as an excuse for violence is that society, friends, and family—and often the mental health community—may view alcohol or drugs as the primary problem. Many people assume that if a substance abuse problem is resolved, the abuse and violent behavior will end. This is a dangerous assumption for the partner of an abusive man. People who abuse alcohol or drugs and act violently have two problems—not one. They need to address *both*.

Unfortunately, substance abuse treatment usually does not address the reasons for a person's violence. In many cases, men will continue to batter when they are sober.

If you think you have a substance abuse problem, take immediate short-term steps—whatever is necessary—to ensure you will not be in a position to act out violently. Then get an assessment on substance abuse and follow the recommendations of your counselor. This may mean going into inpatient or outpatient treatment, followed by aftercare. After completing that treatment you can begin a program dealing specifically with the issues of violence. The two programs have two very different functions, even though some of the issues you deal with will overlap.

A note to women
Some researchers have concluded that a battered woman may stay in

a relationship with a physically abusive man for a much longer period if he has a substance abuse problem. In many cases she is reluctant to leave a dangerous relationship because she feels compelled to make excuses for her partner's behavior. She accepts the rationalization that the abused substance was a contributing factor in his use of violence.[18]

If your partner is both violent and under the influence of alcohol or drugs you risk suffering serious injuries. Call a shelter in your area immediately or use the resource section at the end of this book to find other places to get help.

Anger

Anger is a common human emotion. We get angry at people, events, and ourselves. If someone cuts in front of us on the freeway, if our children do something wrong, if things at work are difficult, if events in the world are troubling, we may get angry. This is a normal feeling and not necessarily a negative emotion.

However, men who batter often cite anger at their partners as the reason for their violence. This discussion in one of our men's groups shows how Calvin uses anger to justify his violence:

Calvin: I decided to come to this group to get a handle on my anger problem.

Michael: What do you mean by "anger problem"?

Calvin: Well, when I'm in a relationship with a woman and she does something that pisses me off, sometimes I get violent. I want that to stop.

Michael: Are you saying that anger causes the violence?

Calvin: If I wasn't angry I guess I wouldn't be violent.

Michael: Does that mean that if you get angry with me right now you're going to hit me?

Calvin: No. You don't understand.

Michael: What don't I understand?

Calvin: There are certain things that get people angry, and then that triggers a violent response. My past girlfriend would say things that got me so angry I became violent. I suppose if you said certain things I could get that angry with you.

Michael: It seems to me you're making a choice when, and with whom, you're going to be violent when you get angry.

While anger does not cause violence, it is an emotion many men exploit when things are not going as they want. People get angry with each other in most relationships, but men who batter typically use anger as a way to control their partners and show displeasure. Most women resist being controlled, yet a man who batters tries to impose his ideas of what should happen regardless of his partner's resistance. He perceives her refusal to abide by the rules he has designed for the relationship as defiance or provocation, and gets angry. His expression of anger is followed by threats, intimidation, and violence. Then he blames the violence on his anger.

A woman who lives with an abusive man quickly learns to watch for mood swings, and either accommodates her partner's rules or resists them. We often believe we need to express our disapproval through angry words or actions. If this becomes a common pattern, we develop a tendency to lash out. Lashing out in turn can bring an initial and often exhilarating rush. Screaming, punching a wall, calling someone a name, or hitting someone lets off steam and gets attention. However, venting anger in such an intimidating way is threatening and unfair to others.

Some people feel bad or foolish after going into a rage and may try to make amends for their behavior. They walk around feeling guilty and powerless to confront this seemingly sudden and uncontrollable rage. Others find a sense of power in unleashing and venting their anger and feel no remorse. They walk around angry at the world, expecting someone to cross them. Then they can vent without taking responsibility.

I am not suggesting you should never get angry. But do find an appropriate way to express anger. As with other emotions, you can feel and express anger in a healthy, nonhurtful manner. But you must have a clear understanding of the patterns that occur when you get angry before you can change them. If your usual response after getting angry is to explode at someone, remove yourself from the situation before you say or do something abusive.

It's important that you not confuse the emotion of anger with your choice of becoming abusive. Explaining your violence by saying, "She made me so angry I _____" is a convenient—but dishonest—excuse.

As you address the ways you deny or minimize your abusive behavior and as you stop blaming others for your violence, you will begin to see more clearly what you really *do* when you become violent. Then you can begin to move ahead and make real changes in your life. In the chapters that follow, you will read about concrete ideas and suggestions to help you to change and heal.

6

Making Changes and Staying on Track

Mark's Story — Letting Go — Taking Time-Outs —
Self-Talk: Learning to Think Positively — Handling Jealousy —
The Danger of Obsession

Our greatest glory consists not in never falling,
but in rising every time we fall.

RALPH WALDO EMERSON

In this chapter, you will read about letting go of relationships that have ended, some important exercises to help you stay nonabusive, including time-outs and positive self-talk, and handling jealousy and obsession.

Mark's Story

Mark, aged twenty-eight, is an environmental engineer and lives in an upper-middle-class suburb of St. Paul. He is presently separated from Jody, the woman he battered. Their divorce is pending. In his story, Mark talks about his abuse and the struggle it has been to put his life back together. At the time of the interview he was attending a domestic violence group in the Minneapolis/St. Paul area.

My parents never fought. Throughout my childhood, I only remember one incident where they had a verbal confrontation. We lived in a nice neighborhood and had a beautiful home. My parents rarely hit us. I think I was spanked on one occasion.

I'm not sure what influenced my violent tendency. I guess it had something to do with my size; I'm not very big. I would get picked on in school a lot and I started to fight back. I started to get into a lot of fights and I think that shaped my attitude about violence.

I felt powerful when I got into fights. It also got me acceptance from the guys I wanted to hang around with. At the time I liked that tough-guy image. I thought it might impress the girls, but in retrospect I think they thought we were being childish.

Jody and I got married right after high school and we were together for about ten years. The first couple of years of our relationship were pretty good. I joined the Marine Corps and Jody and I moved to California. After I got out of the service, we moved back to the Twin Cities.

Looking back, I don't think I really wanted to be married. I was young, and all of a sudden I was married and had a kid on the way. I resented the responsibilities of marriage. I got this job that required a lot of traveling, and that caused conflict. I liked being on the road because I didn't want to be that involved with Jody and I liked the freedom.

One time, Jody called me at a hotel and told me I had to come home right away. When I got home, she told me she wanted me to find a job close to home and that she couldn't stand my traveling anymore. A couple of weeks later the bombshell hit: she told me she'd had an affair. It hit me like a ton of bricks. She said she only slept with the man once and the relationship was over, but the incident changed everything.

After her affair, I started treating Jody differently. What I said went. I'm sure some or most of my behavior was punishment. Even though I tried to put it behind me, I couldn't. I started making all the decisions in the relationship, from what movie we saw to what groceries we bought.

To get back at her, I started lying to her to make her suspicious. Sometimes I wouldn't come home at night to piss her off. When she went out, I would interrogate her when she got home. She had to account for her entire evening, including who she was with and where she went. Sometimes I would check the mileage on the car to see if she was telling the truth.

The first time I was arrested for assault was about three years ago. We were driving home and she wanted to stop and get something to eat, but I refused to stop. We argued all the way home. She kept saying how I always got my way and how I always made the final decision. We got home and she said something derogatory to me. I grabbed her and pushed her into the wall. I was clearly in a rage and she was totally shocked.

She went into the house and called the police. I followed her and hung up the phone but she had gotten through to them. I took the wedding pictures off the wall, smashed them on the floor, and started swearing at her. I broke other things in the house. She went to the other room hoping I would calm down. I grabbed a couple of knives from the kitchen and threw them at the wall, partly out of just being pissed and partly to scare her.

When the cops came, I started to fight with them. I had one of the cops pinned on the floor; another cop maced me. By that time, there were several officers at my house. My daughter saw the entire incident and I know it had a big effect on her, especially when the police arrested me. For some time after that, whenever she saw a police car she would say things like, "Remember when the police came to our house and took you away? I don't like police." I didn't talk to her about the incident and would change the subject when she brought it up.

I spent the night in jail and my lawyer picked me up in the morning. When I got home from jail, I could tell that Jody was nervous. I apologized for what I had done and we talked for a while. I told her I would go to counseling, but I never did. I didn't want to go to a domestic abuse program because of the stigma of saying you've beaten your wife. With my circle of friends, it would be better to have been arrested for bank robbery than for domestic assault.

Both my lawyer and I asked Jody to write a letter to the court stating that the incident was exaggerated, and she did. By the time the case went before the judge our relationship was going pretty good. I was on my best behavior during that time because I didn't want to go to jail. I think the fact that Jody wrote that letter and both of us stated that we wanted to make the relationship work influenced the judge. The assault charges were dropped.

I never thought the violence was that bad. My friends, family, and my lawyer supported me. I would bring up the affair she had had and they would side with me. I guess they felt I was justified in what I was doing and that some men would have done a lot worse. My lawyer would say there's nothing wrong with throwing things around in your own house. With everyone defending me, I felt like the victim of this bitch and of the police who were overstepping their authority.

I was never intoxicated when I abused Jody. In fact, I rarely drank very much. Jody and I went to a marriage counselor a couple of years later. The issue of my violence rarely came up. When the counselor asked specific questions about the violence, both Jody and I would minimize the abuse.

I would smash things in the house when I was angry or when I wanted to scare her. If I became upset at something she'd said, I would step on her foot and put all my weight on her. She would always cry when I did this because it hurt, but I felt justified because I thought she was hurting me by yapping and embarrassing me in public. Sometimes I would pinch her really hard, usually under the table if we were out with people, to get her to shut up. I would tell her I was going to kick her ass and sometimes I would threaten to kill her.

I think the emotional abuse was the worst part of it. Jody was very sensitive about her weight even though she really wasn't that big. I'd call her "fat ass." Sometimes I'd get in her face and say, "You fuckin' bitch, I'm so sick of you!" I'd tell her I hated her and she would go into the bedroom and cry. I would say anything I could think of to hurt her.

I hated the way things were going in my life. I knew what I was doing was wrong, but at the time I couldn't see alternatives. I got into this pattern of being really abusive to her. I mean, it got to a point where I felt almost funny when I was nice to her.

I don't know why we stayed together so long. I guess we both hoped things would change. The last incident occurred about a year ago. Jody had decided to leave. She wanted me out of the house while she was moving out. I came to the house after work. I wanted to talk to her about whether we were actually going to split up. She didn't want to talk and asked me to leave. She was sitting on the floor folding laundry with her back to me. I came up behind her and grabbed her by the hair. I pulled her up off the ground and started shaking her. I demanded that she talk to me.

She was scared because I caught her by surprise. I screamed in her face, "I ought to kill you, you goddamned fuckin' bitch." I pushed her down on the floor and left. She called the police and I was informed the next day that I was charged with assault. The charge was subsequently dismissed after I hired my slick lawyer again to get me off.

Even though our relationship is over, I've still been abusive. Jody is seeing a man and I've questioned the kids about what she's doing, which I shouldn't do. It makes me feel bad that she's already seeing someone else.

My trust with women is pretty low. But I know I need to get on with my life, and I'd like to get involved in a new relationship. I may need to continue in counseling for a while and I'm certainly not going to rush into a relationship until I'm ready. I guess I've really seen the light since being in the program. I don't want anyone else to experience the pain that Jody experienced from me and I don't want the pain myself. Relationships don't have to be like this.

I'm not sure I want to tell a new partner about my past violence. I don't believe I'll ever be violent with a woman again. If things aren't working, I'm confident I'll leave or get help before things ever get to that point. Perhaps there will come a time when I can talk freely about it, but it's too fresh right now.

I feel better today and I'm starting to get my life together. Despite Jody's affair, I really believe I caused the marriage to break up. I'll always be mad about that. I'm trying not to get into a pity thing about where I'm at—you know, the poor-me syndrome. Living alone has not been easy. I'm often lonely, but I'm dealing with it. I know this is going to sound weird, but I wish I would have been sent to the Domestic Violence Program after my first arrest five years ago. I'm convinced my relationship would be alive today because my whole attitude would have changed. It's too bad I had that slick lawyer.

Letting Go

Mark is nearing the end of his domestic abuse group attendance. Unlike the other men who have told their stories, he is still sorting through the past and the hurt. His abusive behavior was relentless and clearly punitive after Jody's affair. For five years he made her pay—and they both suffered.

People often have painful experiences in relationships. Communication breaks down, conflicts surface over children, money, sex, and commitment, and affairs happen.

Sometimes people seek affection and love elsewhere because a relationship is emotionally bankrupt and intimacy is gone. For others, an affair is a one-time thing; afterward, guilt sets in and the affair is seen as a mistake.

An affair in a monogamous relationship can be crippling, as it was with Mark and Jody. Some relationships survive, however, and people rebuild their trust and continue to work on their relationship.

Many men in our groups tell me that, in retrospect, they should have ended their relationships much sooner. The love and intimacy were long gone, but they stayed because of the children, or for fear of being alone, or for financial reasons. Violence adds a confusing component to all this; sometimes it prolongs a dying relationship, and sometimes it hastens its demise.

I do not believe a couple should consider divorce every time their relationship hits some ruts in the road, but I also do not believe in hanging on when it's time to let go. Frequently, at the end of a relationship, one or both parties are ambivalent. Seeing a counselor and being truly honest about your feelings may help clarify whether you want to make the relationship work or not.

If you have battered your partner, however, couples counseling may not be appropriate unless the violence has stopped and your partner feels safe to talk freely without fear of retribution. You should not pressure or coerce your partner to attend counseling. She may need time and support from outside sources—such as battered women's advocates and support or educational groups for women—before she is ready to attend marriage counseling with you. Honor her requests.

Letting go of a relationship is always hard. Confusion over what went wrong and conjectures about how you might have handled things differently can be consuming and debilitating. Do not pretend the feelings do not exist. Feel them and understand that this is a natural process. The feelings will slowly pass and you will get on with your life.

Try, through the process of self-talk discussed later in this chapter, to dislodge any bitter feelings and thoughts about your partner. Those feelings and thoughts are not helpful and get in the way of healing and letting go. Similarly, do not wallow in guilt and shame about the past. Think through the past in phases and do not expect clarity right away. The grieving process may obscure a clear picture of all that worked and all that did not in the relationship.

In subsequent sections of this chapter on self-talk and jealousy, we will explore the letting-go process in more detail. However, if you feel desperate about losing a relationship, seek help from a counselor. Develop a plan to stop focusing on your former partner. Part of the plan may include finding new activities so you do not feel isolated. Counseling and support groups will help you to let go and move on with your life.

▨ EXERCISE: Letting Go

If your relationship has ended, or will end, and if you are grieving the loss, the following exercise might be helpful. These are difficult times, but you need a plan to get back on your feet. Write your responses in your journal or notebook. If you are in counseling, you might want to ask group members or counselors to help you with ideas.

1. List the daily activities or special times that you'll miss when the relationship ends.

_____

_____

Examples:

Having dinner together, intimate times, celebrating special occasions, taking trips, going out with friends together, talking about our day, doing projects together at home.

2. For each example above, try to think of a way you can still get your emotional needs met even though your relationship is over.

_____

Examples:

Spend more time with friends and family, explore new interests, spend quality time with the children, get involved with community organizations or activities, develop new friendships, play sports, read, go to counseling.

3. If you are having negative or hurtful feelings about your partner or ex-partner, think about the steps you can take to avoid harassing or being hurtful toward her and ways you can bolster your spirits in this difficult time.

_____

Examples:

Use positive self-talk and try not to dwell on the loss. Refrain from saying negative things about her in front of the children. Honor the protection order. Respect her decision if she doesn't want contact with me. Refrain from blaming her or myself.

4. Think of ways that you can bolster your spirits. When you feel lonely or depressed look back at this list.

Examples:

Acknowledge that feeling sad is okay. Talk to and get support from friends, family, and group members. Use positive self-talk when I'm feeling depressed. Try not to think about her. Make sure I don't get isolated. Occupy myself with activities I enjoy.

Remember, grieving is natural and there is no set time limit for when it will end. The end of a relationship is much like the death of someone close—you need to grieve and then get on with your life. Time will eventually heal things. Don't get consumed with bitterness, blame of your partner, or self-blame. Make a life-change plan based on this exercise and stick to it.

Taking Time-Outs

Taking a time-out means removing yourself from an explosive situation. This practice may seem simplistic and it is—but it works.

You take a time-out anytime you feel you may become abusive. You make a commitment to remove yourself from a situation that might otherwise result in your intimidating, threatening, emotionally abusing, or hitting your partner.

When people get angry, it's usually because they aren't getting what they want or because someone is doing something they don't like. Taking a time-out does not address the causes of your anger, but it does provide an instant tool to help you avoid situations in which you might become abusive.

When you get angry or agitated, you usually have emotional or physical feelings. On an emotional level, you may feel hurt, defensive, or mad. Your mind becomes engulfed with anger and you feel an urge to vent your feelings. On a physical level, you may feel your fists or teeth clenching together, a tightness in your stomach or neck, tenseness in the body, or headaches.

These emotional and physical feelings are cues that anger and possibly violence are on the way. Pay attention to these cues. When you feel that you cannot express yourself in a nonabusive manner, take a time-out and leave.

You can use a time-out to get away from a potentially abusive situation, such as an argument between you and your partner that is about to begin or that has escalated. Perhaps you have been thinking about present problems or past issues and feel yourself getting angry. Recognize the emotional and physical changes in yourself, listen to what your body is telling you, and get ready to take a time-out.

What to do and where to go during time-outs

First, calmly tell your partner you are taking a time-out, or write a note. You might say, "I'm feeling angry and I need to take a time-out." By stating this clearly you let your partner know you are taking responsibility for your actions and leaving to avoid anger that may result in abusive behavior.

Second, let your partner know how long the time-out will last. You might say, "I'm feeling angry and I need a time-out. I'll be back in one hour." Never stay away longer than you have indicated without calling to let your partner know. This is so your partner will not be scared or startled when you return and also is not left wondering when you might return.

During your time-out, do not use alcohol or drugs. Do not drive. Take a walk; that's usually the best way to relax. You may also want to talk with a friend or someone from a support group, if you are in one. Whatever the conflict, use the time-out to think positively about yourself, your partner, and the relationship. Remind yourself that you are a good person, that your partner is a good person, and that separately or together the two of you will be able to resolve the conflict in due time.

Many conflicts between partners arise over little issues that are blown out of proportion, generally because of the mood one of the partners is in. When you take a time-out for what may be a minor misunderstanding, try to separate your emotion from the issue and tell yourself that your anger, too, will pass.

Sometimes, though, conflicts arise between partners because of major differences or large, unsolved issues. These might include money problems, jealousy, sex, the children, or disagreements about decisions that affect both of you. Obviously, these issues need time, discussion, and negotiation. You should still take a time-out if, during discussion and disagreement, you believe you may become abusive. In this situation, a walk and positive self-talk may be useful in the short term. In the long term, however, you may need to do other things to work out the problem, including setting up an environment where negotiation can proceed fairly, without intimidation and threats and in a true spirit of give-and-take. You may also consider seeing a counselor to help you iron out the problem.

Regardless of the difficulty of the issue, take a time-out every time you recognize your cues. Let your partner know what you are doing, and leave before you raise your voice or do anything that may make your partner afraid.

Although I recommend taking time-outs to the men in my groups, I am also aware that some men use them to avoid working on problems. If you take a time-out every time you have a disagreement, your actions will not only be controlling but also self-defeating. Use time-outs with a constructive purpose in mind.

Time-out Rules

1. Take a time-out when you recognize your cues and before your anger level escalates.

2. Take a time-out when you feel like you want to become abusive; do not take a time-out to avoid conflict.

3. Tell your partner you are taking a time-out.

4. Tell your partner how long you'll be gone.

5. Do not drink, use drugs, or drive.

6. Call a friend or group member for support.

7. Do calming exercises like walking, shooting free throws at a basketball court, or meditating.

8. Think positive thoughts. Do not dwell on the problem that caused you to become angry.

9. If you are still agitated and need more time than you agreed to, call your partner and let her know.

10. Your partner is not obliged to take a time-out; you take a time-out for *yourself.*

11. If your partner indicates that she is afraid of you, stay away. Find an alternative place to stay until things have calmed down.

12. When you return, do not insist that you and your partner should solve or resolve the conflict you were having.

13. If you notice your cues again, take another time-out.

14. Whenever you follow the time-out rules, make a note of the positive way you handled the situation and its results.

An important note

If you are going to use time-outs in your relationship, review this section and the previous one with your partner. You may want to practice a time-out when you are not angry so that you and your partner understand the process and each other's expectations. Your partner needs to know the rules of the time-out so she knows what to expect.

Some programs advocate that both parties use time-outs. Usually, the man has gone through a domestic abuse program and now the couple is learning techniques from a counselor. If you are at this stage of counseling it is very important that you honor your partner's need for a time-out. Don't try to stop her if she wants to take a time-out, and don't harass her when she returns. The above rules can certainly apply to both parties.

Self-Talk: Learning to Think Positively

Self-talk is that internal voice with which you talk to yourself. It is part of an internal thinking process, and in some ways is like a little tape recorder in the mind that continually plays positive or negative messages.

If you feel anxious, jealous, insecure, or angry, you are usually thinking negatively about a situation or person. Maybe things in your life seem hopeless. Then the tape starts playing negative messages: "I'll never get that job—I just don't have the skills." "She doesn't really care about me, I'm wasting my time." "I'm no good—everything I do comes out bad." "I'll never be happy; I might as well stop trying." If you continue to focus on these negative thoughts and don't resolve the problem, you can become seriously depressed. And you may start taking out your negative feelings on others, especially family members.

The use of positive self-talk is a process of replacing negative messages by concentrating on positive thoughts: "I am a good person." "I know I'll succeed if I keep trying." "I have no reason to be jealous." "This problem—like other problems—will pass." You may need to repeat these statements many times to erase the negative thoughts. Positive self-talk, like most changes, takes time, willpower, and concentration.

The following is an example from our group of how positive self-talk can work. Steve's usual response to conflict was to storm around, swear, and yell. I asked him to practice positive self-talk the next time a conflict occurred and to express his anger in an appropriate manner. He agreed.

In one of the following group sessions, Steve told us about how he used self-talk to avoid becoming abusive. He said he was angry because his partner got home late with the car, which meant that he was late for his golf game. In the past, Steve said, he would have been "all over her" as soon as she walked in the door.

I was really mad as I waited for her. I made a couple of calls, but I couldn't locate her. I was getting madder and madder, but I tried the positive-self-talk approach. Every time a negative thought came into my head like, "She doesn't give a shit about me," I replaced it with a thought like, "There must be a good reason why she's late."

I then called my golfing partners and told them that I'd be late and would catch up with them. When Patricia got home forty-five minutes late, I sat at the table rather than rushing to the door. She was nervous when she came in because of my past behavior, but I didn't look angry—at least that's what she said. I calmly asked her where she had been. Normally, I would have been screaming things like, "Don't you know I've got plans?" But I waited for her response, which was apologetic and reasonable. Seeing that she wasn't afraid of me felt good. I guess I don't have to be an asshole every time I get mad.

In another group, Jerry had been making it hard for his partner, Joan, to go back to work. Maryann questioned him about this:

Maryann: Jerry, you were talking last week about how you didn't want Joan to go back to work. What's been happening?

Jerry: We've been talking. I told her I would try to be supportive, but she knows I don't want her to go.

Maryann: Did you tell her that you didn't want her to go?

Jerry: I guess I've been pretty indirect and manipulative. I tell her I'm okay with her decision, but then I tell her I make enough money for both of us. I'm sure I come off as suspicious.

Maryann: Why are you so resistant to her getting a job?

Jerry: Well, she used to work at this restaurant years ago and there were lots of men there. I remember when we were dating, she would go out with her coworkers after work and have drinks and a good time. I don't know, I guess I'm assuming I'll be jealous, and we've had some rocky times, you know.

Maryann: My hope is that you would accept her decision and support Joan. We've been talking about self-talk the last couple of weeks. Maybe the group could come up with some ideas on how Jerry could change the negative messages he has when he thinks about Joan going back to work.

The group came up with the following ideas for self-talk that Jerry could substitute for his negative and suspicious thoughts:

- Joan needs to have her own life.
- She'll be happy.
- If I don't control her, she'll respect me more.
- I have my work life, and she should have hers.
- I don't need to be jealous.
- The extra money will be helpful.
- I need to remember what I've learned in the group.
- I should trust her.

Maryann: Jerry, when the negative thoughts occur, try to use some of these statements. If you need to, repeat them in your mind and believe them.

Jerry: I'll give it a try.

■ EXERCISE: Self-Talk

In your journal or notebook complete the following exercise.

1. Write down an issue or situation with your current or former partner when you were preoccupied with negative self-talk.

_____

_____

Example:
Whenever my partner went out with her friends. There were these two women in particular I didn't care for, so when she was with them I thought the worst. If she came home late or didn't call I would get consumed with rage.

2. Write down examples of positive self-talk you could have used to counter the negative self-talk.

Examples:
I trust my partner. She will be home soon and there's nothing to worry about.

I've been late too—it happens. I need to relax and do something calming. When she comes home I won't be abusive—I can control myself.

When the negative thoughts creep into your mind, use your positive self-talk messages to push the negative ones out. It helps greatly to use positive self-talk when you take a time-out, because during this time you are usually worked up. The best approach to a time-out is to take a long walk, take long deep breaths, and repeat the self-talk statements from your list.

We cannot "will" our problems away, but we don't need to dwell on them and have them consume us. We have no control over certain things in life, but we *can* control our reactions to them.

Handling Jealousy

Men and women get jealous. In fact, jealousy is a very common emotion most of us have experienced, probably quite often. Yet, for some men, jealousy becomes a life-consuming passion that distorts reality. A jealous man questions everything his partner does and feels: her trust, fidelity, love, and commitment. He gets jealous if she buys new clothes, puts on makeup, or gets a new hairstyle. He gets jealous if she talks on the phone, writes letters, or goes out with friends. In our groups these men constantly blame their partners' unfaithfulness for their violence even though their suspicions are often unjustified.

Feelings of jealousy, especially for men who batter, are tied to a belief that you have a claim to this woman—"She's *my* wife." Some men are possessive from the beginning of their relationships. Many battered women have told me that their husbands became extremely possessive right after they both said "I do," immediately becoming jealous or suspicious if their partners' behavior did not conform to their expectations. This does not even give the couple time to discuss what they expect from each other in the relationship.

Jeff told the following story in one of our groups:

Jeff: Arlette and I had been arguing pretty much all night about her going bowling with this group of friends. I didn't used to mind, but there are these women in this group I just don't trust.

Michael: Why?

Jeff: Everyone knows they're pretty loose. One of them is single and the other recently divorced, so....

Michael: So what happened?

Jeff: Well, like I said, we were arguing about her going and I was pretty insistent that she not go. I mean, part of it was her friends, but we had also been drinking and I didn't want her to drive. When she tried to leave, I blocked the doorway. Then she tried to go out the back door and I grabbed her by the arm and slapped her and took the keys out of her hand.

Michael: Was the real issue the fact that she'd had some drinks or that you didn't want her to go bowling with her friends?

Jeff: Both. But I guess I was mostly reacting to her being with those women. Anyway, she was pretty upset. But I think on some level she knew I was right. We talked about it later that night.

Michael: What kind of feelings were you having about her going?

Jeff: I suppose I was feeling somewhat insecure and scared, and had she gone I would have been worried.

Michael: Of what?

Jeff: That being with those women would give her ideas. That maybe she would find some other man there and sleep with him. I don't really know, except I felt insecure.

Michael: So you hit her and stopped her from going. I'm curious. Did those feelings of being scared and insecure go away by forcing her to stay home?

Jeff: That night I didn't have those feelings. But later I had them again because I knew I was depriving her of doing something she really enjoyed. So I've been thinking that Arlette must really think I'm a jerk or something, and then those nervous feelings come back.

In this case, Jeff used violence to control his partner and end a disagreement. He succeeded in one respect, because Arlette did not go out. But looking at the long-term impact of his actions, we see that the very feelings he wanted to avoid—fear and insecurity—were intensified. He told the group he became even more jealous later. He finally accepted Arlette's going out with her friends, in part because he knew she was angry at him for trying to stop her, yet he always made an issue out of it the night she was to go out. Jeff also admitted checking up on her, because his insecurity and jealousy were so intense.

As much as Jeff tried to justify what he was doing, he was aware of his partner's unhappiness, and his mind kept conjuring up the worst. Every time he made an arbitrary decision about her life he imagined her thinking about leaving him for someone who would treat her better. As his insecurity grew he became more controlling. He used a variety of threats, including the possibility of taking his own life. The abuse became an endless cycle until finally his partner left him.

Handling jealousy is not easy, but it is possible. If you continually have jealous feelings, talk to friends, practice self-talk, or see a counselor. The best way to keep from being destructive is to put the situation into perspective. Your partner's right to have friends and spend time as she wishes does not have to make you feel jealous. And if someone finds your partner attractive, it does not have to be threatening.

Trust is earned and develops over time; it cannot be imposed by making demands or controlling another person.

The Danger of Obsession

For some men, the thought of losing a relationship is unbearable, and jealousy becomes an obsession. An obsessive man may think about his partner all the time. He may try to think about something else, yet images of his partner with another person slip into his mind, setting off feelings of anger and pain. He cannot imagine living without this person.

An obsession can be destructive and is often dangerous. We frequently read newspaper articles about an estranged husband killing his ex-wife, family members, and then himself. There is a difference between feeling jealous and having an obsession about someone. If you are jealous, you may be concerned or even afraid that your partner is interested in others or that others are interested in your partner. Jealousy can usually be resolved through honest communication, reassurance, and trust. An obsession, on the other hand, is an intense preoccupation with losing a partner. These compulsive feelings and emotions are usually unwanted, but frequently consume the person who is obsessing.

While a jealous person still has contact with reality, an obsessive person has lost, or can easily lose, touch with reality; he is operating in a fantasy world in which anything is excusable to avoid losing the object of his obsession.

If you find yourself enmeshed in obsessing about a relationship that has ended or may end, if you cannot stop thinking about your partner, or if you feel you cannot live without her, get help at a mental health agency in your community. A counselor can help you sort through your feelings, gain some perspective, and move on in your life. Sometimes, when a relationship ends, you think you'll never get through the pain. Your feelings of loss are real and you need to grieve just as you would if someone close to you died. A counselor can help you cope and get through this period, too.

A note to women

Men who are obsessive about holding on to a relationship can be dangerous. If your partner or ex-partner makes threats such as, "If I can't have you, nobody will," or "If you leave me, I have no reason to live," seek help *immediately*. If your ex-partner follows you, threatens your friends, checks up on you, sends unwanted letters, or calls your home against your wishes, you could be in danger. Seek assistance from a battered women's shelter, obtain a protection or restraining order, or develop a safety plan, which may include going to a safe home or moving to a different area. Call the police and let them know what is occurring. *Never* disregard indications of an obsession, especially if there has been violence in your relationship.

A note to counselors

If you are providing counseling to a man who is obsessing about the loss of a partner, or to a woman who has concerns about a partner's obsession, probe to assess the possibility of danger.

Find out:

1. Is he depressed?

2. Has he threatened suicide?

3. If yes, does he have a plan? Does he possess weapons?

4. Has he threatened to kill her?

5. Is he preoccupied with her or does he follow her around?

6. Is he on medications or has he ever been hospitalized?

7. Is he isolated or cut off from friends and family?

8. Does he believe that he owns her?

9. Does he idolize her?

10. Does he abuse alcohol or drugs?

While any of these warning signs should be taken seriously, usually a cluster of these behaviors increases the danger that an individual may commit a homicide. We cannot predict who will kill, but we *can* be attuned to signs.

If you are providing counseling to a man who has an obsession, you may want to seek further evaluations. He may need to be hospitalized. Get information about your options, which may include notifying authorities. Call the victim and let her know your concerns. Encourage her to call a battered women's program and develop a safety plan. Remember that you have a duty to warn. If you believe your client is a threat to another person, you must take the appropriate steps to protect that person.

Similarly, if you are working with a woman who expresses concern about her partner's or ex-partner's obsession, make sure you refer her to a local battered women's program and assist her with safety options. Your attention and action are critical and may save her life.

7

Staying Together

What Traps a Woman in an Abusive Relationship? —
The Switzers' Story — It May Always Be a Struggle —
Understanding and Accepting Women's Anger — Changing
the Mind-Set — Getting Your Needs Met without Being Abusive

Being human is difficult. Becoming human is
a lifelong process. To be truly human is a gift.

ABRAHAM HESCHEL

What Traps a Woman in an Abusive Relationship?

I first met Chuck and M'Liss Switzer in the early 1980s. We had
appeared on the *Sally Jesse Raphael Show* and the *Phil Donahue Show* to
talk about domestic abuse. The Switzers were there to tell their
story, and I was there to provide commentary on the dynamics of an
abusive relationship. At this time, the issue and prevalence of
domestic abuse was just beginning to surface around the country.

Audience members asked M'Liss a crucial question that day,
one that battered women hear over and over again despite growing
understanding of domestic abuse: "Why did you stay with him?"
Battered women's advocates often turn the tables when they hear
this question, and respond: "The question shouldn't be why does
she stay, but rather why does he batter?"

I've come to the conclusion that both questions are legitimate.
The reasons a battered woman stays in an abusive relationship are
complex, and leaving the question "Why does she stay?" unan-
swered won't deepen our understanding of domestic abuse. Sometimes when I'm training at a workshop I'll rephrase the question
by asking, "What do you think *traps* a woman in an abusive relationship?" People seem more accepting of this interpretation, and it
is probably more accurate.

Trying to synthesize all the reasons a victim stays in an abusive
relationship into a single theory is difficult, and perhaps misguided.

First of all, a woman doesn't set out trying to find a man who will beat her. Girls don't say, "When I grow up, I want to marry a man who will assault and hurt me." The belief that women are masochistic, that they like to be beaten, is purely and simply a myth.

Some battered women will say they should have recognized the danger signs when they first started dating. Violent outbursts, controlling behavior, hyperjealousy, and demeaning attitudes toward women were all indications of potential problems. But for many women, these signals got jumbled in with the positive feelings they had about the men they were dating.

Many women who have suffered domestic abuse grew up in violent families. Many of them say they came to believe that violence—though a carefully guarded secret—was to be expected in a relationship. In other words, this is just the way families are.

Battered women have told me that when they were first slapped or punched they were shocked by the violence. They thought, "How can this be? Why is he doing this? What did I do? What should I do now?" It is this final question that frequently confounds a woman's decision making. Many people will say, "If my partner ever hit me, I'd be out the door in a minute." While some women do leave the first time they are hit (and they probably should), for most, it isn't quite that easy. At workshops, I often have participants list all the different reasons they think a woman might get trapped in an abusive relationship. At least forty different explanations will surface. Here are just a few:

- She's afraid she'll lose her children (he has threatened to take them or gain custody).

- She has accepted his apologies and promises, and believes the abuse won't happen again.

- Divorce is perceived to be wrong in her religion, so she feels pressured to stay married.

- He has made threats, and she fears retribution if she leaves.

- She still loves him.

- She lacks financial resources.

- Her family has pressured her to stick it out ("You made your bed....").

- She feels she's to blame ("If I hadn't done this..." "If I hadn't said that...").

- She believes his threats of suicide.

- She doesn't think she'll ever find another partner.

- She believes the negative things he has said about her (her self-image and self-esteem have been damaged).

- She doesn't have a support system, doesn't know where to go or who to talk to.

- She doesn't know or doesn't believe the police or courts will help.

- She thinks abuse is part of marriage.

- She doesn't want to be perceived as a failure if she leaves.

Usually a combination of reasons will trap a battered woman psychologically, emotionally, and physically in an abusive relationship. Women begin to adjust who they are when faced with abuse; they develop adaptive behavior to survive or to make the relationship function at a level that has some semblance of normalcy.

Then there is the other question—why does he batter? When discussing a battered woman's reason for staying, we must never lose sight of who has ultimate responsibility for the violence. Many men who batter manipulate and play on a woman's fears of being alone, losing her children, being ostracized, or being further abused. As discussed throughout this book, controlling and abusive behaviors are like maneuvers or tactics men use to win arguments and get their way. Some men use blatant behaviors and others are more subtle—the intent is still the same.

In many ways an abusive relationship is like a war in which one country has more armaments than the other. In order to exact concessions from a less powerful country, the aggressor-state will make demands and threats. If this strategy doesn't produce results, it resorts to a show of force, hoping to prove its superiority and accomplish its objectives with minimal losses. If this approach fails, the aggressor-country can unleash all its weapons, until the less powerful country capitulates—and it usually does. This doesn't mean the less powerful country doesn't try to negotiate a way out, or resist the aggression. Sometimes a peaceful solution is found and the hostilities cease, but the threat of violence always exists when there is a power imbalance.

Men who use violence can stop. But battering doesn't end until intimidating behavior, threats, coercion, and the need to control also cease. Repairing a relationship damaged by domestic abuse isn't easy. Restoring trust takes time and may not be possible. For many battered women, the memories are too painful, the anger too overwhelming. They simply don't believe that real change has occurred, or feel they need time alone to heal and sort things out. When battering has diminished a woman's trust and caused a loss of intimacy, she may refuse to invest the time and energy toward reconciliation.

Staying together and trying to work things out can also be difficult for men who have battered. Being confronted by someone who is justifiably angry about the past, living with guilt, and trying to change attitudes and beliefs create a thorny wall to climb over. Some men conclude that it just isn't worth it.

This leads us to the Chuck and M'Liss Switzer story. Chuck battered M'Liss for twenty years, but against all odds they stayed together. They are a violence-free couple today, and their story is what "Staying Together" is all about.

In this chapter we will explore the difficult but not insurmountable challenges ahead for those couples who do want to work things out. The ideas in "Staying Together" are not for everyone—both men and women who have been in abusive relationships must decide. Hopefully, you will both get feedback from counselors, advocates, family, and friends on whether this is the right path for you in light of everything that has happened. But if you do decide to try to stay together, the Switzers' story is inspiring for their perseverance to struggle through the hard issues.

The Switzers' Story

The Switzers agreed to be interviewed for this book because of their fierce belief that we as a society must confront domestic abuse at its roots. Chuck and M'Liss have told their story numerous times on national television and in news magazines. M'Liss published her own book, *Called to Account*, in 1984.[19] She sits on the Board of Directors of the Domestic Abuse Project in Minneapolis. Chuck and M'Liss frequently speak to offenders who have been court ordered into counseling programs. They commit their time and energy and tell their often painful story because they believe that men who batter will relate to their experiences and perhaps see a way out of a bad situation. They have an important story to tell.

Chuck and M'Liss met at the Minnesota Bible College in 1960. At the time, M'Liss didn't recognize the signs that Chuck had the potential to be abusive. Chuck battered M'Liss for more than twenty years before she finally got help.

Chuck grew up in a rural area of Southwest Missouri. He never drank, was obedient in the home, and considered his family to be of good Christian roots.

> I had two sisters and a brother. My father was very abusive toward all of us. When he became violent, he was unmerciful—he would beat the living daylights out of us. He would allege that he'd lost something and then force us to look for it, sometimes for hours—he did this as a game, as a way to control us. He had been in the army and must have gotten some of that mind-control stuff there. He actually ran our house like a prison camp and we were deathly afraid of him. I'm still afraid of him. We really don't have much of a relationship today—we talk only indirectly. I did confront him on his behavior after I completed counseling for my violence, but he denied he ever did any of those things. Strangely, my siblings also deny that any of the abuse took place.
>
> My father was also very abusive toward my mother. The first incident I remember was when I was only about three years old. At this time my mom and dad were roughly the same size. They'd just come home from a family party. Evidently my dad had done some things my mother wasn't pleased with, and there they were, rolling around in the front yard wrestling and throwing blows. Whenever my mom would confront my dad about issues, he wouldn't even respond verbally—he would just decide the best thing to do was to beat her up. He figured that was the way to get her to come around to his way of thinking. And I saw that happen! I got a very clear picture that violence works. It's the ultimate in control. I think our family was as violent as a family can get. There wasn't any screwing around—there weren't any threats, they just went right into it. A conversation was brought up, issues were presented, and blows came next. There wasn't a lead-up time like you often hear about, nor was alcohol involved; he would just beat the living daylights out of my mom with his fists.
>
> After she was beat up, I stayed away from her. If I tried to console her, she would beat the shit out of me, so I left her alone until she was fully healed. I never felt or verbalized any empathy for her.

Violence was just part of the picture. My mom used to beat me and my siblings and I never thought there was anything wrong with it. In our cultural strata, this seemed to be normal—the way you dealt with kids when they misbehaved was you simply beat 'em up.

I know this will sound strange, but despite the violence I did see my parents being loving to each other. I saw them kissing and hugging. I really thought they loved each other. My parents prayed together, went to church together, and had Christian people over to the house.

Usually, it didn't seem like there was a reason for the violence, it would just happen. My brother, sisters, and I would spend as much time in the woods as possible, because it was safer there—when we were home we would be terrorized, beat up, or intimidated so we tried to stay away. Where I grew up, things were very different. If you screwed up in school and the teacher told your parents about your behavior, you got the daylights beat out of you. The violence was part of our life. And it wasn't just my parents. My grandfather beat my grandmother. I remember one time at the dinner table at my grandparents' house. My grandmother had questioned my grandfather on some farm issues, and she raised her voice. He jumped up from the table and hit her so hard she flew into the next room, and that was the end of it. I wasn't shocked by this at all—not the least bit surprised. It seemed like it was part of the culture. My cousins who lived a few farms down the road were constantly coming over to mend their wounds from beatings. That's the way things were.

For most folks, if things got to the place where you thought you couldn't handle something the person was doing or saying, you just beat the other person up. I worked for my dad in his construction business. I remember during lunch breaks—if the subject of family conflict came up, it was a forgone conclusion by all the men at the construction site that you just beat the shit out of the person that was causing the problem, man, woman, or child. That has been my cultural experience all my life, whether in Missouri, the armed services, or here in Minnesota.

I beat M'Liss from the day we were married and didn't stop until I was charged in 1982. All that time, I didn't think there was anything wrong with what I was doing. To be honest, I got off on the violence—it was like a sugar high. My adrenaline would increase and when I was whaling on her it was really like I was intoxicated with a feeling of power. Sometimes the violence was premeditated—I mean, I would actually think about being violent on the way home.

I could easily be sitting in prison for killing M'Liss—it was that close with some of the incidents. When I think back, most of the issues I beat her for were trivial—some incidents I don't even remember why I hit her. One time, I was dragging M'Liss around the house with a belt around her neck because she burned the toast. After the beating, I just went off to work.

Despite what some people say about losing control, I was clearly in control of my actions—I knew exactly what I was doing. I could turn it on, and I could turn it off at will. One time I had beat M'Liss pretty severely—I mean I was in a rage, but just as I was finishing with her, I saw the neighbor come to the door. When I answered the door and talked with the neighbor, I was totally calm. I'm sure he couldn't tell that anything had happened in our house.

M'Liss fought back only once that I remember. I was disciplining our son and she hit me on the head with a pan. I turned to her and said, "Don't you ever do something like that again." There was a clear message that if she ever hit me, I would most definitely raise the ante—inferring that I might kill her, and I might have.

I was very critical of her friends. I was smart enough to know that when she started talking to other people, it brought a new dimension into our lives. I didn't want her to change. To say it in more crude terms, I bought this horse and I didn't want anyone messing with its training. The more she associated with other people, the more she knew, and I thought she would be less dependent on me. I didn't like that at all.

When M'Liss charged me with assault, I was furious and scared. I didn't believe that what I was doing was criminal behavior, but on some level I started to realize that I had a problem. I didn't want to lie about the police report in front of the judge. I went to an attorney. He told me I should plead innocent and that a jury would never convict a disabled vet on a domestic abuse case. However, I was guilty and I pleaded guilty. Being on probation was a humiliating experience. Having to report to this probation officer weekly was hard for me to accept because I'd never been in trouble with the law before.

As a condition of my probation, I was ordered into domestic abuse counseling. At first, I just went and wanted to get it over with—you know, meet the requirements of the court. Again, at this point I wasn't totally convinced that I had a problem, except that I got tangled up with the courts. But, after about four months into counseling and after listening to the other men, I started looking at myself. First I was in groups with just men, and then M'Liss and I went into groups with other couples. It was in the couples groups that my eyes were opened. Listening to other people's stories, especially from the other women who'd been abused—that had a real impact on me. Coming to grips with the fact that my behavior was criminal was very humbling. At about this time, M'Liss had also gotten an Order for Protection, so I ended up living in a rat-hole apartment. I was all alone and I wanted my life back. In order to get it back, I knew I had to take a serious look at myself.

Change has been a long process. I was in groups as a participant for many years and then I cofacilitated a group. I stopped the violence and then started working on other ways I was controlling and abusive. It's still difficult for me to hear about my past violence. I still feel guilty. When M'Liss reminds me of my violence and her pain, it's like digging up the garden in my head. I think the reason most relationships touched by violence don't make it is that men who batter can't acknowledge what they've done. When they stop using violence, they immediately want their partners to forget about it and basically forgive them. That usually doesn't happen. So even today I have a hard time hearing about what I did to M'Liss. I feel like she brings up the past too much. She says she rarely does, but it's still hard for me to hear. The change process is hard and long and never totally over. It's a mind-set—that's how you change.

M'Liss was born in St. Paul, Minnesota, and her parents divorced when she was one year old. After her mother died she was reared through much of her adolescence by her older sister, who was abusive and domineering.

Here is her story:

My mom remarried when I was ten years old. My stepfather was really nice—never abusive to my mother or us kids. Two years later my mother died, and my sister became my guardian. She was really nasty to me. She ruled the roost. She abused me both physically and verbally for the next ten years.

I converted to a fundamentalist church when I was twenty-one years old and ended up going to the Minnesota Bible College. That's where I met Chuck. We dated for a about a year, but he was never abusive until we got married. Chuck was in the Marine Corps and he came back to Minnesota on leave so we could get married. I quit my job, moved out of my apartment, said my good-byes, and was ready for a married life with the man I loved. We were going to drive down to Missouri to see his folks and then head to Tennessee where Chuck was stationed. We spent our honeymoon night in a motel in Iowa. We made love for the first time that night and I didn't have an orgasm. Chuck got enraged. While he was still on top of me, he started hitting me around my shoulders and head with his fists. When he got off, I went to the bathroom and got cleaned up. He was standing at the bathroom door apologizing and saying it would never happen again. I wanted to believe his promise and I really didn't have anywhere to go, so I just let it go. I distinctly remember thinking this must be the way marriage is—so we moved on. It's clear to me now that when we got married I became a thing, Chuck's possession.

The violence was very frequent at first—about once a week. We lived off base and I never thought about seeking help or talking to anyone about the abuse. You simply didn't talk about such things back then and there wasn't any help available. And with Chuck being in the service, I didn't want to get him in trouble. Sometimes Chuck's violence wasn't even related to me—he was just taking it out on me. Anytime I was critical of Chuck, or if I didn't agree with him, he would beat me until I did. It got so bad that if I didn't cook the eggs right I got beat. I even got beat for dropping a fork one morning. I took the car to the car wash and the fender was damaged and I got beat for that. One time we went down to Sears, and he wanted to buy a lawn mower, but I talked him out of it. That night he beat me up because of what happened at the store. Whenever he was unhappy, I got it.

Chuck is a big guy, so he was careful how he would abuse me so it wasn't noticeable. He would choke me with a belt or with his hands, kick me in the stomach, or drag me around by the hair. One time he followed me into the bathroom and threw me through a glass shower door. On one occasion, he hit me on the side of the head causing my inner ear to bleed. I went for medical attention for that injury, but I lied to the doctor when I explained what happened.

I know this will sound strange, but I was always afraid Chuck would leave me. He knew I was threatened by the thought of being alone, so he would always use that as a weapon. He didn't use a lot of emotional abuse or put-downs that a lot of battered women experience—he would simply say I deserved the beatings because of my actions.

We were faithful churchgoers at the time—three times a week. I never talked to the pastor about the violence. I had learned that if you were getting beat you must be doing something wrong. "What are you doing that makes him so mad?" At the time, I felt enough shame and blame that I believed I must have been doing something wrong—why else would Chuck be hitting me?

My self-esteem had always been really low. My sister—my guardian—was abusive. She had me convinced I wouldn't amount to anything, and of course no man would ever want me. So when Chuck wanted to marry me—well, I just held on, violence and all. Somehow,

I worked it out in my mind that this was the way it was going to be. I was determined to be a better wife to avoid getting beat up.

We went to a psychiatrist about ten years into our marriage. The psychiatrist didn't really understand domestic abuse. One exercise he had us do was to plan times when we would be together and tell each other exactly how we felt. Well, telling Chuck how I felt was dangerous. If he didn't like the way I felt, he'd beat me up for it. One time the psychiatrist told me he didn't think Chuck would kill me. That just shut me down because I didn't feel my feelings or experiences were being validated. One time Chuck was beating me up and I managed to get the car out of the garage. Chuck came running after me, bounding over a chain-link fence chasing the car. I was so desperate. I went to a phone booth and called our psychiatrist at his home. I told him Chuck was beating me up and I didn't know what to do. All he said was to call him at his office in the morning.

When the Domestic Abuse Act was passed in Minnesota, I warned Chuck that I would call the police if he assaulted me again. For a whole year after I made that threat, Chuck didn't hit me. That summer, we went up to Canada for a vacation. We were only twenty minutes across the border when Chuck beat me up in the car. After we returned to Minnesota, we went another whole year without any violence. Then we took a trip to Missouri to see his family and he beat me up again when we were out of Minnesota.

It was at about this time I could see that things were really deteriorating. I started getting really scared for my life or the possibility of being maimed. Chuck had stopped apologizing for the violence and his self-esteem had eroded—he just didn't seem to care anymore.

In the winter of 1982, when the violence continued, I followed through on my threat. I went to a St. Paul Police Department precinct in our neighborhood and reported the assault. The police sergeant said, "Can you come back later? We're in the middle of rearranging the furniture." That was not the kind of response I was hoping for, but I did go back the next day and pressed charges. When we went to court, Chuck was escalating up and down with fear that he would lose his job if the assault charge became public. The night before we went to court for the sentencing, Chuck took a loaded Winchester into the bedroom and threatened to kill himself. I tried to reassure him that everything was going to be all right—I told him he needed help. He endlessly blamed me for pressing charges. Things were out of Chuck's control now and he didn't know what to do.

In counseling, we were in separate men's and women's groups where both of us learned about battering and techniques to use like the time-out. They taught us both to take time-outs whenever we felt we were getting agitated. Whenever I started to feel uncomfortable, I would take a time-out and we both would agree that we would come back to the issue at a later time. Chuck would usually respect my wishes to have that time alone.

Things were going pretty well when we were in counseling but then there was an incident. Chuck had wanted to have sex with me and I refused. He hit me in the face. My women's group at the Domestic Abuse Project really encouraged me to get an Order for Protection, and although I didn't want to I agreed to take this step. They rightly concluded that Chuck had to see that there were going to be consequences for his continued violent behavior, despite the progress he had been making.

I wouldn't let Chuck back in the house until I was relatively sure I'd be safe. At first, if I had an issue with Chuck, I would only go to restaurants with him to work things out, because I felt he wouldn't go off on me in a public place. I didn't trust Chuck for a long time. I would challenge him from time to time just to see if he would honor the time-out, to see if he would listen to me, or to see if he would threaten me.

I've had to let go of a lot of the pain. At some point, for me, I had to make the decision that the relationship was more important to me and I had to let go of the resentment and anger. Chuck would have to tell me he was sorry again and again to get it all healed—I didn't know if he could do that. I don't think Chuck has been able to fully forgive himself, but we've continued to work on our issues. For me, the important thing is that Chuck values my opinion, we can compromise, he treats me respectfully. I am happy today. I loved Chuck despite the violence—I wanted the relationship to work and it's working.

It May Always Be a Struggle

If you choose to stay in the relationship after the violence has ended, you must understand and accept that rebuilding your life together will be challenging. Your relationship is like a home severely damaged by a tornado; to repair it, you must first fix the foundation, then restore the rest of the structure. Your success will be determined in part by how long the violence occurred, the nature of the abuse, and your commitment to work through the hard issues.

Interestingly, M'Liss reported that Chuck was rarely emotionally abusive. Most battered women talk about the horrible things said to them prior, during, and after a violent attack. As discussed in earlier chapters, this depersonalization of the victim makes the violence easier for the offender. But for battered women who internalize the cruel and piercing verbal attacks, forgiveness may be difficult. M'Liss may not bear those emotional scars, but she clearly bears others. Reestablishing trust, mutual respect, and partnership isn't easy.

Starting over fresh will have its complications. Friendships and even relationships with family members may have been strained by the violence. Even if you think the abuse was kept secret, people close to you were probably aware of what happened. Some may accept and respect that you are working on your relationship. Others may be judgmental, cautious, and unaccepting—they still may not trust you. Although difficult, talking about your past behavior and the changes you have made may gain you a level of acceptance from your friends and family members, perhaps even some appreciation for being honest and willing to change. Talking can be a humbling experience, but it may also be therapeutic and healing.

M'Liss and Chuck went public with their experience, which has forced them to be more accountable to each other. In any relationship, it is easy to get into ruts and assume that everything is okay, when in fact it may not be. Not everyone who decides to stay with their partner will be comfortable talking publicly about the past, but if you don't, make sure you take the time to check things out with each other. If you sense you are reverting back to old patterns, see a counselor or an advocate. After all the progress you've made, you may be afraid to confront the reality that old behaviors or attitudes can creep back into the relationship. Deal with it before it becomes a problem.

As discussed earlier, a man who batters usually tries to isolate his partner from friends, family members, and others who might give her information and support. He believes she will then be dependent and won't attempt to leave the relationship, despite his abuse. He believes if he makes it difficult for her to be involved in activities, she may give up trying, because fighting is too exhausting.

Obviously, if you're going to stay together, you must give up this controlling and abusive behavior. It is important that you support and encourage your partner. When you do, you'll see dramatic changes in your relationship. M'Liss and Chuck have learned the importance of having independent lives, and they respect each other's needs. They are honestly supportive of each other's aspirations, a key element of their partnership. Trust must be the underpinning of your relationship. For some men this will be difficult, because they still have feelings of jealousy or uncertainty about how secure their relationships really are. If this sounds familiar, go back to Chapter 5 and review the material on self-talk, or see a counselor. Don't slip back into the old way of thinking.

Chuck had not been violent for seventeen years, and according to M'Liss had not been abusive in any way for two decades. Ironically, a few weeks prior to our interview, Chuck became verbally abusive. I could tell this was not an easy thing for either of them to reveal to me. On their way to a speaking engagement at the Domestic Abuse Project, where they discuss their experiences with men who are ordered into counseling, they got into an argument. Chuck started swearing and yelling. It brought it all back for both of them. M'Liss said she was afraid. Chuck believes he could have become violent. He didn't, but it was close. They talked through the incident at length later that evening. As Chuck and M'Liss both admit, the potential is still there, even seventeen years after being charged, even after years of counseling and sharing their story publicly.

M'Liss says that Chuck still gets an attitude. And Chuck is clear that he needs to be very aware of his emotions—he knows he could still be violent.

"I'd be a liar if I said I haven't come close to being violent on occasions," he says. He then adds, "A couple can learn to put the brakes on things when they escalate. For me, it's like driving down the freeway at sixty miles an hour and putting on the emergency brake—the wheels lock up, the brakes are smoking, and you come to a quick and complete stop."

As M'Liss says today, "I'm usually never afraid, but there are times—seventeen years later."

I suppose the skeptic might ask, "How can you call this a success story?" Even though Chuck hasn't hit M'Liss in almost twenty years, he admits he has come close, and she admits to still being fearful at times.

First, I think the fact that they discussed this incident with me is indicative of their level of accountability. They have been and continue to be very public about their experiences. Their ethical expectations of each other require honesty, even if it reveals embarrassing setbacks. Second, the Switzers' lives, like those of Andy, Jim, and other men I interviewed, are in many ways lives placed under a microscope because they have chosen either to volunteer or to work in the domestic abuse prevention field. Their credibility can only be maintained if they are honest and accountable. Third, though I don't intend to minimize the abusive behavior and its impact on M'Liss, Chuck did exercise enough self-control not to use physical violence.

If Chuck had never battered M'Liss, this incident in the car would seem relatively harmless. Couples get into arguments, say bad things they don't mean, sometimes say bad things they do mean, swear, criticize, and use put-downs. Hopefully, in healthy relationships this happens only sporadically. It is a rare couple that hasn't occasionally thrown all rationality out the window in a fit of anger. However, when battering has occurred, arguments should be viewed from a different perspective. A disagreement that results in raised voices and power struggles often brings back old feelings, memories, and fears. This incident with M'Liss illustrates that a victim probably never forgets, and perhaps never should. Chuck and M'Liss both told me they don't believe you ever totally get over the past.

The Switzers and I spent a good deal of the day talking about their experiences. Sometimes my questions brought up sensitive areas that were still a little raw, like this recent incident. Throughout the interview, I was very aware of how respectful they were of each other as they told their stories and clarified things for me. In my years in this field, I have been conned by many men who batter. Being with the Switzers I could see the love, their commitment to each other, and their struggle to stay together and work through the tough issues.

After four hours of the interview, we were all a little tired. We walked down the block to a restaurant and had lunch and talked about relationships, travel, and politics. As we walked back, Chuck told me about some of the new changes in his life—he recently had a second heart attack, which required a triple bypass, yet he was still active and planning on reroofing the house. I'm convinced the Switzers' relationship has been helped by the fact that they talk about the past between themselves and with others. It is therapeutic and keeps them accountable. They also acknowledge that the violent incidents of earlier days are like ghosts—experiences that will forever haunt them, and could recur, if they don't both continue to work on the relationship. I got into my car with my notes and tape recorder. As I drove away, I turned and saw M'Liss and Chuck walk up the sidewalk to their house, arms around each. It was very touching—

they had taken a long and somewhat improbable journey, and they have made it.

Understanding and Accepting Women's Anger

Anger is a domain still reserved for men. In professional sports it seems perfectly acceptable for one player to get mad at—and sometimes physically attack—another. The public accepts this behavior, cheering as both benches clear in a baseball game and the players duke it out. A hockey player may drop his gloves and attempt to land as many blows as possible to an opponent's head before the referees finally stop the fight. Professional wrestlers feign anger to inspire the roars of admiring fans eager for someone to get stomped or have a folding chair slammed over his head. Men are aggressive in the workplace, using real or exaggerated anger to intimidate their fellow workers. This is all part of the male world of anger, violence, and power—sadly, it is expected and accepted.

Men are often excused for displaying anger at home. Fathers have long been expected to be family disciplinarians, with anger part of the role. I remember my childhood days clearly. When my mother's discipline didn't work, she would say, out of total frustration, "Wait until your father gets home!" Sometimes she would actually call him. He would leave work furious and come home to mete out the discipline. He also perfected a glare—we called it "the look." The look meant shut up, or knock it off, or you'll get it big time. That's what dads did, and many still do. In a marriage, men often use their anger to intimidate or shut off discussions. Men who batter use their anger as a warning that violence is right around the corner.

This is not to say that women don't also use anger, or that mothers don't abuse their kids—they do. They also scream, yell, and exhibit anger toward their partners. The difference is that a woman's anger is unlikely to inspire fear in her partner, and unlikely to intimidate him or shut him down.

Men in general don't like it when women get angry. But instead of being afraid they are likely to minimize, trivialize, or deflect. The following exchange is an example:

Eddie: Darcy was really angry when I got home. I was late and she wasn't able to get to her women's group. I admit I was late, but she didn't have to get so bent out of shape.

Michael: Why don't you tell us what you said and what she said?

Eddie: Well, I went downstairs and she was folding the laundry. I tried to explain why I was late. I told her I was helping Jerome with his car so he could get to work. Legitimate, right? So she's giving me the silent treatment.

Michael: Had you tried to call her?

Eddie: No, but I didn't think I would be that late. She just totally overreacted.

Michael: So she missed her group and was angry and she wouldn't talk to you. What happened after that?

Eddie: I apologized. I hate it when she gives me the silent treatment, so I ate shit. And instead of accepting my apology, she goes off on me. She says, "You think an apology makes it okay!" She starts ragging on me about being irresponsible and purposely being late so she couldn't go to her group.

Maryann: Were you intentionally late so she'd miss her group?

Eddie: I knew you were going to ask that. No. I was just late. She goes to those damn groups every week; it won't kill her to miss one. But no, it was not intentional.

Michael: What did you say or do when she confronted you?

Eddie: I guess I just tried to loosen things up a little. I said, "Darcy, you know, you look so cute when you're mad, and you are definitely mad." Then I said, "Come on, lets just drop it and go get something to eat."

Some of the group members rolled their eyes; a few chuckled.

Michael: We'll get back to you, Eddie, but I have a question for the group. What is it about a woman's anger that makes men react defensively?

Devon: I think it may have to do with our mothers. I mean, my mom would scream and kick ass once in a while, but that was my mom. Now you've got this woman who you're involved with on an intimate basis acting like your mom and that's hard to take.

Maryann: So do you mean it's okay for your mother to have authority or the upper hand because she's your mom, but with your partner it's a threat of some kind?

Devon: I think so. I mean, I would kind of feel humiliated unless I stood up to that shit. I suppose it's the macho thing—about being dominated by your woman. If she starts in, you've got to get right back in her face, so she doesn't think she can boss you around.

Michael: So it's a power thing, if I'm hearing you correctly. In Eddie's example it almost seemed if Darcy stayed angry she would have a certain amount of power, and he didn't want that. What about the "You're so cute when you're angry" comment?

Devon: The "You're so cute" thing definitely doesn't work—that just pisses them off more. But I agree with you, I do think it's a power thing. I don't know what the other guys think, but I think men learn how to use their anger to survive. I mean, sometimes you gotta look angry so people don't mess with you. And with a woman, I don't know, you just don't want your wife to be angry, so you shut her up or leave.

We had a lengthy discussion about the nature of anger and why some men challenge and try to stop their partners from feeling this emotion. There are several ways that men—but especially men who batter—block their partners' anger. The following are some examples from groups at the Domestic Abuse Intervention Project:

Minimizing and trivializing a woman's anger

An example of minimizing your partner's anger is when you try to convince her she's overreacting:

- "Why do you get hysterical over such little things?"
- "Why are you making such a big deal out of this?"
- "I don't know what you're talking about."

We trivialize a woman's anger by being sarcastic or using put-downs:

- "Yeah, you're right, you're always right, so you can stop being angry."
- "I do one little thing, and now look at you."
- "What, are you on the rag?"
- "It must be that time of the month."
- "If you would just grow up, you wouldn't be reacting this way."
- "You sound just like your mother!"
- "You're cute when you're angry."

Contesting a woman's anger

An example of contesting your partner's anger is when you compare something *she* did in the past to the issue she's angry at you about:

- "What about when you _____?"
- "As if you've never _____ before?
- "You don't see me getting bent out of shape when you _____, do you?"

Another way of contesting a woman's anger is by refusing to talk things through or turning the tables on her:

- "Well, if that's the way you feel, I'm out of here."
- "I'm not listening to this shit anymore."
- "You don't care about my feelings."
- "Maybe you should go see a shrink to deal with these problems you have."
- "If you didn't hang around with _____ you wouldn't be acting like this."

Being abusive to keep from experiencing a woman's anger

Examples of shutting down your partner's anger by being abusive might be:

- Threatening her—"Shut up, or else."
- Screaming back at her or yelling loudly in her face.
- Using threatening gestures or throwing something at her or at the wall.
- Hitting her.
- Holding her by the arms or putting your hand over her mouth.

If the two of you are going stay together, you need to understand that your partner most likely has significant anger—and it's probably right below the surface. Whether your violence was constant or infrequent, the memories of being battered and humiliated may be unforgettable. Little things, conversations, and anniversaries may remind her of an argument or a beating.

M'Liss told the following story:

> Chuck had beaten me up when we were traveling in northern Minnesota because I'd left a blanket where we'd camped. It was the kind of thing Chuck would get angry about. Well, years later, when Chuck had stopped abusing me, we decided to take a car trip to Canada. When we drove by the park where he had beat me, I asked him if he remembered beating me there, because it brought back painful memories for me. He got really defensive and asked why I was always bringing up the past. It's strange, because I don't bring up the past that much, but he thinks I do.

When men make the decision to change, they often think their partners should totally accept their assurances that they'll never be abusive again. They feel hurt and sometimes get angry when their partners bring up past episodes or question their sincerity. This is the reality of an abusive relationship. To be blunt, if you're frustrated by your partner's mistrust and anger, you've just got to deal with it. In the past, she may have been forced to submerge or temper her anger because she was fearful you would be violent. The anger she felt during those abusive days—and may still feel today—is like a volcano, dormant for years and now ready to blow. It may not explode all at once, but periodically you will feel the eruptions. If you can understand where your partner's anger is coming from, it will be easier for you to accept that her healing will take time.

Many women who stay with the partners who abused them test them to see if they really are committed to nonviolence. M'Liss told me that after Chuck completed counseling she would actually do things to provoke him to see if he would honor his agreement to take a time-out when he was agitated.

■ **EXERCISE:** Understanding and Accepting Your Partner's Anger

1. Remember a recent incident when your partner was angry at you. This should be an example when you *didn't* react to her anger appropriately. Write down this incident and respond to the following in your journal or notebook:

a. What was the issue?

_____

_____

b. Describe your feelings.

_____

_____

c. Describe your thoughts.

_____

_____

d. How did you respond to her anger?

_____

_____

e. How could you have handled this situation differently?

_____

_____

Example:

a. What was the issue?

Tyra got angry at me when I asked her where she'd been. I thought it was a harmless question and we got into an argument.

b. Describe your feelings.

Defensive. Misunderstood. Angry. Picked on. Hurt.

c. Describe your thoughts.

She's saying these things purposely to make me angry. I don't deserve this, she's overreacting. I'm not going to take this anymore, I'm leaving. She better stop.

d. How did you respond to her anger?

I yelled at her and called her a bitch.

e. How could you have handled this situation differently?

I could have not responded to her when she got angry. I could have discussed her reaction with her at a later date. I could have acknowledged to myself that she may have thought I was checking up on her.

2. Now, remember another recent incident when your partner was angry with you. This should be an example when you *did* respond to

her anger appropriately. Write down this incident and respond to the following in your journal or notebook:

a. What was the issue?

_____

_____

b. Describe your feelings.

_____

_____

c. Describe your thoughts.

_____

_____

d. How did you respond to her anger?

_____

_____

e. How did you feel after handling a tense situation in a positive manner?

_____

_____

Example:

a. What was the issue?

I didn't give Jeanne the message that her sister called. I told her I forgot and apologized. She said this kind of thing happens a lot. We started to argue.

b. Describe your feelings.

Attacked. Angry. Defensive.

c. Describe your thoughts.

I thought she was blowing this out of proportion, but I did think that maybe what she was saying might be true.

d. How did you respond to her anger?

Listened to her before arguing. Used positive self-talk and tried to understand why she was upset. Was assertive but not aggressive in my response. Didn't turn her anger around so that now I was angry and blaming her.

e. How did you feel after handling a tense situation in a positive manner?

It felt good to have a disagreement that was settled without our usual yelling and accusing.

Responding to conflict in your relationship may be one of your biggest challenges. Your past approach has probably been to react defensively to disagreements. Physically, your body gets tense, your teeth and fists seem automatically to clench, and you might feel tightness in your chest or stomach area. Emotionally, your brain signals "fight" and you get defensive—ready for whatever she has to say. Odds are, you probably didn't really listen to her, except the words that triggered an angry response from you. Once the conflict started, you would end it on your terms—breaking something, calling her a vile name and walking out, threatening her, or using violence.

That was the old you. If you have made the commitment to stay in your relationship, hopefully a new you has emerged. In your new incarnation, you understand that there will always be conflicts. At the same time, you have a heightened awareness of your reactions, and pay close attention to the tenseness in your body or old negative messages still lodged in your mind. You remember your commitment to remain accountable for your actions. When the conflict starts, you assess the situation and determine whether you can have a fair discussion without becoming abusive. You remember and follow the negotiation rules on page 175. If you sense agitation or if you recognize past cues, you take a time-out and follow the time-out rules you committed to on page 119.

It would be so easy to forget about all this. Many men have gotten into trouble by convincing themselves that the old abusive behavior is all in the past. But as we noted with the Switzers' story, after seventeen years of being violence free, he came close.

It will be hard at first. Your partner may be consciously or unconsciously testing you. As your relationship improves you can develop healthier ways to work through problems. When her fear has subsided, a marriage counselor can teach you all kinds of communication techniques that you will find useful.

Changing the Mind-Set

People don't change the way they think overnight. Education is a process, and we should all consider ourselves lifelong learners. But we can't just will a change in our thinking. Our inward journey needs external information, which is why I'm such an advocate of counseling, education—both formal and self-taught—and time for reflection.

In order to understand algebra, you have to take mathematics courses for some time—in my case, a very long time. To comprehend the complexities of an algebra problem you first need instruction, then time to process the information and practice what you have learned, before that wonderful moment when the lightbulb goes on and you say to yourself, "I think I understand. It all seems so easy now." Men who have battered must be willing to go through a very similar educational process. Those who have made radical transformations in their thinking and changed their behavior first took the initiative to gain a deeper understanding of their beliefs and attitudes about men, women, and relationships. They read and discussed the historical origins of sexism, questioned how sexist thinking affected them as men, and finally began to understand how they came to their own world view. They were willing to be challenged.

Chuck Switzer told me, "I started examining the ethics of my violence. I had to confront my attitudes and beliefs about women. This issue is about sexism—I never thought that women were equal and it was only through the confrontation of counseling that I changed that mind-set."

It was a long process before M'Liss recognized that Chuck was changing. Trust was not something that could be restored because of promises or because Chuck was going to counseling. He'd beaten her for twenty years!

"For me," M'Liss said, "it was when Chuck started listening, honoring my time-outs, letting me express my opinions without trying to control me—that was when I knew he was changing. When he was truly listening to me, and we could finally negotiate as equals."

▓ EXERCISE: Changing the Mind-Set

1. In your journal or notebook, make a list of all the stereotypical and sexist messages you heard as a boy and as an adult male about men, women, and relationships.

Examples:

Men must be tough. Women are weak. Men shouldn't show their feelings. Women are too emotional. The man is the head of the household. A woman should submit to her husband's authority in marriage. It's okay for men to get angry. Men settle disagreements through violence. Women provoke men to use violence. Men have uncontrollable sexual urges. If a woman dresses "provocatively" she's asking for it. Men are the breadwinners. Women take care of the house and children.

2. Briefly answer the following questions:

a. What has been the impact of these beliefs on your life?

b. How have these beliefs affected your relationship with your partner?

c. How has your thinking about these kinds of stereotypes of men and women changed?

Getting Your Needs Met without Being Abusive

Boys are taught to be aggressive. To survive on the playground, in the neighborhood, or within an abusive family system, they are constantly being tested. They tease and taunt, give and receive insults, shove each other and hit each other, sometimes landing the blows and sometimes enduring them. This is a boy's world. To get his needs met, or to be accepted, he quickly learns to be aggressive.

Most boys adjust and survive childhood and adolescence, even though we all lose a bit of our innocence and some of our ability to be vulnerable and sensitive. But, increasingly, boys are using violence to resolve conflict in a much different way than just a generation ago.

Because of easy access to guns, the fistfight is now a bullet to the head. Rejection in school from peers or from girls results in a shooting spree. Boys who commit crimes are consistently being tried as adults and then languishing in our prisons. When they get out, they are often hardened and mean. Our society is failing miserably at addressing this issue, and many in the domestic violence field also fail to make the connection between boys' childhood experiences and their later use of violence in intimate relationships.

A man who batters often perceives arguments and conflicts with his partner as a test of wills, like the childhood tests of "manhood." In our groups, men frequently claim that in order to get their needs met they must be aggressive and not allow their partners to get the upper hand. Being disrespected by a woman is not to be tolerated. During an argument, they might storm out of the house, swear, refuse to talk, refuse to negotiate, threaten, and sometimes become violent. However, it doesn't have to be this way. You *can* be assertive without being aggressive. You *can* get your needs met without being controlling and abusive. You *can* work out your problems in a respectful manner.

Two key elements for being assertive are

1. having the willingness to ask for what you need without being demanding, controlling, or threatening;

2. being able to express your feelings without attacking or shaming.

In discussing the distinction between aggression and assertiveness, Tom described an argument he had with his partner Jamie:

Tom: We got into this big argument on the way home from the Christmas party. I was upset because Jamie brought up an embarrassing issue in front of the people I work with. We've been having a long-standing conflict with our neighbors over their loud parties. Anyway, I got angry and I let her know. She got all upset and there was screaming and crying all the way home.

Maryann: So you were embarrassed by something she said. You said you let her know that you were angry. What specifically did you say to let her know you were angry?

Tom: I just confronted her. I told her, "You know, Jamie, you made me look bad by bringing up the argument we're having with our neighbor." I told her our disagreement was private business. I said, "You shouldn't have brought that up—you screwed up my whole night." And then I just told her the truth. I said, "Every time we're out with people you've got to open up your big mouth." I asked whether she was trying to make me look like a fool.

Maryann: And how did Jamie respond?

Tom: She got really defensive and accused me of overreacting. And then I got even more upset and started yelling back at her. I asked her how she would feel if I brought up some embarrassing things about her in public. I named a few choice things and the next thing I knew we were off to the races. We didn't talk for two days.

Maryann: Not to take away from how you felt at the party or on the way home, but I'm just wondering if there was another way of letting Jamie know you were upset without being so attacking or blaming. I mean, unless she purposely revealed something to hurt you, which it doesn't sound like she did, then it would seem like a mistake. And if that's the case, do you think there was another way of communicating how you felt?

Tom: I don't know.

Maryann: What do others think? Tom was obviously upset and maybe for good reason. Are there other ways to communicate these feelings?

The group analyzed the incident and came up with a number of suggestions. Some group members thought Tom could have eliminated the comment about Jamie having a big mouth. Others thought it was unnecessary for Tom to make assumptions about why Jamie said what she did. Some questioned his need to yell. After getting plenty of feedback, we asked Tom to role-play the conversation he had with Jamie. We asked him to communicate his feelings, but delete the personal attacks. Maryann suggested that Tom substitute the "you" statements with "I" statements during the role play.

After several tries, with Maryann playing the role of Jamie, we ended up with the following:

Tom: Jamie, I would like to talk with you about something that happened at the party.

Jamie [Maryann]: Sure.

Tom: Well, when you brought up that stuff about our neighbors, I was really upset. I thought you were disclosing private business and I was embarrassed that people were hearing it. [Tom said this in calm voice.]

Jamie: Jeez, I thought what I said was harmless. But I'm sorry if I embarrassed you. It just sort of related to the issue we were talking about—you know, neighbors with barking dogs, neighbors who are inconsiderate. I didn't realize you felt this way.

Tom: I appreciate that, but I'm not really proud of this disagreement we're having with the Jensens and I would just prefer that it not get raised in a public forum—because for me it's embarrassing.

Jamie: Okay. I won't bring it up in public again.

Tom: Thank you.

Tom was able to be assertive without being aggressive in this role play. Of course, not every conflict would necessarily turn out this way, but you *can* express your feelings without being abusive. Had Jamie become defensive, Tom could still have remained calm, but also assertive about his need for privacy.

It might be unrealistic at this stage of Tom's work in the group for him to shift to this kind of interchange with Jamie. But if Jamie and Tom choose to stay together, their methods of communication will have to change so that both parties can articulate what they need without being controlling or abusive. Because of the history of domestic abuse in the relationship, Jamie may still be too angry at Tom to try different ways of communicating or resolving conflicts. She may not trust his motives. She may think this is just another way for Tom to control her.

If your partner doesn't want—or isn't willing—to try new communication techniques, you would probably be wise to back off. When she's ready, she'll let you know. Trust is earned, and takes time. Even if your partner doesn't want to try different approaches to conflict resolution, this doesn't mean you yourself can't change. You can eliminate aggressive and attacking responses to issues and conflicts. You can be calm in your approach, yet still assertive. Right now the change process is your responsibility. If you and your partner stay together, you will eventually work out a healthy communication pattern.

You may need the help of a good marriage counselor if you choose to stay together. As stated earlier, you should attend marriage counseling only after (1) the violence and abuse have ceased, (2) you have completed a domestic abuse program, and (3) your partner feels safe bringing up topics ranging from intimacy issues to your past use of violence. Try to find a counselor who is familiar with domestic abuse issues. Tell him or her about your past use of violence at the outset. Be truthful even if it's painful. A good therapist will teach you and your partner effective communication techniques. Getting feedback from someone neutral, whom you both trust, will make your journey together that much easier.

Relationships are not easy. Even the healthiest marriage has struggles and times of uncertainty. Over half the marriages in the United States end in divorce due to incompatibility, irreconcilable differences, and the fact that sometimes people simply fall out of love or want something different in their lives. Divorce is not failure, but it is change. For those who can and want to stay together, I truly believe you have something very special. I hope you take good care of each other, and cherish each other and your relationship.

8

Resolving Conflicts, Strengthening Relationships

Elliot's Story — New Relationships, Old Problems — Egalitarian
Relationships — Sharing the Load — The Issue of Money —
Expressing Feelings — Learning to Negotiate and Compromise
— Developing a Personal Responsibility Program

*Seldom, or perhaps never, does a marriage develop into
an individual relationship smoothly and without crisis; there
is no coming to consciousness without pain.*

CARL JUNG

People have conflicts even in the most stable relationships. How
we choose to resolve our differences is frequently influenced by the
behaviors modeled for us when we were growing up. For men who
are violent, dealing with conflicts requires a willingness to learn
new, nonabusive approaches to conflict resolution.

In this chapter, you will read about starting new relationships
and how to develop equal or egalitarian relationships. We will examine some typical areas of conflict among couples and explore how
violence influences these conflicts and how to deal with them in a
mutually respectful manner.

In the following story, Elliot explains how his attitudes about
women had an impact on how he responded to his partner when
they had conflicts.

Elliot's Story

Elliot grew up in a rural community in Iowa. His father was a strict
disciplinarian and Elliot and his brothers tried hard not to cross
him. Elliot's father was never violent with his mother.

Elliot was married to his wife Claudia for seventeen years.
When he came into our program, he wanted to focus only on the

situations when Claudia was abusive, allowing him to feel justified in his use of violence. Elliot sees his life and his destructive relationship with Claudia differently today.

I grew up with the belief that a woman basically had to know her place. The family was an important unit, and traditional values dictated that the man commanded the respect of his family. My childhood was rather lousy. Dad's values were such that everyone in the family was to work hard like he did, so there was little time for fun. All I ever did was work. I had very few dates with girls in high school because my parents didn't allow dating. That was the early sixties and I guess that's the way things were.

As soon as I graduated, I left home and went to college in Minnesota. All that pent-up frustration came out because I partied constantly. I started drinking a lot and that's when I began fighting. I got kicked out of college and joined the Air Force and ended up in Vietnam.

My self-esteem was very low. My father put me down a lot. He'd say I was no good and I would never amount to anything. I think part of my experience in Vietnam reflected the suicidal tendencies I had. I was depressed when I went into the service. Hell, I even volunteered for "door duty" on helicopters because the job was extremely dangerous. I never sought help for my depression and just dealt with all my feelings with the bottle.

When I got out of the service, I started hanging around a group of people who drank and got into trouble. I was working in construction at the time. My attitudes about women weren't very good. Basically, I felt women were there to be used. My thinking was that if they didn't want to play the game, then they could hit the road—there were plenty of other women. While I was emotionally and psychologically abusive, at this point I had not been violent with women.

I married Claudia in the early 1970s. We were married for seventeen years and were in constant conflict from the very beginning. I never hit her while we were dating. Both of us were drinking quite heavily. Both of us wanted things our own way, so our relationship was a constant power struggle.

I think I wanted to replicate what I knew from growing up. I wanted the kind of relationship my father had with my mother, although I wasn't conscious of that at the time. I wanted to be in control and call the shots. Claudia resisted me, of course. The first time I hit her was when she accused me of looking at other women. She started screaming at me in the car and the argument spilled over into the house, and that's when she slapped me and I hit her back. Whenever she hit me, it gave me a license to hit her back.

I have bad memories about my violence, her violence, and our mutual violence. The way she would start the violence was usually by slapping me. And then I'd slap her back. I never punched her, because of our size difference; I'm sure I would have killed her. The way I would start was by picking her up and throwing her on the couch, bed, or floor.

Sometimes when I thought I was losing a verbal battle, I would pick her up and spank her on the bottom like a child. She was so much smaller than me that I could just hold her between my arm and body and spank her.

I specifically remember one incident when we were in Hawaii on vacation. We were arguing and she hit me several times and then kicked me in the groin. I came up swinging and grabbed her by the hair and slapped her several times. We physically fought for hours. One time, we were having an argument and I was holding our son and she tried to kick me. She was going to try to kick me again so I started to leave and slammed the steel door. She put her arm out to stop me and her arm got crushed. I didn't intentionally try to hurt her; it was just a result of our violence. I took her to the hospital and she had some tendon damage.

I took her to the hospital on another occasion, too, but I was so drunk I don't remember what happened, only that she had a head injury after I threw her. I thought the hospital officials were going to call the police because I told them what I'd done, but they didn't. When they released her, we drove home and that was the end of it for then.

I controlled Claudia in many ways. I was the breadwinner and she wasn't working, so she had to come to me for money. That was a powerful tool because she would feel humiliated having to ask me for money. I'm sure I withheld money as a punishment. I could intimidate her easily. I would hold my fist up and threaten to beat her up. When she was sober she would cower, thinking I would punch her. If she was drinking, my intimidation didn't seem to scare her.

I would call her a bitch because she hated that. I would compare her to other women as a way to put her down. I'd imply that she wasn't living up to my standards.

My son saw a lot of the violence. When he was around, I would try to do or say things that would indicate the violence was his mother's fault.

On a couple of occasions, I would take a gun from the house and leave, hoping that she would see that she'd pushed me too far. I wanted her to think I might kill myself. Well, apparently she did, because she called the police and they took all of my guns. When I first came into the Domestic Abuse Intervention Project, I couldn't seem to focus on me, it was always her. I quit the program and went into alcohol treatment. I then came back into the program because I wanted the violence to stop and to get a handle on my life. I realized by that time, however, that my relationship was not going to work. I'm in a new relationship now and have been married for two years. I don't have the desire or the need to control. I know who I am. I don't need to control her to feel good and I don't desire the power I sought with Claudia. I don't need to win when we have disputes or conflicts.

The most important thing that happened to me in this program was that people listened to me and didn't call me a no-good son of a bitch. It was the first time that people seemed to care. The counselors told me that I had a life to lead and that I could make changes. It was a revelation.

I try to apply some of the tools I learned in the program. I take time-outs and try to use self-talk when I feel myself reverting to old patterns. I'm much more aware of my feelings.

My new partner and I make decisions together, although I guess I still see myself as head of the household. I think it's more of a perception than reality. I guess there's still some male stuff I need to look at—like when we get into the car, I drive.

I still meet with some of the men from my group to continue focusing on issues I need to work on. I've come a long way and I feel good about that.

Elliot describes his relationship with Claudia as a constant power struggle. Many forces kept them in this destructive and unhappy relationship. Elliot's belief that he is the head of the household in his new relationship points to a belief that he holds on to about the roles of men and women, despite the groups and programs he has been through. However, he maintains that his life is different today and that his change is an ongoing process.

New Relationships, Old Problems

Elliot made a decision not to get involved with someone immediately after the breakup of his marriage. He wanted to work through some of his problems. Many men, however, get into a "rebound relationship"—they become involved with someone new right away. This way they don't have to experience the pain and grief of losing a relationship or confront the hurt they caused their previous partner.

In our groups, a man in a rebound relationship will report how everything is great with this new woman and how different she is from the partner he just left. He explains how this person does not have the same problems and defects that he believes his former partner had. This is a common trick of denial. Comparing his past relationship with his present one allows him to subtly justify his past abusive behavior.

However, when men jump into rebound relationships, they usually do not take the time to sort out the mistakes of the past. Because they aren't experiencing major conflicts in their new relationships, they don't believe they need to make changes. In the early stages of the relationship the man and his new partner are usually on their best behavior. When people are dating, they often try not to reveal flaws and they overlook character deficiencies because they want the relationship to work.

The problem for a man who has battered is that he often reverts to familiar ground. He finds someone he really likes and immediately wants to possess and control her. When she resists, he uses what has worked before—threats, intimidation, and violence—to get what he wants. Ultimately, the cycle of violence begins all over again.

If your relationship has ended, take some time before you get involved with someone else. It is important to work on the issues that led to your violence before entering into a new relationship. As Anthony explains below, giving yourself time to sort things out can have positive results. You don't have to wait as long as he did for a new relationship, but the point he makes is clear.

> I thought about getting involved after Vickie and I split. I certainly had a lot of opportunities, but I'd been violent with two women and didn't want to do it again. I kept going to the group. Then I went to a support group so I could continue to work on my issues. It was five years before I really believed I had come to terms with all this stuff. I'm now in a really good relationship and I'm glad I waited.

Participating in counseling or a domestic violence group can be helpful. You do not have to attend many sessions, and going does not mean there is something psychologically wrong with you. A few sessions in which you are honest can be valuable and you may get the kind of feedback you need. The sessions can provide insight about what you need to change and work on.

Sorting out your prior response to conflicts and clarifying the beliefs you had about women and relationships will help you know what to be aware of in the future. If someone videotaped an argument you had with your partner and played it for you, I'm sure you could pick out precisely where you made mistakes and how you could handle the situation differently now. This is the kind of feedback and insight counseling and support groups can give you. Here are some issues and techniques you may still need to work on:

- Confronting your possessiveness and jealousy

- Letting go of always being right and having things your way

- Trying to be less critical

- Finding ways of being more intimate

- Practicing communication and negotiation techniques

For some, the thought of living alone is scary. However, living alone does not mean you have to be lonely. Meeting new people, connecting with old friends, and finding activities of interest in your community can enrich your life. You could choose to live with friends or find a roommate, if your finances require it. The important thing is to *take your time* before entering a new relationship. Work on your problems and make sure you're confident that you will remain nonabusive in your new relationship.

Egalitarian Relationships

In egalitarian, or equal, relationships, couples work through traditional gender expectations. Often, people who have been in relationships in which there were bitter and divisive struggles around gender roles and equality want new role definitions and freer, healthier interchanges with their new partners.

Women who previously were in traditional relationships may now seek something different. They are often quite clear about what they expect and what they are willing to accept. Similarly, a new consciousness is emerging in a growing number of men. They see egalitarian relationships with women as a path to liberation rather than as the loss of control.

What do I mean by "liberation" for men? Here are some examples. Egalitarian relationships permit men to go beyond feeling *obliged* to share in child care; they may *desire* the responsibilities of shared parenting and the rewards of being involved fathers. In egalitarian relationships, men *encourage and support* partners who are pursuing new careers and community involvement. These men are likely to feel less threatened by their partners' aspirations, because they see that mutual development, growth, and support from each other enhance the partnership.

Such relationships were not common in my youth, and I suspect this was true for many of my generation—the baby boomers. My mother fulfilled the traditional female role. When she did enter the job market, her position with my father changed because she became less dependent.

Men in our groups frequently say they have equal relationships. But as we begin to discuss roles and household responsibilities, a different picture emerges, as is shown in the following exchange:

Michael: Lloyd, you say that you and Patty have an equal relationship. Tell us how that works.

Lloyd: Well, I think it's pretty equal. I do a lot of the yard work and stuff with the car and she does most of the housework.

Michael: So you mow the yard once a week and she does the cleaning, cooking, and child care.

Lloyd: It's not like I'm forcing her to do this stuff, but she's better at a lot of it. Look, I've tried to help out when she asks, but she's never satisfied with the way I do it. I mean, she doesn't like the way I fold the towels—you know, they have to be folded into three perfect sections. So she doesn't want me to do the laundry. And let's face it, most women can cook better than men, so she does that. With child care—well, after all, she is the mother. It's not like I don't help out, but there are certain things she can do better than me and certain things I can do better than her.

Some of Lloyd's explanation may be accurate. Patty may want to assert control over the household areas she feels are her domain. When a person does not have much power or many options, that person will want to hold on to areas in which she has some control. In other words, your partner looks for a niche to call her own.

Some men in our groups have admitted they do a sloppy job folding laundry, cleaning, or cooking on purpose so their partners will perceive them as incapable of doing these chores. Pretending incompetence is an old childhood strategy that worked while growing up, so many men think, why not use it now? Television shows and movies constantly reinforce the image of the incompetent male in the household. Living up to those limited expectations allows men to avoid responsibilities.

Yet today many men realize the importance of equal partnership. They have examined failed relationships and see how their definitions of roles for men and women became obstacles. In these past relationships, struggles and conflict over unfair role definitions and work distribution took the place of friendship and intimacy.

Because egalitarian relationships are new territory, you may stumble and experience confusion. A commitment to making the relationship work and communicating expectations and needs are critical for success. We have all the tools we need to make an equal partnership work; we just need to use them.

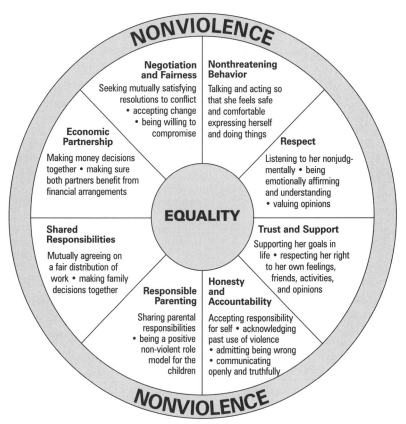

The Equality Wheel was developed by the Duluth Domestic Abuse Intervention Project. (If you have difficulty reading the wheel, see the text reproduced in the Appendix.) As you can see, there are many elements to an equal relationship. Consider this wheel from time to time. Are you relating to your partner in a manner that reflects the positive elements of the wheel? If not, review the Negotiation Guide on page 175, and practice some of the exercises in this book—especially "Negotiating Roles," later in this chapter—to get back on track.

Sharing the Load

While society has changed considerably in the last generation, the division of labor in many homes has not. The majority of families today cannot survive financially on one income, and both men and women must work. Yet women still clean, cook the meals, do the laundry, and provide most of the child care. Arguments often occur when women express resentment about this unequal—and unfair—load.

Men who think taking out the trash and occasionally doing the dishes are the only household responsibilities they need to fulfill are being unfair. Yet in our groups these men often describe their partners as "nags" who are always "bitching." In one group, Herman discussed an argument he had with his partner Roberta.

Herman: This woman is really something, man. I mean, last week, almost every day she was ragging on me. She says I don't help out enough. I swear, it's like living with my mother sometimes.

Michael: Two things before we proceed. Does this woman have a name?

Herman: Yeah, Roberta is her name.

Michael: This word ragging. I hear men use the word a lot. Men often say that if a woman is upset she must be "on the rag," or "it must be that time of the month." To me that term is used to belittle women's anger and is a derogatory statement about a woman's menstrual cycle.

Herman: Shit, it's getting to the point where you can't say anything anymore. Okay, how about if I say she was nagging?

Michael: Would you ever say a man was nagging?

Herman: Let's just say she was in my face.

Michael: Okay. So she was in your face because she feels you aren't doing enough around your home. Is there any truth to what she is saying?

Herman: Ever since she went from part-time to full-time at the hotel where she works, she expects me to do all this extra stuff at home. I work hard all day. I know she works hard, too, but cleaning rooms isn't as stressful as a steelworker's job.

Michael: So even though she's working full-time, you expect her to do all the household stuff too?

Herman: You're starting to sound like her. Look, if she asks me to do something, I do it.

Michael: It's quite obvious you're going to continue to have conflicts around this, Herman. I mean, if she has to ask you to do your part, I'm sure she'll be resentful. Is there any way you can sit down with her and figure out a plan? You know, kind of divide up the responsibilities?

After a lengthy discussion, Herman admitted that the position he was taking wasn't fair. He agreed to sit down with Roberta and work out a plan for them to share the load.

When we speak about sharing the load in an egalitarian relationship, we're not talking about something like cutting an apple in half, everything fifty-fifty. Some people think equality means you do the dishes one night and I'll do them the next night; you clean the house this week and I'll do it next week; you bring the kids to soccer this month and I'll do it next month; we take turns paying bills and going grocery shopping.... Egalitarian relationships don't have to be that rigid.

The following exercise will help you understand how to share responsibilities in a relationship. If your relationship has ended or is ending, the exercise may still be worthwhile. Use it to review your past relationships, and to develop insight that will be helpful in future relationships.

▓ EXERCISE: Negotiating Roles

With your partner, make a list of your joint and separate responsibilities and obligations:

_____

_____

Now write down who always, or for the most part, does the following:

1. Pays the bills

2. Cooks the meals

3. Buys groceries

4. Buys the children's clothes

5. Feeds the children

6. Cleans the apartment or house

7. Repairs things in the home

8. Washes and puts away the laundry

9. Takes care of the car

10. Arranges social contacts

11. Other _____

The purpose of this exercise is not to judge, but rather to assess who does what in the relationship. Use this list to figure out together the responsibilities you and your partner need to modify so the relationship is more equal.

Often, couples get into ruts regarding responsibilities, but don't express their displeasure to each other. Consequently, resentment grows. If these feelings are not communicated, your resentment tends to spill out during other disagreements. So it's better to deal with this issue directly, clearly, and fairly.

As you and your partner complete the above exercise, you may find that sub-issues come up under each category. Each of these should be dealt with. One partner may also try to hold on to certain responsibilities for reasons of his or her own. For example, parents often disagree about disciplining children, school grades, setting boundaries and curfews, and values involving parental decision making. If one partner holds on to a major share of responsibility for the children in order to influence these decisions, this needs to be addressed as well.

Whether you and your partner have lived together for years or for months, take time periodically to make a list of your joint responsibilities. Talking about and modifying these responsibilities can be an important and perhaps relationship-saving exercise. By looking at each other's needs and listening to each other's concerns, you pave the way for healthy future negotiations about problems and issues that have not yet surfaced. You may have to reevaluate the way you share responsibilities, but you will find the journey to true partnership that much more rewarding.

The Issue of Money

Someone once said that money is the root of all evil. Money causes people to react in strange ways. Nations go to war over it and individuals go to jail trying to steal it. We work the majority of our lives to earn enough of it to survive—and couples often disagree about it.

We live in a money-driven, market-oriented society in which most of us need money for the necessities of life, and most of us do not have enough. The pressure to make money to live affects everyone. So, of course, it is a source of stress and conflict in even the healthiest relationships.

Our views about money are shaped by our upbringing. If you grew up in a household with limited resources, that is likely to have an impact on how you deal with money. If you saw your parents scrimp to get by, you might mirror that experience. Or you might try to do the opposite even if you don't have the resources. If yours was a family of means, you may have received very different messages, which will undoubtedly affect your attitudes about spending and saving.

When I grew up in the 1950s and 1960s, my parents went from having nothing to reaching middle class, the American dream. Even though our family had greater opportunities than some families today, my mother always reminded us children of how hard my father worked for every dollar when we received our weekly allowance. When I became an adult, I adopted an attitude of "you can't take it with you," partly in response to my parents' worrying and my own feelings of guilt. Yet, as much as I tried to get away from my upbringing, my parents' voices still echoed in my mind. Consequently, at different times in my adult life, I have been overly concerned about not having enough money or dwelt on financial problems.

When you enter into a relationship with someone, you have to combine both of your ideas about spending and saving. If your priorities and values are different, conflicts occur. In some traditional relationships, men believe that all the decisions about spending money should be made by them. Even in relationships in which the woman also works, the man may assume decision-making responsibility because of this belief, and because money is power. Controlling the money usually gives a person more authority in the relationship.

Victims of domestic abuse often report that, besides the fear of threatened violence, what kept them locked in an abusive relationship was their lack of financial resources.

In one of our groups, Frank related the following story about money:

> When we got married, there really wasn't any discussion about money. Jackie wasn't working at the time, so I obviously was supporting the family. I would give Jackie some cash every week to buy groceries and have some spending money. When she went back to work and started making her own money, we had all kinds of disagreements because she felt she should be able to spend her paycheck any way she wanted. She wasn't making very much, but I thought her pay and mine should be put together. I guess I was suspicious of what she was doing with the additional money, because I started accusing her of having affairs and plotting to leave me. That's when the physical violence got really bad. Jackie got a protection order and is seeking a divorce.

The experience of Frank and Jackie is not unusual. During our group session, it took a long time for Frank to understand how humiliating and dependent Jackie felt because she had to ask for a few extra dollars to buy herself or the children something. Though he finally acknowledged how Jackie may have felt, Frank refused to yield on what he believed was a fairness question, making statements such as, "Women are just out to screw men." His hurt and anger about Jackie leaving him kept him from seeing how his violence affected her and how he used money to control her.

When the discussion of economic control comes up in our groups, men frequently say that they "give" their paychecks to their partners, so women really have financial control. When group members discuss disagreements they have had over money, the examples are similar to the experience Rick explained in group.

Michael: Rick, you were talking about an argument you had with Angie last week about money. You said you think she's always blaming you for the amount of debt you both carry. Do you think she's really blaming you, or is it just that she's concerned over your financial situation?

Rick: I understand her concern and I realize she wants to get a handle on our expenses. I mean, I don't like to be in debt either. But I do feel she uses a very blaming tone when she brings up examples of things we didn't need to spend money on.

Michael: Why do you say that?

Rick: Well, she usually mentions the things that *I've* bought, or says that *my* priorities aren't right. Like she'll say we shouldn't have gotten the motor for the boat, even though she knows how much I like to fish, and that I charged a bunch of tools at Sears that we're still paying for. Yeah, I think she brings these things up in a blaming way when we get into it.

Michael: You said earlier that you understood her concerns and that you also have concerns about your debt. Can you see any way you could resolve this?

Rick: I don't know. It seems that whenever we talk about it, we usually end up fighting.

The issue of money in relationships is complex and difficult for couples to sort out. Sometimes, trust issues that get raised call the entire relationship into question. When two people become a couple, do their funds become one? If one person makes more money is that person entitled to a greater say in how it is spent? Who gets to decide?

There is no one set of rules to follow when dealing with money issues. Couples have to sit down and decide what feels fair to them. Both people must take into consideration the forces that shape their partners' opinions and beliefs, and their own. The goal should be a compromise. Remember that one aspect of partnership is a commitment to sort through the tough decisions in a respectful and fair way.

▓ EXERCISE: Handling Money Problems

If you get stuck in a money conflict, try the following exercise. Even if you are not presently in a relationship, think about a money problem that you had in a past relationship. Write your responses in your journal or notebook.

1. Describe clearly, simply, and as fairly as you can the money problem you are having.

_____

_____

2. What do you think is your partner's perception of the problem?

_____

_____

3. When and where do you and your partner usually argue about this issue? For example, what time of the week, day, or month? Do you argue on the phone, at home, in public?

_____

_____

4. Do you think it is possible to reach a compromise that works for both of you?

            Yes _____ No _____ Maybe _____

5. If yes or maybe, what can you do safely—without controlling, provoking, or blaming—to initiate a discussion in which you and your partner negotiate a solution to this conflict?

_____

_____

6. If no, what can you do to handle this conflict safely over the long term?

_____

_____

The following is an example from Erwin in one of my groups:

1. Describe clearly, simply, and as fairly as you can the money problem you are having:

I think she's too uptight about money and blames me for us being in debt.

2. What do you think is your partner's perception of the problem?

She thinks I'm not concerned enough about our financial problems and that I'm willing to spend money we don't have.

3. When and where do you and your partner usually argue about this issue?

Usually at the end of the month when the bills have to be paid.

4. Do you think it is possible to reach a compromise that works for both of you?

Maybe.

5. If yes or maybe, what can you do safely—without controlling, provoking, or blaming—to initiate a discussion in which you and your partner negotiate a solution to this conflict?

The group helped Erwin with some possible solutions:

a. Discuss budgets and money commitments at the beginning of the month rather than when the bills are due and both people are anxious.

b. Discuss major projects or purchases that may need to be made during the year and attempt to reach agreement on priority items.

c. See a financial counselor.

The issues surrounding money don't have to be as complicated as you make them if you can come to a cooperative arrangement. There has to be give-and-take and a willingness to compromise. Most of us have money problems at some time in our lives. For many, living from paycheck to paycheck is a reality. Others are unemployed or underemployed, and have limited resources. Regardless of your economic struggle, working together with your partner to make ends meet is far more preferable—and successful—than working against each other.

Expressing Feelings

I remember observing a men's group and noticing a chart on the wall called a "feelings" chart. On it were named about a hundred different feelings. The group leaders said they used the chart because the men in the group had a hard time identifying what they were feeling. I thought, so it's come to this—we can't tell anybody how we feel and we need a chart?

I think as men we know exactly how we feel. Many feelings may be going on at one time, which causes confusion, but we know what we are feeling. Most of us don't like to talk about or acknowledge our feelings because it makes us vulnerable. And, as we discussed in Chapter 1, vulnerability in men is considered a sign of weakness.

The following discussion took place in one of our groups:

Dan: Barbara asks me questions sometimes about our relationship and I just kind of freeze. My responses are usually vague. I know she wants me to say more because she keeps asking me questions and seems frustrated. She says we don't communicate.

Michael: This seems to be a common theme. Why is it so hard for men to communicate?

Lance: I think it's upbringing. When I think of the way we played, us boys as compared to my sisters, it was totally different. My sisters would talk and talk about their friends. They would be really upset if they got into arguments. I could never understand how they put so much time and effort into sorting things out in their relationships with other girls. For us guys, hell, if you got into a fight with another guy, you just said "Fuck him" and moved on with your life.

Michael: That's kind of sad, isn't it? Do you think that upbringing stuff has an impact on our relationships today?

Dan: It's partly upbringing. Barb always wants me to go deeper with my feelings. I don't know if I'm afraid to go deeper on an emotional level or I'm afraid to be that vulnerable, especially with a woman.

Michael: You think you'll be hurt?

Dan: Maybe. I just wouldn't know where to start or how to do it.

Frank: I think part of it is that you don't want to hurt her. You know, I wasn't very happy in our relationship but was hanging in there for the kids and stuff. If I was really honest, I'd hurt her. I think men can express themselves but choose not to.

Michael: Does anyone else think that men choose not to share feelings?

Frank: I can't speak for all men, but I think they do. I know in past relationships I would purposely not talk to her, to keep her guessing.

Michael: Keep her guessing?

Frank: Sure. She never knew what I was thinking about her or the relationship. I always had the upper hand. Kind of a control thing.

We see that the reasons men don't express their feelings are varied. For some men it is a fear of vulnerability, for some confusion, and for others it is a tactic to control their partners, as Frank did. Many men express feelings after committing a violent act. Some cry and ask for forgiveness. This expression of remorse or shame is often sincere. At other times it is simply another tactic to relieve personal responsibility for the violence, or to calm her anger.

Men in our society are conditioned not to express feelings or cry. Most men can remember a childhood experience when they were told, "Stop crying, be a man!" The problem is, the more men repress their inner feelings, the more difficulty they have expressing themselves in intimate relationships.

In one of our groups, Carlos talked about a painful childhood memory.

Carlos: I remember coming home from school one day feeling like shit because some of the kids were picking on me and I'd started to cry. I must have been about seven or eight. I mean, this was big-time humiliation. I went home and my parents knew something was wrong, so I told them what happened. My dad just said I shouldn't take any crap from them and now it's only going to get worse because I showed them I was weak. My mom wasn't much better. She said she'd call the school if it happened again.

Maryann: What did you *want* them to say?

Carlos: I just wish they had acknowledged what I was going through—you know, just let me know they understood.

Maryann: What would have happened if they had asked you how you felt?

Carlos: My parents weren't like that with me and my brothers. You know, they had the idea that it's a rough world out there and you gotta be tough. I think they meant well, but I'll never forget how alone I was with all that stuff.

Most men can relate similar boyhood experiences of being all alone with their feelings. In most homes with fathers, Dad takes the detached role, believing he is providing good modeling for his sons. Would it have been so difficult for Carlos' parents to ask, "How do you feel about it?" or "I bet you feel pretty lousy, don't you?" It would have been much better for Carlos if his parents had acknowledged his feelings, or at least let him know that he was understood.

Parents usually do what they think is right. They prepare boys to become men—but what are the criteria for becoming a man? "You have to be ready to compete, because it's a dog-eat-dog world out there." "You have to be ready to kill, because your country may call you to fight in war." "You have to be ready to win, because men are failures if they lose." "You have to be in control, because men are supposed to be powerful." These messages leave little room for emotions and feelings that aren't tied to winning, fighting, and being in control.

The problem is that the feelings men experience are often repressed, for our own survival, but they don't go away. The explosiveness of men's anger (a feeling generally allowed and understood) is usually primed by their many submerged feelings, but what we mostly see is just the anger. Many men use alcohol or drugs to mask or numb other emotions, but the numbness is usually temporary.

As Bernice states, you never know what to expect with a man who holds his feelings back and then explodes:

> Living with my partner was like living under siege. He would beat me up about once a month. It was almost like things would build and build within him. He usually wouldn't tell me what was going on inside. But I could almost predict when all this rage would build and culminate in him battering me.

What should men do with the feelings they experience? What do you do when you feel insecure, overwhelmed, scared, or unhappy? Men need to find appropriate and positive ways of expressing these feeling to friends and family members, as well as to their partners. Perhaps they should start by talking. They may not release all their pent-up emotion by talking, but at least they won't feel so alone.

One caution: If you are still in a relationship with the woman you abused, you need to exercise control over how and when you express your feelings. Your partner may still be afraid of you and may not understand how you have changed.

Can your expression of feelings be counterproductive for the relationship? There is a distinct difference between talking honestly about what is going on in your life and using your feelings to manipulate or control your partner. For instance, talking about how you *feel* jealous or *feel* insecure about your partner going out with a friend in order to keep her from going is controlling. Though you should be able to talk to her about these feelings, if your intent is to make her feel guilty and not go, you are indirectly imposing your will on her.

Repressing your feelings and thoughts is also unfair to your partner, as she does not get to know the real you. As your current relationship gets healthier, or in your new relationship, you will need to make decisions about your level of intimacy. Being in touch with your own feelings and caring about your partner's feelings are an important part of this. There is an element of risk, because intimacy requires a certain level of vulnerability. This is not easy for men.

You may think that not showing emotion or talking about your feelings makes you stronger or in control, but in the long run it affects your mental health and increases the possibility of explosive outbursts. We all have fears, experience pain, get frustrated, or feel insecure. Denying your feelings robs you of experiencing fully all that life has to offer—the good *and* the bad, the pain *and* the joy.

Learning to Negotiate and Compromise

How do we settle conflicts? For thousands of years world leaders, mediators, counselors, and peacemakers have grappled with difficult issues and tried to reconcile opposing views. From children on the playground to presidents of great countries, we argue, debate, and quarrel. We will always have disagreement and conflict in relationships, yet conflict doesn't have to be hurtful and individuals certainly don't have to resort to abusive behavior to make their point.

A fair way to resolve conflicts in a relationship is to agree on guidelines for discussing difficult issues. For men who have been violent in the past, this is crucial. Following is a fifteen-point guide you and your partner can use to help you resolve conflicts and problems fairly and respectfully.

Negotiation Guide

1. Regardless of how angry or hurt I feel I will remain nonviolent.

2. If I disagree with my partner's position I will still be respectful toward her.

3. I will remain seated during the discussion.

4. I will not yell, scream, or use my voice in an intimidating manner.

5. I will not threaten my partner in any way.

6. I will not use put-downs, call my partner names, or be sarcastic or belittling.

7. I will not bring up past incidents to prove a point.

8. I will avoid blaming or shaming statements.

9. I will strive not to get defensive.

10. I will listen to my partner's position and refrain from interrupting.

11. I will commit to work toward a compromise.

12. I will be willing to explore my own issues and take responsibility for mistakes I have made.

13. I will respect my partner's wishes to end the discussion.

14. I will be honest.

15. I will talk about my feelings but will not use them as a way to manipulate my partner.

Couples have spontaneous disagreements in restaurants and movie theaters or at the homes of friends and family. It is usually better not to try to resolve conflicts over difficult issues in public because you cannot talk frankly, it is often embarrassing, and you may find yourself disregarding the Negotiation Guide for arguing fairly. On the other hand, for some couples a public setting is the best place to talk things through. One couple told me that discussing an issue at a restaurant worked for them because they didn't want to risk the embarrassment of raised voices in public, or where people might know them. If you are in counseling, you might want to discuss these issues with your counselor.

Before discussing the issues you disagree about, both of you should agree on a good time to work on the problem. Make sure you have enough private time without interruptions from kids, business, or phones. One of you should state your position without being interrupted, regardless of how long it takes. When that person is finished, the other starts. Remember the Negotiation Guide!

After you have both had an opportunity to talk about your position, try to see where you are in *agreement*. Are the areas of disagreement significant or can you find a way to compromise? Remember, if you are stuck there is nothing wrong with seeking assistance from a counselor in your community.

Some disagreements can be resolved quickly; others are more complicated and may involve painful issues. Not talking about these problems is *not* the solution. You may not resolve the issue that day or that night, but you can begin the work.

If you are still in a relationship with a woman you have abused, she may not want to work on the same issues as you do. Her trust in you may be diminished. She may still harbor anger and resentment because of the abuse, and may be confused about her feelings. The following discussion occurred in one of our groups:

> **Bob:** I don't get it. Jessie always wanted me to talk more with her. You know, talk about my feelings. Well, now when I want to, she either doesn't want to or gets pissed.
>
> **Michael:** What do you do?
>
> **Bob:** Nothing. I let it go. But I'm getting frustrated. I mean, I feel like I'm making changes and I want to work on our relationship, and she's resisting.
>
> **Michael:** You know, Bob, you really need to give Jessie time.

After all that's gone on you can't just expect her to adapt to your agenda. Sometimes when a woman is healing after abuse she gets in touch with a lot of feelings, including anger at the man who hurt her. You need to give her as much time as she needs.

Arguing fairly takes two people committed to working things out. Bob has been learning things in the group and wants to work on the relationship. Jessie may or may not want to work things out, but she is clearly not ready. The Negotiation Guide may not work right now for women who have been battered.

Regardless of how your partner responds, *you* can still commit to the Negotiation Guide. Because of your past history of abuse it's important that you set high standards for yourself. If your partner says something hurtful or inappropriate during a discussion, it isn't necessary for you to match her. Once you take that step, you begin the slide down the slippery slope to not caring what you say and do, and you may become abusive.

Settling differences requires three basic things:

1. The desire to listen to the other person

2. The willingness to compromise

3. The fortitude to work things out, regardless of how difficult the task

Sometimes we're so convinced of the correctness of our position that we build walls around ourselves. Or we may be hurt or offended by what the other person is saying and our response is to hurt back. Being able to listen to another person's feelings and thoughts on an issue is a skill worth possessing. It takes practice and determination. On certain issues it may be difficult to compromise and reach a place where both people feel comfortable. Sometimes you may have to leave things alone for a while. And not everything is open to negotiation, as we see in the following group discussion:

Maryann: Art, you said last week that you had a disagreement with Ginny about going back to school. You said you worked out a compromise. What happened?

Art: Well, basically we agreed she would wait until we were in better shape financially before she went to school.

Maryann: When will that be?

Art: As soon as I get the raise I've been promised. Maybe next year.

Maryann: And Ginny is okay with waiting? You said before that this has been a long-standing issue with the two of you, and that she really wanted to go back to school.

Art: I think she was disappointed, but after we discussed the pros and cons, she basically agreed with my position that we couldn't afford it right now.

Maryann: So you're saying there were no alternatives like school loans?

Art: I don't want us going into that kind of debt. I mean, she doesn't even know what kind of degree she wants. She just wants to go back to school. There's no way I want to be saddled with several thousands of dollars of school loans.

Art believes he and Ginny worked out a compromise, but in actuality he just put up a roadblock that was impossible for her to go around. He later admitted that other issues about her going back to school disturbed him, but when confronted he would always bring it back to the money issue. He was convinced that he was being rational and that his position was right. However, the fact that Ginny accepted the money dilemma as a reason for their decision does not mean a fair and mutual compromise had been worked out between them.

A major issue for couples often arises if one partner wants to make a change in his or her life. Changing jobs, going back to school, joining an organization, or pursuing new friends can become problem issues if one partner feels the status quo of the relationship will be disturbed. Change can be scary. For men who have been violent and are still in the relationship with the partner they abused, the feelings about such change may be even more pronounced.

Many men in our groups talk about feeling insecure about their relationships. A man who is insecure acknowledges the pain he has caused, and wonders why his partner would want to stay with him. When his partner expresses an interest in doing something different, he becomes suspicious. He *wants* to believe he is entering into true negotiation over a change that affects both partners and the relationship but, instead of encouraging his partner's aspirations and supporting the change, he becomes manipulative and controlling. Obviously, for his partner this is one more indication that the man is not ready to change.

Compromise does not mean that one party has to sacrifice or change to accommodate the other person's needs. If you follow the points in the Negotiation Guide, you should be able to resolve conflicts in a respectful way that honors each partner's freedom to make decisions and takes into account the impact of these decisions upon the relationship.

A man who has been abusive in a relationship is used to getting his way. As men, we have all been socialized to compete and win; this impacts the way we disagree and argue, especially with women. Part of your journey must be a willingness to let go of always calling the shots, and always needing to win. This is not easy for many men. As boys we are expected to compete and succeed. Remember the coaches refrain, "Winning isn't everything, it's the only thing." For many men, this was our experience as boys growing up in this culture. And to lose to a girl was the ultimate humiliation.

Larry told the following story in one of our groups:

> There was this big girl in our fourth-grade class and she would get into a lot of fights with girls and with boys. One day, I remember getting egged on to fight her. We really went at it and I think I fought her harder than I'd ever fought a boy. She ended up pinning me. For weeks I got shit about getting beaten up by a girl—it was the worst humiliation.

Much of this book deals with how men use power and control in relationships, and how we settle conflicts. To say that women aren't also controlling would not be true. When a woman wants her way she can often make a stronger argument than a man can. When girls are growing up, they are socialized to work out problems in very different ways, and their verbal skills are usually more developed than boys' because of this expectation. Consequently, in adult relationships, men feel threatened when they think they're losing arguments or can't articulate what they're feeling and thinking. It is at this point that a man will often resort to behavior he knows will provide leverage in resolving the disagreement. Yelling, making threats, being intimidating, name-calling, and violence can bring about a quick end to an argument. But, as most men who batter eventually come to realize, this behavior has grave consequences. If you've made the commitment not to be abusive, you have to find a fair process for negotiating and resolving disputes with your present or future partners.

▮ EXERCISE: Negotiation

Complete the following exercise on negotiation to help evaluate how you've handled conflicts in the past. Even if you are not in a relationship today, think about an incident in your past relationship when you could have negotiated with your partner, but instead tried to control the situation by becoming abusive. Write your answers and thoughts in your journal or notebook.

The examples are from Mitch, a man in one of our groups.

1. Write down an incident when you became abusive during a conflict.

_____

_____

We argue about money a lot. There were a bunch of charges on our credit card and I confronted her. She claimed we needed everything she charged. I told her I was going to cut the cards up unless she got some self-control. She told me to fuck off, so I grabbed her purse, took the cards, and left.

2. Think about the way you handled this situation. Even though you were upset, how might you have negotiated this conflict in a fair and nonabusive manner?

_____

_____

I shouldn't have brought up the issue when I was angry. I should have waited until I was calm and suggested a time to talk. We could have discussed the way we were both feeling about money and I could have reassured her that I would not get upset. We could have both agreed to the points in the Negotiation Guide before discussing the issue.

The Negotiation Guide (page 175) is primarily for you. You can also share with your partner the following Fair Discussion Guide, which we use at the Duluth Domestic Abuse Intervention Project. She may agree that this format could be useful to resolve problems. If you are still in the relationship with the woman you've abused, don't pressure her to use this guide.

Fair Discussion Guide

1. A good discussion needs two people ready to talk. Don't force a discussion.

2. You know each other's weak spots. Don't use them to hurt your partner.

3. Before you begin the process of negotiation, you must first be committed to a fair process. You must be ready to:

- Listen—try to understand what the other person is saying.
- Work toward a mutually satisfying solution.
- Hear things you disagree with or find painful, without reacting abusively.
- Accept that some things may need to change.
- Find a neutral person you both trust to help with the discussion.

4. Review these rules together and add any that you both decide are important:

- Talk quietly and calmly.
- Keep the discussion free of manipulation or mind games.
- Stick to the issues at hand.
- Set time limits for discussion.

5. Define the problem—it may be different for each person. What is negotiable? How does each person perceive and define the problem?

Who else will be affected and how?

6. Identify goals, both short-term and long-term. What needs to be part of an immediate and then a final solution? If a compromise is needed, list several long-term solutions you both think are fair.

All of this may seem difficult at first. Your habitual reaction to conflict may be to simply lash out—if someone says something you don't like, or does something that makes you angry, you're ready for battle. Hopefully, if you're reading this book, you know there must be a better way. The exercises and guides in this book really do work if you use them—not just once in a while. At first, trying to use the rules and suggestions in the Negotiation Guide or Fair Discussion Guide may seem a little awkward. But when you resolve a conflict with these tools without being controlling or abusive you will feel better about your partner, yourself, and your relationship.

Developing a Personal Responsibility Program

A Personal Responsibility Program is a layout for your future. You've now made the commitment to be nonviolent and nonabusive, but how will you ensure that you are putting into practice all that you've learned?

There are three basic components to designing a Personal Responsibility Program for your new beginning:

- Commitment: What are you willing to commit to do differently?

- Accountability: How and to whom will you be accountable for past and future behavior?

- Assessment: How will you evaluate the progress you have made?

Commitment

If you have completed all or most of the exercises in this book, you have already done a fairly thorough evaluation of past situations in which you were abusive with your partner. By now, you recognize that you always had alternatives to violence. You acknowledge that you've made some bad choices, and wish you could go back and change history. Obviously, you can't. But what happens when similar issues and conflicts come up today, especially if you're staying with the woman you battered? How will you deal with disagreement? How will you interact with your partner without being abusive and controlling? How will you manage the negative emotions that may be just below the surface? Who will you turn to when you need help to ensure that you honor your commitment to your partner and to yourself to stay nonviolent?

▒ EXERCISE: Commitment

This exercise will help you outline a plan for handling disagreements and arguments with your partner. Write your responses in your journal or notebook. Following are two examples, but you can list as many trigger issues as you think you need.

1. Think of the kinds of trigger issues that were the most difficult for you in the past, and then write down concrete steps you will take to ensure a nonabusive response when conflict arises with your partner.

a. Trigger issue:

_____

_____

b. Concrete steps to not become abusive:

_____

_____

Examples:

a. Trigger issue #1:

I get upset when we get an overdraft on a check or when we don't have enough money at the end of the month to pay the bills. I blame my partner because she handles the bills.

b. Concrete steps to not become abusive:

Discuss this issue with my partner when I'm not agitated. Seek solutions together. Use positive self-talk if an overdraft comes in the mail. Take a time-out if I still feel upset. Make a commitment to my partner and myself not to blame her.

a. Trigger Issue #2:

I get angry and defensive when my partner criticizes me.

b. Concrete steps to not become abusive:

I will recognize any physical or emotional cues that tell me my anger level is escalating. If it is escalating, I will take a time-out. I will ride my bike to reduce my stress and negative feelings. I will not get defensive. I will think about what my partner has said rather than rehearsing the way I am going to respond back to her. I will set up a time with my partner to talk about the issue she has raised. I will suggest that we use the negotiation guide to deal with this issue. When we go to counseling, I'll bring up how we both use criticism in our relationship.

2. Ten things that I will do to ensure that I remain noncontrolling and nonabusive.

_____

_____

_____

_____

_____

_____

_____

_____

_____

_____

Example:

1. I will not use violence or any abusive behaviors against my partner.

2. I will take a time-out when I feel agitated, and follow the time-out rules.

3. I will work on my problems with my partner and commit to the rules in the Negotiation Guide.

4. I will work on letting go of always wanting to control situations.

5. I will commit to an exercise program to reduce stress in my life.

6. I will use positive self-talk when I'm getting upset.

7. I will take responsibility for my behavior.

8. I will expand my support network when I get out of counseling.

9. I will go back into counseling if I need help with issues.

10. I will work on having a more equal relationship with my partner.

Accountability

If you have battered, accountability means you are answerable to your partner, to children who observed the violence, to people who have been affected by your violence—including friends, family, counselors, and group members—and to yourself. This can be hard.

Native American tribes have historically used a community intervention process to deal with criminal or antisocial behavior. It is born of the idea that a crime against an individual is also transgression against the community. Today "sentencing circles" or "restorative justice" allow people in a Native American community to confront the perpetrator of a crime with an eye toward atonement and rehabilitation. Victims of the crime and others in the community confront the perpetrator by explaining how the criminal act affected them. The experience can be helpful for the victims and the perpetrator alike. The perpetrator is expected to make amends through some form of restitution. If the behavior continues or if the perpetrator fails to meet the conditions of the sentence, additional and harsher penalties may be imposed. At the heart of this concept is an understanding that when people are harmed, the person who caused the harm must assume responsibility for his or her behavior. Promises that the behavior won't happen again are not sufficient. The idea of accountability is that the person who caused the harm will take certain steps to provide assurances that the behavior won't recur, which requires a plan. This is an important process for men who batter.

▨ EXERCISE: Accountability

In your journal or notebook, develop a plan to be accountable for past and present behavior for the next year.

1. List the people you believe you should talk to about your past use of violence and your future goals of being nonabusive.

_____

_____

Example:

My wife Annie, my ten-year-old daughter Caroline, and my mother-in-law Sara Jane.

2. Outline what you want to say to be accountable for your past and future. Set a date to talk to each person.

_____

_____

Examples:

To Annie, I will acknowledge that I am solely responsible for my past use of violence. I will discuss with her how I rationalized what I did. I will admit that my abuse was wrong. I will tell her that I understand that she may be distrustful because of my past behavior. I will apologize. I will tell her that I'm committed to being nonabusive and noncontrolling and that I will follow some of the exercises in this book and what I've learned through counseling groups. I will talk to her on _____ .

To Caroline, I will apologize for hurting her mother. I will explain to her that what I did was wrong and there is no excuse for my behavior. I will tell her that I've learned a lot about myself through counseling. I will promise to never be abusive to anyone in the family. I will apologize for putting her in the position of having to witnesses my violence and abusive behavior. I will tell her that I hope I can win back her trust. I will talk to her on _____ .

To Sara Jane, I will acknowledge that I am responsible for my past use of violence. I will admit that what I did was wrong. I will tell her that I understand that she may be distrustful because of what I did to her daughter. I will also apologize for being defensive and verbally abusive to her when she confronted me about my behavior. I will tell her that I'm committed to being nonabusive and noncontrolling. I will tell her that I will go back to counseling if I start reverting back to my old ways. I will talk to her on _____ .

Assessment

How will you evaluate whether your changes are making a difference? How will you know if some of your actions have had unintended negative results? You will need to get some honest feedback. But before talking to your partner or counselor, you need to have a way to measure the things that have changed and the areas that still need improvement. If you are still in a counseling group, ask your counselor or facilitator how long you should wait before assessing your progress. Some men may want to assess their progress every three months and for others a six-month assessment period makes more sense.

This assessment is for your benefit. If your partner doesn't want to participate, honor her request. If she does participate, you may hear things that make you feel uncomfortable. Remember your commitment. Trust the feedback you are receiving. This is a long-term process and—despite your efforts—everything you want to happen won't just magically occur.

▓ **EXERCISE:** Assessment

The first thing to do is to review the ten things you committed to in the exercise on commitment earlier in this section.

In the past three or six months, how would you rate your accomplishments in achieving your goals? Give yourself a grade. If your partner is willing, ask her to give her impressions prior to grading.

Example:

1. I will not use violence or any abusive behaviors against my partner. . . **A**

2. I will take a time-out when I feel agitated, and follow the time-out rules . . . . **B**

3. I will work on my problems with my partner and commit to the rules in the Negotiation Guide. . . . . **B**

4. I will work on letting go of always wanting to control situations . . . **C+**

5. I will commit to an exercise program to reduce stress in my life. . . . . . **C**

6. I will use positive self-talk when I'm getting upset. . . . . **B**

7. I will take responsibility for my behavior. . . . . **B+**

8. I will expand my support network when I get out of counseling. . . . . . . **D**

9. I will go back into counseling if I need help with issues. . . . . *Didn't feel I needed to*

10. I will work on having a more equal relationship with my partner. . . . . **B**

If you are still in counseling you might want to review your assessment report with your counselor or other group members. It is important to generate some ideas on how you might improve in certain areas, so feedback is valuable. If you seriously and genuinely adhere to the three components of a Personal Responsibility Program—commitment, accountability, and assessment—you will not only realize notable changes, you will also have a sense of security that your new life is heading down the right path.

9

Healing

Dave's Story — Dave's Story Five Years Later — Support for
Changing Men — New Definitions of Masculinity — Health and
Balance — Dating: How Much of the Past Do We Reveal? —
Talking to Your Children about Your Violence — Beyond Personal
Change: Educating the Community — Staying on Course:
Your Lifelong Commitment

*I'd like to get away from earth awhile
and then come back to it and begin again.*

ROBERT FROST

In this chapter you will read about men changing, redefining masculinity, and getting and staying healthy on many levels. We will also examine issues related to staying accountable in relationships, talking with your children about your violence, and keeping your commitment to living a nonabusive and nonviolent lifestyle.

Dave's Story

Dave grew up in a violent home and was abusive in the majority of his relationships with women. After going through substance abuse counseling, he made a commitment to himself to get the help he needed to end the violence in his life, and volunteered to participate in the Duluth Domestic Abuse Intervention Project. He went on to work with chemically dependent people and run a group for abusive men.

> The first time I saw someone getting hurt was my mom getting beaten by my dad. He punched her in the head, kicked her, and pulled her across the floor by the hair. I was about five or six at the time.
>
> There was a lot of violence in our house, involving uncles, aunts, and parents. Usually the violence occurred when people were drinking. I'm sure those early experiences shaped my thinking. It's

strange, though, because although my brother saw all that stuff too, he never used violence. My parents' verbal message to us was not to be violent and to treat others with respect—especially your elders. Yet that's not what I saw growing up. We were told to never talk about the violence at home because it was a family matter.

My dad would whale on us kids. He worked for the railroad and he would often kick us with steel-toed boots. I remember him standing over me after beating me and saying, "I'll kill you, you little son of a bitch." And I think the only reason he stopped was because he just got tired.

I always wanted to be accepted by my dad, but never was. Whenever my mother tried to stop him from beating us kids, she got beaten herself. I remember sitting with her and both of us were crying. I asked, "Why can't we move out?" She said, "Things will be okay," but they never were okay. I've always been angry about my childhood.

My partner, Lori, and I grew up in the Duluth area, but we ended up in Chicago. I was twenty-five and she was only fifteen when we moved in together. I was drinking a lot. Lori provided the things I needed—a clean house, someone to make my meals, and sex. While we had set up house, we weren't really that committed. I didn't want to get married to her, but the relationship was convenient.

The first time I hit Lori was when we first started dating. Even though we both had other relationships, I still saw Lori as mine. When I drank, I would end up fighting with men who were showing an interest in her.

I told Lori I didn't want her friends coming over to the apartment unless I was there. The fact that other men were interested in her became an obsession with me. Sometimes I almost goaded her into telling me about her feelings toward other men. It didn't matter if what she said was right or wrong—it was always wrong.

It was almost a sadistic thing, like I was a military interrogator with a cigarette in his mouth asking these questions. With her being only fifteen, I was able to manipulate her with the questions. I would be in a good mood and ask her questions about men, and she would think it was okay to tell me about past relationships or men that she still found attractive. Then I would slap her. She would cry, not knowing what I was doing. I would hit her and apologize and then start the whole process over again. I must have slapped her at least two dozen times one night.

The abuse got worse. I moved from slaps to punches and even hit her in the stomach when she was pregnant. My violence included pulling her hair, pushing, and kicking her in the back when she was down. Early on I never hit her in the face because I didn't want to look bad to family and friends.

She knew I was a perfectionist and always kept the house perfect, even with three kids. And while she wasn't that beautiful, she had an incredible body. Sometimes I would look at her and think this is someone I really want to be married to. Other times I would look at her and just glare.

I never trusted people, especially women. I always thought that women tried to get men to look at them or make a pass at them even if they were attached or married. I remember one time Lori was in this bowling league and she wanted to get a new outfit. I went with her to the store and helped her pick out this really sexy top. She had such a beautiful body, and I told her how great she looked in it and that she should get it. Eight hours later I was saying, "You son of a bitch, I saw the way you were crossing your legs." Then I accused her of wearing provocative clothes even though I had picked the clothes out.

Lori never really fought back, except sometimes she would kick at me when I had her down, and sometimes she would throw things at me. When that happened I would really nail her, usually using my fists, or I would kick her square in the ass. If she ran from me, I would kick her in the back.

I was always able to get Lori to forgive me. I guess I had a gift for talking, because I would say, "Things are going to be better," and be really sensitive and then this smile would come over her face and she would say, "I know that wasn't really you."

When I look back on my violence today, I realize I really wasn't out of control. I knew where to hit. I would usually avoid hitting her in the face. Numerous times I would have Lori pinned in a corner or be on top of her with my hand around her neck, but I always knew when to stop. Often I would blame my violence on the alcohol. I would say things like, "You know what I'm like when I'm drunk."

Toward the end of the relationship she would say things like, "Why don't you let me go home to my parents? You can see the kids anytime." When she talked like that I would get really nervous, because even though both of us were unhappy I didn't want to be alone. I would promise her things, like we would get married.

The more I thought she was going to leave, the more controlling I became. I would check the phone bills to see how many calls she was making and to where. And then there was this neighbor friend of hers I was really suspicious of, because I thought she was telling Lori things. I would tell Lori I didn't want her to go over there anymore. If she was talking on the phone I would stand in the doorway and glare at her or look at my watch and then interrogate her after she hung up.

I'd go up to her just like my dad did to us. I could scare the hell out of her. Actually, at that time everyone was afraid of me because they'd seen me going off on people, and as small as I was I would beat the hell out of anyone. At home I would slam my fist on the table and there would be instant quiet. It gave me a certain feeling of power. I would just look and get what I wanted, and I liked that. I got to watch any TV program I wanted. Lori was always trying to keep the peace, just like my mom. She would always ask me what I wanted and I liked that feeling.

Of course, I was frequently emotionally abusive. I would call her a whore, slut, cunt, and a goddamn pig. I knew which words or put-downs hurt the most. The worst was calling her a goddamn pig. I would say, "Look at you, you goddamn pig, you ugly son of a bitch, who the fuck would want you? Go look at yourself in the mirror!" She would start crying and say, "How can you say you love me and say these things to me?"

The worst incident I remember was when we were living in the Twin Cities and the family was there—her mom and stepdad and my dad. I had been in a car accident several weeks before and my leg was in a cast. She had decided that she wanted to be away from me for a while. Anyway, I thought she was getting "smart" because her mom was there. When her family started to leave, I got up, grabbed Lori, and threw her down. I started whaling on her in the same way I would fight a man—ready to kill. I was on top of her, punching her everywhere about twenty times, until her dad managed to pull me off. That was probably the scariest incident. I knew, after that, that I needed to deal with my violence.

She finally left me and moved back to northern Minnesota. I moved to California. I would call her and ask her to come back to me. One time when I called she hung up on me. That day I flew to Minnesota from San Francisco and slapped the hell out of her. The cops came and took me away, although I was never charged with anything.

In the late seventies, I came back to Minnesota. I was still drinking pretty heavily. I went out with two different women briefly. One I abused; the other I didn't. Then I entered treatment. I met Carol after treatment, when I was getting my life together. I opened up a TV repair shop in a city outside of Duluth and we moved in together and things were going really well. I even told her about my past abuse.

I hit her once and she said if I ever did it again, she would get an Order for Protection. She had been battered before and made it clear to me she wasn't going to put up with it again. Carol was afraid of me. I would drive the car really fast, which would scare her. She would be screaming, "Stop the car!" But I wouldn't. Carol finally got an Order for Protection.

I started to go to these abuse groups partly because I wanted Carol to see that I was ready to make some changes. The longer I was in the program, the more I changed. My relationship with Carol ended, however.

I knew I had to make a lot of changes. I needed to let go of the jealousy. In my current relationship I accept my partner having her own life and her own friends. I'm also more supportive of my partner and willing to listen to what she's saying, rather than just reacting.

Of course, quitting the alcohol and going through treatment forced me to look at myself. I've started to focus on my good qualities, my kindness, my ability to be gentle—things women I dated said I possessed, but I never believed them.

I really feel okay with who I am. I've had to change the way I think about men and women. In the past, I believed that women were supposed to be submissive, and I would pick women who I knew wouldn't be resistant. My attitude toward women has changed.

I remember in the group this counselor said, "If nothing changes, then nothing will change." It sounded strange, but it made sense to me, because I needed to change.

I've talked to all my children about my alcoholism and violence. It's not easy to come face-to-face with the fact that they were afraid of me, and that they did things similar to what I did as a child, such as trying to stop their father from hitting their mother. I think it's important for former batterers to talk to their children. They all say how scary it was for them and how angry they were. It wasn't easy to talk to my children about this stuff, but for me it's been important.

We go back in the past, not to relive the past, but to find out about the destructive patterns that still get in the way. I've told my present partner about my past. I still take time-outs from time to time. Once you've battered, you always have to be aware of who you are, where you've been, and what you're capable of doing.

I feel great about where I'm at today and the changes I've made. When I talk about my experiences today, I often say, "Once a batterer always a batterer." And I don't mean that in a negative way, like you can't change, but rather it's similar to being an alcoholic. I still read literature on alcoholism and attend AA, and I need to pay similar attention to the patterns I developed around controlling women and how I handle conflict. The things I learned eight years ago—taking time-outs, sharing, letting go of the need to control, and being more accepting of who I am—are things I continue to work on.

If I let negative and destructive thoughts enter into my life, I think I have the potential to revert back. But I'm able to see the signs now. When a red flag or warning sign comes up, I know what to do and it's easier for me to recognize them.

The most rewarding thing now is for me to give back to others who are abusive what I've learned, and tell them how I've changed. It keeps me healthy. Change is a long process, but you can never stop.

Dave's Story Five Years Later

I sat down with Dave five years after our initial interview. I wanted to find out what had happened in his life during this period, what obstacles he had to overcome to remain violence free, and how he viewed his life today.

Dave is still working in the chemical dependency field and conducts classes for Native American men who have battered. He has been married for the past six years.

I first asked Dave whether his past use of violence had an impact on his children.

On talking to his children about his past

My adult children have all had experiences with chemical dependency and domestic abuse. My two girls have been in abusive relationships. Even though we've talked about what it was like for them growing up in our household, and how their lives have been affected by my violence, they've made some bad decisions, just like I did. My daughters have both been in treatment. I continue to talk with them about what I know about substance abuse, but they aren't ready to make the changes necessary to get sober.

My son Joe, however, has been sober. For a while he was having problems with his girlfriend. I talked with him at length about the choices we all make and the importance of being respectful in relationships. We've talked about his childhood experiences—watching me abuse his mother. He understands how he may have been influenced by what he saw as a child, and he recognizes his own behavior is abusive, even though he hasn't physically assaulted his girlfriend. I try to use my life and my mistakes as a way for my kids to learn and gain perspective on their own attitudes and behavior. I do what I can to help them. I wish I could erase what happened in the past, but I can't—I can only be there for them today.

On his current marriage

I have a great marriage today. The only problems Roxanne and I have are issues surrounding her children, who live with us. A lot of it has to do with adjustment and my feelings that her children aren't respectful of my privacy. But I talk about these issues with Roxanne and I recognize that my responses are often overreactions. I have a friend who's also a counselor, and he gives me good feedback—I find it helpful to talk about issues and my feelings rather than holding resentments inside.

Roxanne had been in an abusive relationship in the past, so her awareness is high. We talk a lot about our relationship, checking things out. Jealousy has always been an issue with me and even though I've worked really hard on changing aspects of my life, I still get jealous with Roxanne. I find myself at times asking her where she's going and feel like I still need reassurance from her. But, I don't get jealous like I did before, because I feel so different about myself today. I'm so much more self-confident.

I'm not a young man anymore. I'm sixty! And for Native American men, life expectancy isn't that high, nor is it very high in my family. So, I made a decision that I want to have the best possible life. Having a healthy relationship with Roxanne is very important to me, so I want to make sure she's happy. Also, being in recovery helps. I try and live by these words [Dave points to a framed saying on the wall in his office]:

"And acceptance is the answer to all of my problems today. When I am disturbed, it is because I find some person, place, thing, or situation, some fact of my life, unacceptable to me. I can find no serenity until I accept that person, place, thing, or situation as being exactly the way it is supposed to be at this time. Nothing, absolutely nothing, happens in God's world by mistake. Until I accepted my alcoholism, I could not stay sober. Unless I accept life completely on life's terms, I cannot be happy. I need to concentrate not so much on what needs to be changed in the world, but what needs to be changed in me and in my attitudes."

I use this saying in my work with men who batter because even though it deals with alcoholism, it applies to domestic violence and relationships. It's hard for men to accept that they can't change their partners.

I believe Roxanne has the right to do whatever she wants. If she wants to go somewhere with her friends, I don't have the right to stop her, and I don't want to control her. I accept her as a person and respect her decisions—and she accepts me and the decisions I make.

On a close call

There was one incident where I came close to violence. We had gotten into an argument over issues with our kids' problems. Roxanne put one of my children down in a negative way and I got furious. I called her names and swore at her. On a scale of one to ten, with ten being a total rage, I was pushing a ten, but I had enough self-control not to hit her. We talked about it later and she said I looked pretty scary. I apologized and never blamed her—but I know my capacity for violence is still there, and maybe always will be there. That was the only time I came close to being violent again.

On making his relationship work

Almost every day when we get off work, Roxanne and I have coffee and discuss our day. We talk about issues like money, the kids, work, our relationship—we make sure we have this special time. This is very different for me. In the past, I had a difficult time communicating, especially talking about my fears and insecurities. I kept everything inside. But now, by Roxanne and me being committed to having this special time, communicating has become so much easier.

I try to live my life in a way that keeps me in balance. I like the equality of my relationship with Roxanne—the way we communicate. I try to take care of myself emotionally and spiritually. I'll go to a pow-wow for spiritual enrichment and I try to keep learning things by reading. I still go to AA. I've had heart problems, so I try to keep healthy physically, although this is an area that could stand some improvement.

On men changing

In my work with men, whether it's a substance abuse or domestic abuse group, I stress that recovery means change—and for change to occur things must be different. Sometimes, the change doesn't all come at once, but as long as a process for change is occurring there is progress. When I think back on my own life, I always wanted to be in a healthy and loving relationship. To do this, I had to change and keep changing. I'm happy in my life today. This discussion five years after our first interview has been hard, because my life is going so well, and I don't think about my own situation in the way I did before. But remembering the past shows me how far I've come—and I'm proud of that.

Support for Changing Men

Struggling with the issues discussed in this book can be hard. Some men might claim the analysis and self-reflection I ask of the reader only bring shame and guilt about one's maleness. The opposite is true. Awareness and understanding of sexism and the willingness to make changes are liberating. However you define your own masculinity is okay, but being a man doesn't mean you have to be sexist, or to support sexism. Men who are comfortable with their masculinity don't feel the need to defend sexist beliefs and locker-room sentiments.

Develop a deeper awareness by talking to people, both men and women, about the issues discussed in this book. In most communities men are getting together, albeit in small numbers, to talk about masculinity, men's violence, and healing. Some join men's organizations in their communities. Others work with civil rights and human rights organizations, because the issues associated with violence against any group of people are very similar. Some men work with domestic abuse programs, facilitate groups, and volunteer at shelters and schools that are addressing community violence. Stay involved— it will remind you of where you've been, and how far you've come on your journey.

If you have battered but have not been ordered into a domestic abuse program, or if you fear you have violent tendencies, volunteer to attend a program in your community. Go for the information and get the help you need before your abusive behavior escalates. I know many men who have built solid friendships through these programs. Like the relationships alcoholics often build to help with sobriety, similar friendships can help men who batter. Together, these men grapple with personal issues and support each other in their commitment to remain nonviolent. This support can be very important.

Your commitment to change may require you to give up certain friendships or activities, much like an alcoholic gives up a social situation in which there is the temptation to drink. Going to a bar, party, or social function where other men tell sexist jokes or devalue women soon becomes objectionable to men trying to change their lives. You may want to confront these men, tell them you don't appreciate their sexist comments, and try to educate them. Or you may just decide you prefer to be around men who don't see the humor in sexism.

Several years ago I was at a YMCA to play racquetball. After the game I was sitting in the sauna with six or seven men, and one of them began telling sexist jokes, to the delight of the others. When I said I thought his jokes were sexist and insensitive the sauna became uncomfortable. The man told me to "chill out," and said, "They're only jokes." Someone else said, "It's not like there's any women here to hear the jokes." I left wondering if I had overreacted. Then I thought, would I have been quiet if someone made a racist or anti-Semitic joke? What was the difference? And what difference did it make that no women were there? Because I've recognized how destructive sexism is to women, I cannot remain silent. This doesn't mean I confront every man or woman who does or says something sexist—sometimes it simply isn't worth it. Confrontation can sometimes make things worse. But, when I can, I try to educate in my own way. I know I always run the risk of being rebuffed. I also know my words may challenge some people along the way. The best approach is to engage people in discussions, without shaming them. Shaming makes people defensive and they usually become combative and closed to new ideas. The rule I try to follow is this: keep your sense of humor, and don't be condescending.

Hopefully, like many of the men in this book, you will seek out friendships that are not superficial. Although talking about sports or cars is fine, there is more to life than box scores or overdrive transmissions. You will want relationships with men and women in which you support each other's growth and change in a *true* spirit of friendship.

Men who are committed to change should not rely on women for all their support. They should make the changes for themselves. They should take responsibility and undo a system of violence that generations of men have constructed. Their rewards will be healthier relationships, children who value equality, and the knowledge that they are part of a revolutionary process that someday will bring about a more peaceful world.

New Definitions of Masculinity

Our masculinity is defined by our culture—whether we like it or not. The messages and expectations we are exposed to shape who we are.

For many men, the thought of being sensitive or caring is scary, as Ralph discussed in a group:

> After that last group, when we talked about what it meant to be a man, I really thought about all the comments that were made. Last

weekend I went down to the bar to watch the Vikings' game. I watched the men around me. They all seemed lonely and content with their booze and football talk. I sat down with a few buddies and had a beer. We talked about the game and hunting. I tried to get them talking about some more personal things, but all that came out was Ben's divorce and how he thought he was getting screwed. Then we talked about who might make it into the play-offs.

This type of superficial conversation is typical of the patterns of "male bonding" men learn from childhood on. "Sensitive" boys are teased and ridiculed by their peers if they don't conform. This taunting emphasizes stereotypical male interests, and serves to keep us from developing complex self-images and forming deep relationships.

Look at these definitions of man in the *American Heritage Dictionary:*

Man: 1. Any adult male human being, as distinguished from a female. ... 5. A male human being endowed with such qualities as courage, strength, and fortitude, considered characteristic of manhood.

If courage, strength, and fortitude are the sole characteristics of manhood, that leaves no room for men to be compassionate, gentle, and nurturing. It is because of narrow stereotypes like this that men in growing numbers are seeking a healthier definition of masculinity, an emerging understanding that allows them, as men, to feel and give.

Allowing yourself to be sensitive and nurturing does not diminish your masculinity. Allowing yourself to feel makes you more human and compassionate. You become a better father, a closer partner, and a stronger friend. In fact, in many ways allowing yourself to feel helps you gain *greater* courage, strength, and fortitude.

The idea of changing can be frightening. It's much easier to stay the way we are. So many men in our groups are living lives that lack fulfillment, hurting others and themselves, and modeling a destructive path for their children. It doesn't have to be that way.

In my interview with Cassie, she said, "I think on some level my partner really wanted to change. He would tell me he planned to get help but he wouldn't follow through. Things would go along pretty well and then something at work would happen and he would take it out on me. Because he never got any help, I don't think he saw any other way of living."

Some men are threatened when we talk about redefining masculinity. They're concerned about what they may have to change or give up. We discussed this issue in one of our groups.

Neil: I don't know if I believe men need to change. I agree that we don't need to be so violent, but basically I like being a man.

Michael: I don't think it's an issue of whether you like being a man or not. But I think there are ways we get socialized that have a negative impact on how we live our lives. I mean, why are we here?

Tom: We're here because the court said we had to be here.

Gordy: I know what he's saying and I agree to a point. We grow up in a culture where men are supposed to be a certain way. And I think violence is a big part of growing up male. I think, too, that controlling women is ingrained in us.

Michael: If what Gordy said is true, are there ways we can redefine masculinity, keeping the positive stuff and throwing out those qualities that are destructive?

Gordy: I think we can. You know, I think back on my childhood and I feel bad. My father never said he loved us kids, even though I know he did. He purposely was distant and never gave us approval. I almost think he was incapable of telling us.

Michael: That's sad.

Neil: Yeah, but fathers have to project that image of strength. I mean, I have a hard time saying that stuff to my kids. Just because I don't say it doesn't mean I don't have those feelings.

Michael: I think this discussion demonstrates the point I'm trying to make about how our culture defines masculinity. It also speaks to what we are losing as men, husbands, and fathers.

We should be proud to be men. Throughout history, men have countered the tide and fought against oppression and injustice. Gandhi, Cesar Chavez, Martin Luther King Jr., and many others have resisted violence as a means to settle conflict in their struggles—the opposite of what might be considered a typical male response. Men aligned with women during the suffragists' movement in the United States at the turn of the century; this struggle culminated in the passage of the Nineteenth Amendment giving women the right to vote. Many men who fought in the Vietnam War came back and joined other war resisters to bring an end to that conflict. Men and women protested and struggled peacefully against insurmountable odds during the civil rights movement in the 1960s, which led to sweeping changes combating discrimination.

Today, many men are working to confront violence in their own communities. With the rash of school killings committed by boys, and rampant inner city gang violence usually perpetrated by males, men are recognizing the importance of working to resensitize society and especially males to the impact of violence. Dave Grossman, in his book *On Killing*, discusses the ways the military desensitizes men to killing through systematically training soldiers to dehumanize the enemy. He further questions what makes today's children bring guns to schools and use them when their parents did not. He hypothesizes that in our modern American society a systematic process is defeating the age-old psychological inhibition against violent, harmful activity toward one's own species.[20]

Clearly, some of the violent behavior exhibited by young males can be attributed to child abuse at home, observing family violence, and other social factors. But, as James Garbarino points out in *Lost Boys*, nearly 30 percent of high-school-age boys carry a potential lethal weapon in school as part of their normal routine and 12.5 percent carry a firearm to school. This easy access to guns and a willingness to use them to settle conflicts is tragically disturbing. Garbarino describes what happens when boys are taught not to exhibit fear or vulnerability and how accumulated inner damage all too often results in aggressive behavior. He especially notes that the school environment and boys' peer groups play powerful roles in influencing a child's behavior.[21]

School shootings and gang violence also point to the very male characteristics and male training that have been discussed in earlier chapters. Failure of boys and men to live up to the unrealistic expectations of being male in our society leads to feelings of powerlessness, isolation, and rejection. In one school shooting, the young male assailant had been rejected by several girls and decided some of his fellow students should die. Was this just an aberration?

When girls and women are hurt or rejected they handle their emotions very differently than men do. You don't often see a women picking up a gun and killing her family members, then turning the weapon on herself. Nor do you often see a woman committing carnage at her place of employment because of a slight, or because she lost her job. We don't see many girls taking out their aggression on students and teachers and committing premeditated murder. While female violence and female gang violence is increasing, the number of murders committed by girls and young women pales next to the everyday killing by boys and young men of other males, sometimes for the most minor indiscretions.

As fathers and men we owe it to society to change this disturbing reality. Men and women are making incredible contributions in every community in the United States. Most readers of this book have a lot to offer, because you've been there—you know the cost of violence.

Men *can* define masculinity for themselves. Our new definitions can include many important qualities. Within all men is the ability, and often the desire, to be sensitive and caring. We can be loving husbands and fathers. Our loving inner self can emerge when we reject the old masculine characteristics—control, anger, and domination.

Health and Balance

I first learned about the idea of living in balance and harmony from a Native American man named Marlin Mousseau. Marlin grew up on the Pine Ridge Indian Reservation in South Dakota and now works with abusive men in Wisconsin. Marlin developed Project Medicine Wheel, a process designed to help abusive men in the Native American community understand their use of violence, and to motivate men to live in harmony and balance, and use traditional Indian ways for healing.[22]

Marlin states that an individual is made up of four basic essences; emotion, body (the physical side), spirit, and mind (the intellectual side). If one of these areas is not functioning or is unhealthy, the person is out of balance and is not living in harmony with the world. I think men are frequently out of balance. We, unfortunately, have little guidance or support to change our unhealthy lives.

The emotional side

Men in our groups often say they don't know how to talk on a truly emotional level. This is because they have been socialized not to talk about their feelings. Gradually, they become afraid to show their true selves and their emotional side becomes disconnected from the whole. The longer men refrain from expressing their feelings the more difficult it becomes to change.

Occasionally, I have chosen to withdraw in an intimate relationship by withholding my feelings or not talking about what is going on in my life. Sometimes, I'll give just a hint of what is going on or what may be disturbing me. Every time I hold back there is a consequence. I become more distant and the relationship suffers.

Men need to open up emotionally. We need to talk about what we're really feeling. Talking about emotions should not be limited to partners, but should be a precondition to new friendships with women and men. People usually *want* to talk about their lives on a less superficial level, but do not think they have permission. We feel that if we open up, our friends, family members, or intimate partners will think there's something wrong with us, that we're too needy or self-absorbed. Talking on a deeper level takes practice and can never be a one-way street. You must genuinely care about what the other person is saying, thinking, and feeling, too. Your concern and response will be reciprocated. You don't need to solve each other's problems, just to be there for each other.

The physical side

On the physical level, we would all benefit from being active, staying in shape, and putting the right nourishment into our bodies, but we often resist. Many Americans are out of shape, which is a harbinger of future physical problems. Men often ignore health problems and overwork themselves, thinking they are invincible.

An exercise routine takes discipline. Exercise is not only good for the body, it is also emotionally uplifting. Yet there always seems to be something else to do or some excuse. Many times I have left my workplace feeling I had absolutely no energy to exercise. All I wanted to do was to go home, watch the news, eat, and go to bed. I forced myself to go to the gym and, almost always, I enjoyed the exercise and felt reawakened and pleased I had made the effort.

Balancing your physical side also requires monitoring what you put into your body. We hear how important it is to eat a healthy diet, change bad eating habits, and eat in moderation, yet we frequently ignore the advice. Men especially think they can abuse their bodies without consequence. Many men think that cancer or heart disease will happen to someone else, or that there's always time to change. Some men continue to smoke despite the enormous medical evidence that tobacco use causes heart disease and cancer. They engage in unsafe sex even though they know the risks of AIDS and other diseases. They drink to excess and consume dangerous drugs regardless of the physical and psychological effects. Some men believe they are indestructible. Don't make these mistakes. Instead, care about yourself.

If you are not involved in an exercise routine, commit to it now. Join a Y or an exercise club and find the routine that feels good and is fun. Buy some running shoes and power walk or jog. Play basketball, racquetball, or tennis. Lift weights, dance, or join an aerobics class. As the saying goes, *Just Do It!* At least three days of working out per week will keep your weight down, increase cardiovascular activity, and make you feel better.

The spiritual side

When I mention the spiritual level, I am not referring to going to church or temple every weekend; that is your personal choice. I am talking about the need to get in touch with the world around you. This feeling of a connectedness can occur in nature through meditating, walking in a park or in the woods, or sitting by a creek. Some people pray, chant, sing, or listen to music as a way of getting in touch with what is important about life. Everyone can find his or her own source of spiritual light.

Several years ago, I went to a retreat where I learned about meditation. We were asked to focus on the impermanence of life and the limited time we spend on the earth. I remember feeling quite sad during this meditation, a sadness that had much to do with my own inner feelings at the time. I was confused about the pain in the world and wondered about the purpose of my life. I had no answer. Today, when I think back on that time and the focus on impermanence, I realize the message. In the short time we are here, we need to live our lives with significance and purpose. We do not necessarily have to do something earth shattering, just live with more compassion and love. It was an important lesson for me.

I forget that lesson a lot. I choose to live a spiritually unbalanced life because the world around me seems so cold, unloving, and angry. The collective pain of families and communities spills out all around me. I easily become withdrawn, and insulate myself by becoming cynical, self-absorbed, and uncaring. When the pain I see in my work overwhelms me, I know I am spiritually out of balance. Like most things in life, the imbalance is a choice. I can choose to slow down, put my life in perspective, and take the necessary steps to reconnect with what is really important.

The intellectual side

On the intellectual level, men have been trained in particular ways. I think people often have a difficult time being open to new ideas. We get locked into thinking a certain way and refuse to hear opposing views. Listen, for example, to other men discuss politics. The debate takes on an almost warlike character, with each person determined to win. I'm not suggesting that we be afraid to debate or give up some principled positions. But when we refuse to listen to other ideas, we become hardened.

You don't have to be a rocket scientist to nurture your intellectual side. Simply be open to information and ideas. Allow yourself time to reflect. To broaden your intellectual horizons, take a class, join an organization in which ideas are shared, or volunteer in your community.

Unfortunately, television has become the dominant source of ideas and information for many people. While there is certainly entertainment value in television, too many individuals and families have become glued to their sets. TV sitcoms, movies, or sporting events often take priority over discussing ideas with family members or reading books.

Staying in balance is not easy. I am frequently aware of being out of balance. I remember going through a stressful time after I moved from Duluth to the Minneapolis/St. Paul area. I left a relatively small town, friends, and familiar territory for a large metropolitan city. I was emotionally drained. I lacked motivation and changed habits. I stopped exercising and became depressed. I finally went to a counselor to sort things out. On an emotional level, I needed to address my grieving about the move. On a physical level, I needed to develop a plan to take better care of myself, which included exercise, rest, and a good diet. Slowly, I worked my way through the depression.

EXERCISE: Health and Balance

Awareness and the motivation to seek a healthier life are within your reach. The following exercise will help you to assess your present state and determine the steps you might want to take to live a life that is more in balance. You can either think about your responses or write them in your notebook or journal.

1. Briefly write about how you feel about each area of your life today.

Emotional: _____

_____

Physical: _____

_____

Spiritual: _____

_____

Intellectual: _____

_____

2. Write some specific problems or deficiencies under each category. For example, drinking too much, lacking a purpose, or being out of shape, hot-tempered, stuck, or withdrawn.

Emotional: _____

_____

Physical: _____

_____

Spiritual: _____

_____

Intellectual: _____

_____

3. Write some things you can do differently to bring these parts of your life more in balance.

Emotional: _____

_____

Physical: _____

_____

Spiritual: _____

_____

Intellectual: _____

Learn to recognize when you are out of balance and figure out ways to make healthy changes. Embarking on lifestyle changes is hard and the results are not instantaneous, but you *will* notice a difference. And it's worth it.

Dating: How Much of the Past Do We Reveal?

Many men do not tell a new partner of their past abuse. Although I understand the reasons for this reluctance, I think it is important to be honest in a new relationship. Telling your new partner about your past is a way of being accountable for your actions. Your new partner should have the right to confront you if she senses you are becoming abusive. She should have the right to insist that you make changes or seek help.

Peter described his experience in one of our groups:

> When I told Lydia about my past, I was scared she was going to run. She seemed a little shocked at first, but I think she really trusted my commitment to nonviolence. Once I made the decision to tell her, I knew I had to be totally honest about everything. Afterward, I felt incredibly free—as if a ball and chain had been removed from my leg.

Being honest about the past can be hard and sometimes humbling, but a major barometer of change is your commitment to accountability. Many men who have told their stories in this book have indicated that staying violence free is a lifelong commitment. They are continually aware of how they interact with women to avoid backsliding into past abusive behavior.

The following discussion about honesty in a new relationship took place in one of our men's groups:

> **Daniel:** I don't see why I need to tell my partner about my past relationship with Jill. It's over. I want to get on with my life.
>
> **Maryann:** What do the rest of you think?
>
> **Matthew:** I told my new partner about my battering. In fact I tell her what I learn in these groups. She was a little surprised when I told her, but I'm glad I did. I don't want to repeat what I did to Molly. I mean, I really want this relationship to work. I'm committed to being honest about everything with her, and her knowing about my past will help keep me honest.

If you are in a new relationship, you and your partner will be exploring each other in many ways. When you tell her about your past abuse, she may not state all she's thinking or feeling, and it may take time for her to sort through her reactions. It wouldn't be unusual for her to be cautious or even test your commitment to nonviolence. Your awareness of her need for caution can help establish trust in the relationship.

If you are living a violence-free life with a woman, check in with her sometimes about how you have handled certain situations, especially conflict. For instance, you might want to ask if she has felt fearful during a discussion. Ask if your body language or voice was intimidating, so you can correct that behavior the next time you disagree.

"It's important for me to know if Connie is afraid of me in any way, or if she feels I'm exhibiting past behaviors," said Don in one of our discussions. "She's told me that on certain occasions she's withdrawn or backed off because she could tell I was getting irritated. It didn't feel good to hear that, but I need to know about it if I'm going to continue to change."

Talking to Your Children about Your Violence

Children often assume the blame for things that go wrong in their families. I remember my parents having a big argument late one evening. I strained my ears to hear if it had anything to do with us kids. My immediate thought was that I had done something wrong. My next thoughts focused on whether my parents might get a divorce. I kept thinking how I might intervene. At six years of age, I felt responsible for making things right between them.

In families in which there has been violence, children feel enormous responsibility and therefore guilt. And it is in these families that parents are unavailable, leaving children nowhere to turn and no one to talk to.

Some research indicates that in families in which there has been domestic abuse toward a spouse, the risk that the children have been abused is higher than usual. If you have been abusive to your children or think your discipline is becoming abusive, seek help from mental health centers in your community.

Some of the men I interviewed for this book indicated that they talked with their children about their violence. Their motivation was to apologize and offer assurances that they were changing.

Look for an appropriate time to talk to your children, but never force them into talking. They may not be ready, and the experiences they have had with you and your violence may be too fresh and painful. They may not feel safe with you, and pressuring them to talk might cause further harm.

If you talk to your children, be honest. Explain that what occurred in the past was *your* responsibility. Reassure them that they were not to blame. Let them know that you are taking steps to change and that your past abusive behavior was wrong. Admitting your violence to your children will not be easy, but they will respect your honesty even if they can't articulate a response.

When you make the decision to talk with your children, never talk about your abusive behavior in a way that implies your partner or ex-partner is equally responsible. In no way should you blame your partner. Too many parents have done grave damage to their children by pitting one parent against the other and forcing the children to take sides.

Remember that your children may not be ready to have this discussion. Smaller children especially may feel uncomfortable. Do not pressure them. It is far more important that your present behavior demonstrate the changes that you have committed to.

Beyond Personal Change: Educating the Community

Never doubt that a small group of thoughtful
and committed citizens can change the world.
Indeed it's the only thing that ever has.

MARGARET MEAD

Many men have gone public with the fact that they were abusive. They make that decision for a variety of reasons. For some men, telling others of their abuse is a way of staying accountable. For others, the motivation is to help other men by sharing their experiences and their process of change. For yet others, going public is a way to participate in changing society by confronting the attitudes and beliefs that foster violence. Some men speak in schools or community clubs, do public service announcements, or volunteer to work with domestic violence programs. Some teach their sons that violence is not the answer to conflicts.

I know one man who speaks at police training sessions on domestic assault in Minnesota about his years of battering. After listening to him, the police officers have a clearer understanding of the dynamics of an abusive relationship. As a result, they can intervene more effectively in these cases.

We can address violence against women in our community in many ways. Men can take a more active and visible role in confronting sexual and domestic assaults. We can join neighborhood crime watches, participate in antirape marches, and organize community meetings. We can initiate dialogue in our schools, churches, local governments, unions, professional association meetings, and community clubs. We can write letters to newspapers and talk to our friends; publicly confront judges who refuse to take domestic abuse cases seriously; lobby our mayors, state legislators, and congress for tougher laws to protect women who have been abused.

As fathers, we can teach our sons and daughters that attitudes or behaviors that degrade girls and women in any way are wrong. We should be able to talk clearly and with conviction to our children. We can help shape their thinking about men, women, equality, and violence. We need to remind them that if they witness inappropriate behavior on the bus or in the school yard or park, they do not need to participate.

Men can *and should* take the initiative to confront violence in homes and communities, because most violence is instigated by men. Women don't usually kill people; they perpetrate less than 15 percent of the homicides in the United States. When women do kill, it is often in their own defense, notes Angela Browne, author of *When Battered Women Kill.*[23] Gang violence, fights, and domestic and sexual assaults are by and large a male phenomenon. It should be our responsibility to put an end to it.

Women have struggled for years to end rape and domestic violence. They have organized movements, fought for resources, lobbied for legislation, and spoken out about the magnitude of these problems. Men who ally with these movements should support women's leadership. If you plan or seek funding for a program or an event, talk with and work with women's groups in your community.

I'm convinced we can make a difference. I believe we will see more and more men speaking out and confronting sexism and men's violence. We can make a difference today, so that future generations will not have to experience the violence and abuse that occur in homes throughout this country.

Staying on Course: Your Lifelong Commitment

I had promised my wife Kathy I would never hit her again. I really made an effort to apply the things I'd learned in my group and the self-control techniques I'd worked on. I was determined not to repeat my past behavior. We were having an argument about something, and I leaned across the table and yelled, "Now you listen!" She was startled and I was kind of shocked that I did it. I felt the same rush I used to feel when I battered her, and I was aware of her fear. I saw how easy it would be for me to slip back into old behaviors.

As Earl discovered, drifting back into familiar patterns of responding to conflict, anger, and agitation with abuse is a real danger for men who have used violence in the past. The instantaneous response of the victim to an abusive act and the subsequent power one achieves can be intoxicating. The conflict ends, and it ends on your terms.

Most of the men I interviewed for this book told me they work continually to avoid backsliding. Whenever they feel hurt, jealous, or angry, their first thoughts are to react in a way that will bring an immediate response. Being intimidating was so much a part of how they handled conflict in the past that it remains almost an automatic reaction. Yelling or grabbing their partners would make their partners afraid and put them on the defensive. If they resisted, these men could always resort to more violence.

To avoid this all too familiar path, men who lead violence-free lives practice some of the exercises outlined in this book. They maintain a persevering attitude of self-control. There can be no "slips," just like an alcoholic cannot go off the wagon for even a night.

Am I asking for perfection? No. I'm asking only that you remain nonviolent and that you monitor yourself to determine if you are using abusive behaviors.

Remember, acknowledging positive and healthy responses to problems and conflict resolution is important, too. Do not underestimate your achievements. The new path you are taking for yourself as a changing man is important.

For those of you who are still with the partner you abused, you should be especially aware of your response to disagreements. Your partner's fears may stay with her for a long time. If you are in a new relationship and you have told your new partner about your history, she may also be hesitant or nervous when you get upset or angry. Getting feedback from her can be helpful. Your partner, however, is under no obligation to give you this feedback. If she feels safe and is willing, be certain to take advantage of her help.

Part of your commitment to nonviolence may involve exposing yourself to new ideas and challenges about masculinity and the socialization that shapes men and women. Your new awareness can open doors to a different way to view the world and interact with others. Changing men try to share their lives. They become active, not only to contribute, but also to keep growing on a personal level.

Your commitment to change cannot be temporary; it must become part of who you are. At first, you may not get much support from friends, family, or coworkers. But you'll know your new path is the right one to be walking down. You'll feel better about yourself.

Try to be a true friend to other men. When you see or sense that a friend or family member is being abusive to a partner, make it your business to intervene. Choose an appropriate time to talk to that person and strongly encourage him to get help. Use your own experience as a guide; tell your story and tell him what you know. He may reject your attempts, but you may also plant a seed that may be nurtured when he is ready to confront his problems. You can be understanding but also be honest.

Lastly, don't be afraid to seek help. You should not feel ashamed of seeing a counselor to work on issues that come up in your life. If you were physically sick, you wouldn't hesitate to see a doctor. A therapist or counselor can be a good neutral party to talk to; asking for help is not a sign of weakness but an acknowledgment of your desire to be healthy and in balance. If you feel depressed at times, have trouble coping with or resolving problems, stress out, or feel stuck, seek help. Attend a support group or consciousness-raising group. If there is none in your community, organize one.

As you change, you will soon recognize the rewards. Your relationships will improve and you will feel differently about yourself. When you make this lifelong commitment, you are making a personal statement about who you are and your capacity to change. Will you make mistakes? Sure you will. But your willingness to learn from your mistakes and grow will make the journey you have started more valuable as you reach your goal.

Conclusion

A journey of a thousand miles must begin with a single step.

LAO-TZU: THE WAY OF LAO-TZU

Violence gives a man who batters temporary power and control over his partner. He ends an argument, vents his anger, or punishes. But at what cost? Although he often gets his way, he also hurts and destroys in the process. Violence and abusive behavior become a cancer, consuming the victim and perpetrator alike, and usually killing the relationship.

A man who batters tries to justify his behavior, yet the terror in his partner's eyes is always there as a reminder that he—and no one else—has done something hurtful and abusive. Men who batter say, "I don't understand," but they do. There *is* no excuse. In their attempt to avoid responsibility they dig in their heels and try not to feel or remember. They turn on a kind of psychic numbing to have peace within themselves. A friend once told me that a man who batters looks in the mirror, sees that his face is dirty, and wipes the mirror to get it clean. Yet, some men *do* face the problem head-on and make commitments to change. You have met some of these men in this book.

And what of the women in this book? They are survivors. They have struggled to understand all that has happened and they are healing. I try to imagine how they must have felt as the blows and kicks bruised their bodies. What were they thinking when they saw the rage and hatred in their partners' eyes? They must have wondered how the men they chose with love as mates and husbands could do these horrible things. Were their spirits broken? Would they ever trust a man again?

I also wonder about the children of the men and women in this book. Have they already been infected by what they have witnessed? Will I see their sons in future groups for men who batter, or will the cycle be broken with this generation?

Much of this book has been about men taking personal responsibility for past behavior. These men have learned not to blame others and have reached a state of awareness so that positive change can take place. How many men will take the initiative? Many will enter new relationships and remain nonviolent. Many will not learn from the past and will be doomed to repeat it.

At times, over the years, I have been discouraged working in this field. I thought that with new laws and increased societal awareness domestic violence would be on the wane, but it is not. Domestic homicides are a daily occurrence. Emergency rooms continue to receive victims. And the little secrets in so many of our homes continue.

Yet, through it all, I remain hopeful. Many men who have battered, including the men I interviewed for this book, have made significant changes in their lives. They have grown and recognized how their past beliefs and attitudes toward women have contaminated their relationships and led to violence. They have seen the hurt they were causing and have said, "No more!" With the help of programs and concerned individuals, they were able to change. They still struggle, but they are personally rewarded for their commitment to living a nonviolent life.

Now that you have completed this book, don't stop here. Set some goals for your life, and practice what you have learned. Ask for help. Use the exercises in this book to keep you focused on your objectives. *You will change, if you want to change.*

One final message to men reading this book: *get involved.* Domestic violence, for too long, has been considered a women's issue. It isn't.

What communities and men can do

- Fathers can model for their children successful egalitarian relationships with women by being respectful, sharing responsibility in the home, and demonstrating how conflicts and disagreement can be resolved without being abusive.

- Invariably, our children are exposed to negative perceptions of females and males. Fathers and mothers can help their children understand about sexism in our culture by explaining why sexist jokes and degrading names are wrong, and by discussing the positive aspects of gender equality.

- Boys especially need to understand that differences can be resolved without violence, that you don't and shouldn't always get your way, and that you don't always have to win.

- In far too many communities men commit acts of violence against women without consequences. Men who batter are more apt to change if they are held accountable for their behavior by friends, family, and the community.

- We must challenge the way men are defined in our culture and stop glamorizing violence. Movies, television, and sports portray men as tough, violent, unfeeling, always in control, and not like women. From a very early age, boys are bombarded with these conflicting signals and expectations of what it means to be male. These messages encourage violence and the devaluation of women.

- Most men who batter know their behavior is wrong. If you have a friend who is battering, don't be silent—help is available. If you are using violence or are becoming abusive to your partner or your children, get help—it is out there, and you *can change.*

- Men can constructively confront other men about sexism, exploitation of women, and violence. Men can be true friends to other men by showing a different path, free of abuse and violence. This may seem risky to some men, but it is one way to change the negative attitudes and beliefs that far too many men have about women and relationships.

- Governments, nonprofit organizations, and community institutions need to commit resources to ensure that our communities are safe havens for victims trying to get out of abusive relationships. Battered women's shelters, advocacy, counseling, and training for interveners all cost money, but it is money well spent. For men who have battered, maintain your change path by volunteering in your community—whether you talk about your past behavior or not, you have a lot to offer.

Today we can *all* make some serious commitments about how we want to lead our lives. It is up to all of us to change a little piece of the world.

Appendix A

An Overview for the Practitioner

Part 1. Working with Men Who Batter

Ron's Story — Expectations of Counseling — The Theory and
Practice of Offender Programs — The Duluth Curriculum —
Does Counseling Work?

> *Almost anything you do will be insignificant,*
> *but it is very important that you do it.*

MAHATMA GANDHI

Ron's Story

Ron grew up in Cleveland in the 1950s. He experienced domestic
violence firsthand by observing the actions of his father, stepfather,
and mother. He developed a substance abuse problem at an early
age, traveled from city to city, joined the United States Marine
Corps, and subsequently went AWOL. When he left the service he
again traveled, and ended up in the Midwest. He battered the
woman he was living with and was ordered into the Domestic
Abuse Intervention Project in Duluth, Minnesota, in the early 1980s.
Ron was ordered into one of my early groups. Unlike a lot of court-
mandated offenders, Ron was open to examining his life—he
wanted to change.

Here is Ron's story:

> My father was a very violent man, though he left our family when I
> was only four. I have painful memories of this period of my life in
> spite of how young I was. One time, my dad was angry at me

because I'd turned on our gas stove. So, I guess to teach me a lesson, he put my hand on the fire of the stove top—I have the scars to remind me of him. My parents divorced shortly after that time and my mother remarried a few years later. When I was around eight, my mom became a binge-drinking alcoholic. At this point the domestic violence between my mom and stepdad began and escalated. The trouble usually would start when my mom would come home, or sometimes when she wouldn't come home from the bars. There was a lot of violence. I would lie to my stepdad on her behalf so she wouldn't get beaten. Because of the violence, I was confused as a child. I would alternate blaming my mom for her behavior and then blaming my stepdad for his actions. It was a difficult spot for a kid to be in.

Sometimes, I would hide in my bedroom with a baseball bat hoping my stepdad would come in so I could nail him. He was a huge guy, but I don't remember being afraid. There was one occasion when I thought he was going to kill my mom because this time a knife was involved. From my bedroom I heard him say, "Pick up the knife, you cunt, and I'll cut your fuckin' throat." I came out of the bedroom and got between them, and they actually stopped fighting.

One time we were all sitting at the kitchen table eating and my parents start arguing again. The table got knocked over and the legs were sticking up. My stepdad grabbed my mom by the hair and was slamming her face against the table leg that was sticking out. Her jaw broke and her eyes were blackened from this incident. The police were called and they arrested my stepdad. Whenever she fought back, she really got it and that's what happened that night.

I felt like I was living in a dreamworld. The strange thing is I never thought anything was really wrong with our family, because despite the violence, most of the time things around the house were very peaceful. My stepdad was a good provider and Mom was a great housekeeper. We had a lot of family outings. My parents could be very loving, but about every four months there would be a blowup. When my mother's alcoholism got out of control the violence got more frequent. When I was around thirteen, I started to understand that things weren't quite right in our family.

We lived in the inner city of Cleveland. I was really a big kid, so I didn't get messed with, but even though I had physical size I was afraid of violence and avoided it. When I was sixteen, I left home and became a full-blown alcoholic and drug user. Oblivion was my goal. I lived with various family members for a while, but that didn't work out. Believing I needed to do something with my life, I joined the United States Marine Corps and was stationed at Camp Lejune, North

Carolina. I was drinking a lot and soon went AWOL. When I was apprehended, I was forced into substance abuse treatment, but I didn't buy the program, and continued to drink. I started to get into fights with men, usually in the bars. I fought because I didn't like feeling frustrated and because I didn't like being fucked with. I was very opinionated and bullheaded. If I got into an argument with someone, and I felt threatened or challenged, we'd be fighting.

When I was released from the service, I hitchhiked through the Twin Cities on my way to Seattle. The police picked me up because I was intoxicated. I decided to go into treatment, since a program was offered. When I got out of treatment, I met Clarice, the woman I would live with and batter. Clarice was afraid of me right from the beginning. I would scream in her face and terrorize her. We would usually fight over little things, but when I wanted the upper hand I would punch holes in the walls or slam things around the house to scare her. One time I put her over my knee and despite her resistance I gave her a spanking. This wasn't just a spanking; it was a beating. I was stone-cold sober when I did this to her. I thought of Clarice as almost childlike, and if she fucked with me, she was going to get it. I would usually apologize after I assaulted her and then I would tell her how much I loved her. During my apologies, I'd usually minimize the incident and blame her for getting me so upset. It was really easy for me to turn things around and then say to her, "You're lucky I don't leave you."

Even though I felt Clarice had it coming, I did feel bad when I was abusive. Because of my experiences as a child, I had sworn I wasn't going to abuse women, but like so many men who grow up in violent households I became a batterer. I don't believe alcohol was a factor in my behavior, because I battered Clarice when I was sober. When I hit her, I actually experienced an adrenaline high. There's a certain feeling you get when you have that ultimate power over someone—it's difficult to describe.

The worst violent incident occurred when I got home from a fishing trip and Clarice wasn't at the house. I had a feeling that something was up. I thought she might be at her mother's, so I drove to her mom's house and sure enough she was there. I demanded that she get in the car, but she refused, so I put her over my shoulder and carried her out, and forced her into the car. Her mother was screaming and asking Clarice if she wanted her to call the police. Clarice yelled back that she did. When she said yes, I was in a total rage. I felt betrayed that she told her mom to call the police, and I hauled off and punched her several times in the face. We argued in the car and when she threatened to leave me, I stopped and punched her in the face some more. I drove away again, but she continued to argue with me, so I again stopped the car and started to beat her. I felt I could scare her back into her place—that she would tell the police everything was okay. I thought this strategy would work, because she'd covered up for me when I'd beaten her in the past. But this time was different. A car drove up behind us and Clarice jumped out. She ran to the other car and the people let her in before I could really react. She was badly beaten up and they took her away. It didn't appear there was anything I could do about the situation, and I knew I was in trouble, so I just decided to go home. I went to bed, and the next thing I knew the police were in my bedroom. I was charged with a felony.

I had no idea Clarice was going to leave me. I found out later that she was in contact with battered women's advocates at the shelter and they had helped her figure out a plan for leaving me. I was given three years probation and ordered into substance abuse treatment and the Domestic Abuse Intervention Project. I thought of myself as sort of a tough-guy when I came into your group, but when I think back, I was far more open than most of the other men. From the very beginning, I wanted to discuss my violence—I wanted it to stop. I knew I needed help and being forced into counseling gave me the opportunity.

At about this time, I enrolled in college and befriended people at the school. Ironically, I started dating an advocate from the shelter. I was honest with Arlene about my past use of violence and my experiences in the group. I talked with a lot of my friends about what was going on in my life. I wasn't ashamed that I was in the abuse classes; in fact, it seemed the more I talked, the freer I became.

Early on in my relationship with Arlene, I did become abusive. Most of the abuse was of a threatening nature. I would scream at her; I never hit her, but on one occasion I restrained her. She wanted to leave an argument, and I wanted to finish it, so I grabbed her by the arms and held her. I know she was afraid of me during the early years of our relationship. Arlene stuck with me at that time, because I think she saw the progress I was making and she knew I was working on my issues. Still, I was unpredictable and I knew I was capable of reverting back to using violence. One time, Arlene was late and I was furious. I wasn't sure what I was going to do when she got home, so I called this guy I'd gone to group with in the past. I told him I was feeling really upset and kind of crazy. We talked about what was going on, what I was feeling, and why my thinking was mixed up. That conversation and his support really helped calm me down.

I'm committed to not being violent or abusive with Arlene. I'd like to believe all my abuse is in the past, but I still don't totally trust myself. Fifteen years after getting ordered into counseling, I know I still have issues with women and relationships. I went into therapy for a long time to work on my childhood stuff a few years back. It was hard and painful, but I learned a lot about myself. That experience was important to me. I think about my violent history, the kinds of struggles men and women have in relationships, and I try to understand how my past has influenced me today. As long as I continue to talk about these issues and as long as my thinking is challenged, I know I'll be okay. It's about awareness and remembering where you were, and of course, how you want to live your life in the present and in the future.

Expectations of Counseling

Beginning in the early 1980s, offenders convicted of committing domestic assaults were ordered into counseling or domestic abuse classes. Many people in the battered women's movement questioned the value of court-ordered mental health counseling in domestic assault cases. They felt the offender had committed a crime, so he should do the time. The reality was, and still is, that the already crowded criminal justice system won't put most first-time or even second-time batterers in jail, except for short periods. Hence, the courts have found that mandated counseling in lieu of jail is a realistic sanction. Probation orders, diversion agreements, and court orders require the offender to attend counseling or education classes for a period of time, usually with a stipulation that failure to complete the program, or reoffending while in the program, will result in a more severe penalty.

In many jurisdictions, law enforcement and the courts have adequately responded—and levied consequences—when an offender violates his probation or a civil protection order. However, in far too many communities domestic assault cases are still relegated to the back burner, and a violation of court order results in a slap on the wrist, leaving advocates, counselors, and many in the court system frustrated. The offender soon realizes the system has no teeth, and he thumbs his nose at the entire process. When this occurs, victims are at greater risk, because the batterer thinks he can continue his abusive behavior with impunity.

Before setting up an offender program or offering counseling, it is important for practitioners to work with battered women's programs to ensure that agencies within the justice system have policies and procedures in place that centralize victim safety and offender accountability. While some states have standards outlining minimum requirements for providing services to offenders, most do not. If you are starting a program, I would urge you to obtain the manual *Accountability: Program Standards for Batterer Intervention Services* published by the Pennsylvania Coalition Against Domestic Violence.

Additionally, if you are starting an offender program or looking to improve your services, do a little research. Identify those programs in your state that have established good working relationships with the criminal justice system and battered women's programs. Some will have descriptions of their models, or can answer questions, so you won't need to reinvent the wheel. The National Training Project in Duluth, Minnesota, has several manuals and books on strategizing, organizing, and designing an effective coordinated community response to domestic assault cases; see the "Recommended Books" section at the end of this book.

Major concerns have been raised by advocates in the battered women's movement regarding court-mandated counseling. As practitioners, we have an obligation to address these concerns in a responsible manner. The following are some of the criticisms:

- Counseling programs siphon off limited community or government dollars, leaving shelters and advocacy programs without adequate funding.

- Counseling programs can provide a false sense of security to victims, resulting in some women staying in abusive relationships when it might be safer to leave.

- Research of counseling programs indicates that half of the court-mandated offenders will recidivate within five years.

- Counseling may give the wrong message to men who batter regarding the nature and causal factors for their use of violence.

- Practitioners may be prescribing treatment or counseling that will either blame the victim or hold her partially responsible for the violence.

- Counseling programs that don't have solid relationships with shelters or don't have policies that make victim safety central to their work may be putting victims at risk.

Current practitioners as well as those contemplating starting a program would be wise to discuss these issues with battered women's advocates. Many domestic abuse programs around the country do great work. They work closely with shelters or have a victim advocacy component as part of their overall program. Effective programs have written agreements with the courts and are part of a coordinated community response to end violence. Whether your community has a good, mediocre, or poor network of counseling programs in this field, it behooves us all to examine our practices and even our motivation for providing services.

The very nature of counseling implies that something is going to change. We presume that a court-ordered offender will alter his behavior once he's involved in the counseling or educational process. The sad reality is that many offenders don't want to change, see little wrong with what they did, and would batter again if a similar situation occurred. We can't always tell at the outset of counseling whether the offender who subscribes to the belief that his behavior was justifiable will change those attitudes after attending our groups. Nor are we certain the offender who appears remorseful and open to counseling will stay nonviolent. We simply can't predict. We should give every man who walks into our groups an opportunity to change. We should believe in him despite his attitude, and do our work professionally, with his partner's safety always in mind.

Many women whose partners are in our programs desperately want the violence to end, and believe they can salvage their relationships if only their partners will change. A victim may rightly feel frustrated or ripped off if her partner is simply going through the motions to satisfy the courts, if he doesn't want to change, or if he becomes more abusive during the counseling process. Effective domestic abuse programs provide advocacy to partners of offenders so they know what is being taught in the groups or classes. This is an opportunity for women to talk about the progress—or the lack of progress—their partners are making. Some women lower their expectations that their abusive partners will change and reevaluate their relationships.

Evaluating the success and analyzing the outcomes of counseling programs is not an exact science and is never easy. Do we base success solely on recidivism—arrest, protection order taken out, self-reporting—or do we evaluate the partner's perception of changed behavior? Should we accept evaluations of programs that claim high rates of success after assessing the offenders' behavior after only one year, or do we need to examine the sustainability of treatment over a period of years?

We should be realistic about counseling. When an individual man completes his required number of group sessions, we can never be sure he won't be back. We must accept the fact that many men who complete our programs will batter their partners again, or assault new women in their lives. Over the years, I have seen men come back into my office with new stories and sometimes new rationalizations. Some are truly ashamed; others are simply resigned to their predicaments. Usually, but not always, reoffenders have been charged at a higher level of assault and some have now done jail time. I find myself hoping these men will finally "hit bottom," like the drunk who wakes up in a detox center and is finally ready to undertake the challenges of getting sober.

Despite the many setbacks those of us in the field experience regularly, we should also acknowledge that counseling—in concert with other change factors in a man's life—can have a dramatic effect. Some of the men I interviewed for this book have made major life transformations. Most admitted they were resistant when they entered the program, didn't believe they had a problem, and were just going through the motions to appease the court or their partners. Something happened for them. I wish I knew the precise ingredients, but I can only provide a theory.

A man who batter begins to change when events converge in his life. Usually an arrest, having a protection order taken out against him, or losing a relationship provides the impetus. Sometimes he must suffer unpleasant consequences and loss over and over before he is willing to take a long, hard look at himself. But when a man who batters makes the commitment to change, resistance to new ideas dissolves and honest self-reflection can begin. He then must explore:

1. His beliefs about being male in this society

2. His beliefs and expectations of women and marriage

3. His core beliefs and values about violence and the need to control

4. What he ultimately wants in his life

If he allows himself to experience the vulnerability of being human, the batterer may come to realize his abusive behavior is ultimately self-defeating and he will do almost anything to change. Not every man is willing to have his life and everything he believes in twisted inside and out—it's hard and often painful. Some men make changes on their own; most need the information, challenges, and support only a mandated group can provide.

The Theory and Practice of Offender Programs

The philosophy and practices of counseling programs for domestic abuse offenders are a continuing source of contention in the United States. It's tempting to say, "Whatever works," but the issue is more complex than that, especially if we hold to the notion that victim safety must be central to our work. Later in this chapter, victim safety issues will be examined more thoroughly.

Most offender programs base their work with men who batter on one of four theories, discussed below. Most programs share a common goal—to stop the violence—but differ significantly in their approach. Programs that profess high "success" rates should be viewed with a hefty dose of skepticism. As the men in this book have stated, the change process takes years, and for most the process is ongoing today. Men who have been abusive and controlling during most of their adult lives will not be transformed after a six-month program. What we can hope for is a cessation of physical violence, a reduction in controlling behavior, and a willingness to continue changing.

Following is a brief analysis of the theories and practices of counseling programs, and how these theories are put into practice.

"Psychological" Theory

Americans have an appetite for viewing social problems in psychological terms. To help understand and explain criminal behavior in all its various forms, we have created a symbiotic relationship between the criminal justice system and the mental health community. The courts assume the antisocial behavior they see every day must have a psychological basis. They often turn to psychologists, psychiatrists, therapists, and social workers in the mental health community to work with offenders who are incarcerated or under some form of court supervision. In domestic abuse cases the courts in increasing numbers send offenders to mental health centers for evaluations and/or treatment.

Although mental health practitioners today have a deeper understanding of domestic violence than their predecessors a generation ago, they still too frequently do a disservice to both the victim and the offender. Well-meaning mental health practitioners, in part due to their educational and professional orientation, have labeled battered women as masochistic, codependent, passive-aggressive, having a poor self-image, or exhibiting learned helplessness. A battered women must construct an explanation for why she got involved in an abusive relationship, and why she stayed, and must justify her process for coping and survival. Rather than exploring the historical precedents for wife-beating in our culture, many practitioners assume the victims' choices reflect a psychological abnormality, a defect, or an underlying pathology.

Similarly, mental health practitioners also perceive domestic violence offenders as suffering from psychological disorders. They diagnose men who batter with depression, poor impulse control, low frustration tolerance, fear of intimacy, fear of abandonment, or borderline personalities. Some men are labeled passive-aggressive, psychopathic, chemically dependent, or—my favorite—having an intermittent explosive disorder.

Inherent in the Psychological Theory is a perception that the client—offender or victim—has a mental illness. In fact, most mental health centers utilizing third party insurance payments must provide a diagnosis consistent with the American Psychological Association's *Diagnostic and Statistical Manual of Mental Disorders (DSM-IV)*. Once the diagnosis is made, the clinician provides treatment based on certain assumptions. For instance, if the clinician believes a causal factor for the offender's violence is fear of intimacy and low self-esteem, he or she may work with the client to identify the genesis of his fear of closeness, and explore ways for him to feel good about himself. If the clinician believes a causal factor for the violence is shame or family-of-origin issues, then he or she will work with the client to understand the roots of his shame and explore the pain and anger manifested from family experiences.

The assumption in both examples is this: if the offender wasn't insecure or shamed, if he had worked through his family-of-origin issues, then he wouldn't batter. However, plenty of seemingly secure men with strong self-concepts beat their wives. Sean Connery admitted to Barbara Walters on national television that sometimes you need to slap a woman to put her in her place. Aristotle Onassis was stopped by the police after assaulting a woman in his car. He told the police he had stopped beating her because he was tired. These men don't seem overly insecure.

Focusing on individual psychological aspects of the offender at the expense of challenging the beliefs and attitudes most offenders have about women, men, and marriage will not produce significant changes in behavior. This is not to say that some men who batter don't have mental health problems that need to be addressed—the question is whether the court should order therapy for a man who has beaten his wife. Similarly, by focusing on the individual psychological workings of the victim—psychotherapy predicated on her need to change—we may neglect to assess the danger of her situation, or attempt to treat the relationship through marriage counseling before the violence and intimidation has ceased. The question isn't whether a battered woman has a mental health problem, but rather what is in her best interest while she is being battered, and how she can best extricate herself from an abusive and perhaps life-threatening situation.

This description of the Psychological Theory and discussion of the mental health community is not intended as a general criticism of an admirable field. Many mental health practitioners are clear and informed about domestic abuse issues. Unfortunately, others still have little contact with battered women's advocates, have weak policies regarding reoffenses, are insufficiently trained in the dynamics of abusive relationships, and provide marriage counseling at inappropriate times.

Institutional practices don't change easily. If victim safety is to be the cornerstone of our work, we must exercise caution by pursuing ongoing training, working in collaboration with shelters and the courts, and being open to evaluation.

"Relationship Conflict" Theory

Some practitioners trained in family-system approaches believe both parties in a relationship contribute to domestic violence. While careful never to say the victim is responsible for getting beaten, they often imply that her behavior provided an impetus for his reaction. The practitioner then assumes the couple is engaging in mutual combat, or that the wife has provoked her husband by below-the-belt arguments, aggravating and escalating the confrontation. Practitioners will sometimes describe this scenario as a "dance" between the partners, and deem the violence an interpersonal transaction.

If the goal is to repair the relationship through marriage counseling, the clinician will try to help the couple resolve conflicts in a nonabusive manner, work with them to explore ways to redistribute power in the relationship, and teach healthy conflict resolution and communication techniques. These goals are certainly valid when the threat of violence isn't present. However, the question comes down to, "When is it *safe* to provide marriage counseling to a couple if battering has taken place?"

Dangers to the victim

Marriage counseling, quite simply, can be dangerous to a victim of spousal abuse. If a woman freely discusses relationship issues before important criteria are met, she risks physical and emotional retribution by the man who abused her. Victims speak of been beaten in the parking lot of a therapist's office, in the car, or later at home after a counseling session; this anecdotal evidence should convince any practitioner—despite his or her level of training—of the dangers of marriage counseling in abuse cases. And from a practical standpoint, how can you help a couple redistribute power when one person isn't ready to relinquish control?

Some people say marriage counseling is never appropriate in abuse cases. I believe this position is also misguided—some couples *do* stay together. However, practitioners should follow clear guidelines and agencies should adopt strict policies to protect victims. As stated earlier in this book, marriage counseling should be provided only when the following criteria have been met:

1. The man has successfully completed a reputable domestic abuse program that focuses on changing sexist beliefs and attitudes about controlling women.

2. A practitioner is convinced that the battering—violence, coercion, threats, intimidation, and psychological abuse—has ceased.

3. The battered woman has worked with a victims' advocate and has developed a safety plan to get help if her partner becomes abusive.

4. The battered woman feels safe.

5. The practitioner has discussed the risks associated with marriage counseling privately with the woman, and feels relatively sure abusive acts will not take place as the result of these sessions.

Messages to the couple

Many offenders who are ordered into our program are upset when we won't make a marriage counseling referral for them. They protest and argue, "How can we work on our problems if we aren't in counseling together?" Offering marriage counseling at an early stage of intervention implies that the couple is having marital problems, and it gives the offender a rationalization for his behavior. He will usually use the counseling sessions against her. He might say, "Remember that we are both in this together." "You know that it takes two to tango." "If you hadn't _____, then I wouldn't have to hit you." "Remember, the counselor said _____ about the way you handled that situation."

In marriage counseling, when a battered woman tells her story, she might say she feels some responsibility for the violence. She might say, "I shouldn't have said that," "I should have waited to talk to him about this," "I could see he was in a bad mood," "I shouldn't have gotten up in his face." Her interpretations of events may provide the offender enough crawl space to escape responsibility for his actions. The clinician may then unintentionally collude with the offender, offering an implied acceptance that his behavior was an understandable reaction to an interpersonal conflict, despite qualifying statements that the violence was nevertheless wrong.

Some states now have standards describing the qualifications for mental health providers, and some courts are somewhat more enlightened than others when they order offenders to counseling. Many judges will only refer offenders to programs that (1) are identified as part of a community collaboration, (2) have adopted policies and procedures centered on victim safety, (3) hold offenders accountable for violating court orders or any rules of the program, and (4) have a clear working relationship with battered women's programs.

In many communities, however, offenders are simply sent to a treatment provider recommended by the court or chosen by the offender. One-day treatment programs are sometimes offered as an alternative to traditional programs lasting six months or longer. It is inconceivable that a man who batters would make substantive behavioral or attitudinal changes after a daylong class, other than being inconvenienced for that day. In some cases the defense attorney, the offender, or the couple tells the court that they are already in marriage counseling and requests that they be allowed to continue. Unless educated on domestic abuse dynamics, judges and probation officers get conned into believing the offender's motivation is sincere and will fail to recognize the dangers of court-mandated marriage counseling.

I am a strong believer in counseling and psychotherapy. Many offenders can be helped by individual therapy, and couples who choose to stay together will benefit from marriage counseling. However, it is important for agencies and clinicians who do this work to expand their horizons. Victim safety should be a professional imperative. Collaboration with battered women's programs, understanding danger signs, adopting and following policies that hold the offender accountable, granting limited offender confidentiality, and agreeing to some criteria for determining when and if marriage counseling is offered are critical for the practitioner.

"Anger Causes Violence" Theory

In the Anger Causes Violence Theory, the practitioner views the client as having poor impulse control or having adopted patterns of reacting to conflict or stress with aggression. The inherent assumption is that the offender's stress and anger build until an incident triggers a violent outburst.

Practitioners who subscribe to this theory believe anger management techniques can be taught to the offender so he won't batter. The focus is on teaching him to be aware of physical and emotional cues when he's upset or angry. Physical signs might be tightened fists, clenched teeth, or rapid breathing. Emotional signs might be stress, anxiety, or feeling hurt or put down. Offenders are taught de-escalation techniques. The time-out—when the offender removes himself from a conflict if he feels he might become abusive—is perhaps the most effective strategy. Other techniques include meditation, deep-breathing, and self-talk.

Anger management techniques within a holistic intervention approach can be effective, and most domestic abuse programs teach such techniques to both the offender and the victim. However, anger management alone usually won't stop a batterer from using violence; it may provide an intermittent respite when religiously practiced, but fundamental behavioral change will only occur when the offender begins to change his beliefs and attitudes about men, women, and marriage. Time-outs, if used effectively, will calm a tense situation, but they won't resolve issues. A man who batters is likely to admit that eventually, when the issue or disagreement won't go away, he will resolve the conflict by making a threat, using forms of intimidation, or being violent. Maybe not in every instance, or over every conflict, but his need to control a situation and settle things on his terms frequently wins out, and he resorts to violence.

While perhaps not intended, the Anger Causes Violence Theory is supported by another theory—The Cycle of Violence. Dr. Leonore Walker, an important voice in the domestic abuse prevention field, views the Cycle of Violence as a typical scenario in abusive relationships.[24] She describes a tension-building phase during which minor escalating incidents occur, including verbal abuse. As the offender's stress escalates, an acute incident usually follows, resulting in the victim being physically beaten. In the next step of the cycle the couple moves into a honeymoon phase. This stage, or so the assumption goes, is seductive to both parties; they experience emotional closeness, the offender is remorseful and contrite, all is forgiven, and he is given another chance. Then the cycle starts all over again.

This well-known theory accurately explains the dynamics between some couples, at least early on in abusive relationships. Some battered women will say they knew things were never going to change when their partners stopped apologizing. But for many abused women, the Cycle of Violence never fit their reality. This is important to acknowledge.

A woman we interviewed explained the following in a film we produced in Duluth:

> My husband and I were at this bar where he was playing pool. He had gotten upset with me because I wanted to go home and he didn't. The next thing I knew, he told me to go outside with him, which I did. When I got out into the alley he grabbed hold of me and punched me in the face with all his might and said, "There you go bitch, now go home." Clearly shaken, I picked myself up, dusted myself off, and

went home. The next day I had this huge fat lip. When my husband came downstairs, I expected an apology or some kind of recognition of what he'd done—you know, like "I'm sorry, I was drunk" or "I don't know what got into me." But when he saw me he never said a word, he never even acknowledged what he had done.

For Holly, there was no honeymoon phase. The Cycle of Violence doesn't apply in cases like hers, and neither does the Anger Causes Violence Theory. Holly's husband was angry, but his violence wasn't about losing control or escalating anger. He was agitated and wanted her out of his hair. His behavior was methodical; he was basically saying, through his fist, "I will go home when I want, and I don't want any hassle from you." Case closed.

The Cycle of Violence seems to presuppose that an abusive man's anger will escalate. It assumes the offender wouldn't reach the acute stage and use violence if he could just control or manage his anger. The theory of a tension-building phase implies that, unless interrupted, the stressors active in the offender will inevitably produce a violent outburst. But if this were always true, how do we explain the many irrational violent attacks by an offender for very trivial issues? How do we account for the offender who wakes his wife up in the middle of the night to beat her for no reason? While anger is a powerful emotion, and usually precedes a violent attack, it does not cause the violence. Perhaps more important, a man's anger or stress doesn't explain why his partner is the target of his violence, when he might be equally angry about something or someone totally unrelated to her. Why doesn't an offender assault his boss, coworkers, friends, or a stranger on the street?

The Anger Causes Violence Theory gives men who batter the wrong message. When we started the Domestic Abuse Intervention Project back in 1981, we initially ran anger control groups for court-mandated offenders. Because we adhered to the Anger Causes Violence Theory, men would come to groups and explain their reasons for attending in terms of anger: "I'm here because I can't control my anger." "I've got a short fuse and got into trouble with my girlfriend, so the judge told me to come to this group." "When I get provoked, I lose it and get violent." "I've got an anger problem, so I'm court-ordered to this program." "My probation officer thinks I need to get hold of my anger." These explanations don't address the intention and purpose of violent and abusive behavior. Perhaps more problematic, the Anger Causes Violence Theory puts the burden on the victim to change her behavior so she doesn't provoke her husband. She is taught to recognize when her partner's anger is beginning to escalate, and to do things to lighten the tension. *What an awesome responsibility to put on a victim.*

Anger management should be part—but only part—of a treatment plan for offenders. In one program I was associated with, victims reported that the most noticeable change in their abusive partners, early on, was a commitment to take a time-out when they thought they might become abusive. These same women also indicated that they didn't recognize significant behavioral and attitudinal changes in their partners. Anger management is only one piece of a larger puzzle. For a man to stop battering, he must go much deeper in his understanding of who he is as a man, his core values, and why he wants a woman in his life.

"Male Beliefs of Women" Theory

I remember traveling in British Columbia some years back. I had been scheduled to conduct trainings in several cities, so I decided to rent a car and enjoy the beautiful scenery as a break between events. As I traveled down a highway, I came upon a construction site and stopped my car as directed. The road crew person told me it would take about a half hour before the road would reopen. Since I wasn't in a big hurry and the landscape was beautiful, I parked the car and walked over to the river adjacent to the road. Soon a truck pulled up behind my car and the driver got out. The truck driver heard the same explanation I did about the road, and decided to come visit me where I stood by the river. He was a big guy—about six foot four— and weighed around 270 pounds. He wore a Harley vest that exposed several tattoos. As he approached, for some reason I spit on the ground. I guess it was sort of a reflexive male bonding thing I learned in my adolescence.

We started to make small talk. I asked him about his job as a trucker and the current state of affairs in Canada. He filled me in on both subjects. Then he asked me what I was doing in British Columbia. I thought for a minute—do I really want to tell this guy what I do for a living and then have to talk about domestic abuse?

"I'm sort of a social worker," I said, then tried to change the subject. "How 'bout those Maple Leafs?"

He answered, "They'll stink again. A social worker, eh. What kind of family troubles do you work on? "

I figured he wasn't going to drop the matter, so I told him. "I worked with wife-beaters."

"Wife-beaters," he said with some surprise and amusement.

"Yup," I said.

There was a slight pause in the conversation; then he looked me square in the eyes and said, "You wanna know why women get beat?" He seemed so confident.

"Why?" I asked.

He said, "I'll tell you why women get beat. They get beat 'cause they don't listen."

And then he spit. And then I spit and pondered for a moment. I thought, should I confront this guy? There's no way he can out-argue me on this subject. After all, I read, lecture, train, and write about domestic abuse. I eat and drink this stuff. Then again if I did confront him, I could be putting my life in jeopardy by having a philosophical debate with a guy who had "One Way—My Way" carved into one arm and "Instant Asshole Just Add Alcohol" on the other. I thought about what he said about women not listening and I realized that, in an odd sort of way, he was right. His explanation distilled the thinking of most men who batter into one observation. When I think about the hundreds of men I've worked with over the years, except for incidents of true self-defense, men batter (1) to get their partners to stop doing something they disapprove of, (2) to stop their partners from saying things or to end an argument, (3) to punish their partners for something they've done. It really is that simple.

I tell this story because every time we try to come up with psychological theories or explanations for why a man who batters is violent, we shortchange victims and offenders alike by providing a rationalization. We treat and work around the edges, missing the *'cause they-don't-listen* explanation behind every story.

Essentially, the Male Beliefs of Women Theory is based on the premise that men batter women because they believe they are entitled, on account of their gender, to call the shots, end disputes, and control relationships. There are variations of this thinking, but belief in male superiority and authority is a central theme for many men, and especially for men who batter.

This is not to say that all men who have used abusive behaviors in their relationships believe males are superior to females. Some men find themselves in power struggles with their partners. A small percentage could even be described as battered men, and protection and advocacy for these men should be no different from what is provided for battered women. Occasionally couples engage in actual mutual violence; in these situations both parties need not only counseling but legal sanctions to protect them from future acts of violence. Still, the vast majority of men in offender programs harbor sexist beliefs about women and relationships, and use violence to maintain power and control.

Practitioners who believe in the Male Beliefs of Women Theory are considered feminist based. Their programs usually are identified as batterer intervention or domestic abuse programs, and typically use educational or psychoeducational models. Some combine education with group therapy. Often these programs work closely with or are connected to battered women's programs. EMERGE in Boston, the Domestic Abuse Project in Minneapolis, the Domestic Abuse Intervention Project in Duluth, RAVEN in St. Louis, AMEND in Denver, and ManAlive in Marin County were some of the early programs.

Staff members at batterer intervention programs focus not only on eliminating the physical and sexual violence, but also on reducing and ending the myriad other abusive behaviors that constitute battering. In these groups, men who batter are asked to examine their beliefs about relationships. They also explore the intentionality of their violence and think about how their sense of entitlement is manifested in patriarchal thinking. Challenging beliefs and attitudes and helping men who batter think more critically about their behavior is central to this model. The groups are designed to help men construct a different kind of relationship, one based on egalitarianism and respect.

The classes or groups are facilitated by male and female group leaders. Group leaders eschew the notion that offenders are mentally ill. They view battering as a function of the social construction of families and the influences of our culture. For many programs the primary focus is on victim safety, with offender rehabilitation secondary. Some programs are appendages of the court system or at a minimum have a close working relationship with probation departments.

Criticism of this approach comes from the perspective that the gender-based analysis is oversimplified by focusing on social-cultural factors at the expense of other issues. For instance, research indicates that child abuse or observing domestic abuse as a child is correlated to future violent behavior, yet many programs using psychoeducational models avoid in-depth counseling. Some people criticize the psychoeducational model for being too confrontational. Others have questioned whether examining various abusive behaviors in detail in the groups unwittingly gives men who batter new ideas for battering.

As the coauthor with Ellen Pence of the curriculum *Power and Control: The Tactics of Men Who Batter,* used by many batterer intervention programs in North America, I clearly have a bias.[25] Over the years in this field, I have used an anger-management model as well as something akin to an AA or self-help approach in my groups. In the mid-1980s many of us at the Duluth Domestic Abuse Intervention Project began having serious reservations about the groups we were running. We asked a hypothetical question: If a group of battered women were watching us conduct our groups, what would be their observation? We concluded that most would think we were missing the boat, not only in our analysis, but also in our approach. We came to the conclusion that a structured educational model with a feminist analysis would not only be more effective, but also more honest for offenders, victims, and practitioners.

This approach stresses that men make choices when they are violent or abusive. It helps them see that their abusive behavior is purposeful and not caused by provocation, psychological problems, or alcohol or drugs. Programs using this model, through the following core elements, offer men the opportunity to change:

- The groups help batterers understand how their beliefs and attitudes about men and women are steeped in sexism and reinforced by our culture.

- The groups provide a framework for breaking through denial, minimizing, and blaming of others.

- The groups help men who batter understand the impact of their violence on their partners, children, and themselves, and increase empathy for those they have hurt.

- The groups help men see that the painful feelings they often experience are tied to their beliefs and actions. When a man who batters understands this connection he begins to see how his partner's resistance to being controlled frequently makes him feel more vulnerable, insecure, shamed, and angry.

- The groups help men who batter see that they always have

alternatives to using violence and help them develop plans to stay nonviolent and nonabusive.

- The structure of these groups promotes dialogue between all group members and group leaders. While the group is challenging, it is never shaming.

- Victim safety is central to this approach. Most programs using this model either have a victim advocate working with the victim or have a relationship with the shelter to ensure that victims understand the program, the resources available to them including legal remedies, have support from other women, and can discuss progress or the lack of progress that their partners are making, in a safe environment.

The Duluth Curriculum

The educational process in the Duluth curriculum is based on the work of the late Brazilian educator and author Paulo Freire. Freire formulated a theory for the education of illiterates based on the belief that every human being is capable of looking critically at his or her world despite the level of oppression he or she has experienced. Through dialogue and critical thinking, the student develops an awareness about the world, even if the world is his or her own neighborhood. The awareness leads the student to a personal transformation and then to the emergence of what Freire would call a critical consciousness. Students distinguish what is created by nature from what is created by the culture and they begin to understand the impact of socialization on the oppressed and the oppressor. They become more reflective about the world around them, raise questions about the inequities in their society, and ultimately struggle against oppression.

So why do we use this approach in our groups for men who batter? Initially, we used the Freire model in groups for victims of domestic violence because battered women can easily recognize themselves as living within an oppressive structure. The educational process was so powerful in women's groups that we started experimenting with adaptations of the techniques in our groups for men who batter. We thought that if we, as group leaders, could engage the men in our groups, we could provide an environment for dialogue and critical thinking about men's lives and their beliefs about women and marriage.

To effectively use the Duluth curriculum the group leader should:

- Have a fairly clear understanding and philosophical analysis about the history and nature of men's violence against women; otherwise the dialogue will simply turn into a discussion without any challenges to sexist thinking.

- Have a significant amount of training and have worked with a skilled and experienced colleague for some time.

- Feel comfortable entering into dialogue with group members and facilitating critical thinking. Dialogue requires the group leader to be genuinely curious about the group members' belief systems without colluding, and without having a predetermined ending point in the dialogue.

- Have the confidence and skill to pose questions and engage group members in understanding the moral and ethical contradictions of their use of violence and the oppressive structures they have usually constructed in their relationships with women.

- Help men who batter become more reflective about their life and challenge their world view about what it means to be male in our society, and what they want a woman in their life for.

Dialogue is not an easy process for most group leaders. As a former teacher, I can attest to the way I was taught to teach in college. Freire talks about traditional education as *banking education*, which essentially is a form of indoctrination. With the traditional educational model, the student simply repeats back what the teacher presents. Without an opportunity for dialogue and critical thinking the student will not analyze the material being presented. In groups for men who batter, a man may listen to a lecture, complete an assignment, and listen to a group leader's feedback. But the man will likely repeat back only what you hope he will say. It is questionable whether an altered consciousness will ever emerge through a traditional educational process, because the group member isn't being challenged to investigate and analyze the very belief system that guides his world.

There is always a fine line between dialogue and colluding. Dialogue would completely shut down if you confronted every sexist comment a man makes in the group. A skilled group leader will always find ways to reintroduce sexist comments made by group members, and put them into a context that is challenging for the whole group.

The Duluth curriculum is political in nature and therefore may be uncomfortable for practitioners schooled in family systems or other psychologically based methods. However, the nature of oppression in some families, especially those touched by domestic abuse, *is* political—it is very similar to structural forms of oppression based on race, religion, or class. Not all batterer intervention programs use this approach, and some practitioners who have the Duluth materials use only some components. Group leaders using the Duluth curriculum or other models owe it to the men in their groups and to the women these men have abused to immerse themselves in a deeper analysis of battering. Reading, dialogue, and training should be ongoing for all of us doing this work.

The Duluth curriculum is designed for thirty-three sessions and covers the following themes:

1. Respect

2. Trust and support

3. Honesty and accountability

4. Responsible parenting

5. Shared responsibility

6. Economic partnership

7. Negotiation and fairness

8. Non-threatening behavior

9. Sexual respect

10. Nonviolence

These areas constitute the foundation of an egalitarian relationship (see Equality Wheel, page 163).

In contrast, the following behaviors—what we call tactics to control—constitute the foundation of an authoritarian relationship (see Power and Control Wheel, page 89):

1. Intimidation

2. Emotional abuse

3. Isolation

4. Denying, minimizing, and blaming

5. Using children

6. Using male privilege

7. Economic abuse

8. Coercion and threats

9. Sexual violence

10. Physical violence

The goal of the curriculum is to convince the men in our groups to reject the authoritarian structure and replace it with the egalitarian structure. The groups usually spend three weeks on each theme. A series of video vignettes shows situations in which conflicts become abusive. Group members scrutinize the vignettes in Week One by observing and identifying different abusive and controlling behaviors in the scene and then discussing the intent of these behaviors. They calculate what beliefs the man in the vignette might have, and the group leaders then ask the group members if they share any of those beliefs. The questions posed by the group leaders provide the basis for dialogue, and as long as the process is effective the dialogue continues. Group members discuss what feelings might be driving the person in the vignette, the ways in which he minimizes or blames others, and the impact of the abusive behavior on the victim, children, and himself. Finally, the group sorts through alternatives to the abusive behavior.

In Week Two, group members analyze their own situations based on the theme for that week. This personal examination of an individual man's behavior affords a much greater opportunity for meaningful dialogue and critical thinking—the group is no longer analyzing a fictitious person, but their own lives and their own examples.

In Week Three, role plays and exercises on alternatives to abusive, violent, and controlling behavior are explored and practiced. At this point we also teach men self-care—how to take time for themselves and diffuse their anger and self-hate. I've come to the conclusion that most men who batter are unhappy and have negative self-images, in part because their abusive behavior has resulted in negative consequences and losses. They know their partners and often their children are dissatisfied with them. On some level, they know their partners would leave if they could, and will when they get the chance. While the focus of the group is on changing men's beliefs and behavior, helping men who are changing to become better and healthier individuals is also an important goal.

Note: For information on the Duluth curriculum *Power and Control: The Tactics of Men Who Batter,* or for training in this model, call the National Training Project in Duluth, Minnesota, at 218-722-2781.

How Well Does Counseling Work?

Our own research in Duluth has shown that physical violence usually diminishes while the offender is in a group, but other abusive behavior tends to escalate. This trend seems logical if we assume the intent of the offender is to maintain control in the relationship. As mentioned earlier, our studies indicate that over 50 percent of offenders will recidivate. The high rate of recidivism may seem discouraging, but it is no different from the outcomes of substance abuse and other treatment programs. We have to remember that 95 percent of the men are court-ordered into the groups—they wouldn't be there otherwise. We have long maintained that the most effective evaluation of domestic violence programs—with or without counseling—is how the victim perceives the various levels of intervention. In other words, how safe and autonomous does she now feel after calling the police, obtaining a protection order, using a shelter, getting support from an advocacy program, or having her partner ordered into a counseling program?

In Duluth, where there is a relatively tight coordinated community response to domestic assault cases, about 75 percent of women who access the justice system, utilize the shelter and legal advocacy, or have their partners ordered into counseling report that they feel safe five years after intervention. Because many abusive relationships end in separation, some battered women may be feeling safer because they no longer are subjected to violence and other abusive behavior. Conversely, many men who have battered will go on to batter a different woman and end up back in the system, which may explain the variance in offender recidivism and the ratio of victims who claim that intervention has made their lives safer.[26]

Outcome studies on counseling programs for men who batter vary. Some studies examine the recidivism rate based on whether the offender has been rearrested or had a protection order taken out against him. Other programs contact the partners of participants to evaluate changes in offender behavior; still others rely only on self-reporting of the participants. Some programs assess behavioral changes after a few weeks and others after several years. Some have little contact with victims. Assessing only the cessation of violence may give a skewed picture of success if the offender is still employing other abusive behaviors that may not be illegal, but result in the same end as violence.[27]

One program claimed an 80 percent success rate, but only examined the offender's conduct over the one-year period after counseling, when other factors—such as the novelty of counseling, and the deterrent of probation and court requirements—may be influencing behavior. More research needs to be conducted in this area and outcome studies must be examined within a broader context.

Similarly, the model and length of a domestic abuse program will remain controversial. A recent study of four different offender programs observed no significant differences in the outcomes of short-term programs of three to four months and longer programs of nine months.[28] Furthermore, if counseling is deemed too expensive for the number of men making changes, the community must decide what the appropriate sanctions for an offender should be. Community service and other alternatives may be more cost effective, but many men will lose an opportunity for rehabilitation. As stated earlier, if you knew which men were going to change at the outset, making these policy decisions would be a lot easier.

Part 2. The Fundamentals of Offender Programs

The Principles of an Offender Program — Intake, Orientation, and Screening — Partner Orientation and Safety Procedures — The Role of the Group Leader — Rules, Fees, and Program Policies — Related Groups and Programs — Standards and Monitoring

The Principles of an Offender Program

It is inadvisable to accept court-mandated offenders into your program without clear policies. These policies should address what the consequences might be if an offender does any of the following:

1. Uses violence or makes threats while he is in the program

2. Violates conditions of his probation or a civil protection order

3. Fails to attend group sessions

4. Is uncooperative and violates any program rules

Without mutually agreed-upon policies, the court may fail to pay attention to the offenders you refer back for violating program rules or for using violence. When the court fails to act, it gives the offender the message that the justice system doesn't take his assaultive behavior seriously, which may embolden him in the future. Furthermore, it gives other group members the idea that they don't need to attend the group or that they can use violence without repercussions.

Meet with administrators in the probation department and work out specific policies and a process for ongoing communication. Try to attend a judges' meeting or meet with the chief judge to explain the importance of your policies. Judges usually won't sign onto a policy, because they can't be perceived to be influenced by special interest groups regardless of how benevolent the cause, but most judges will understand and respect the policy objectives you have agreed to with the probation department, and most judges want their orders obeyed. Always stress that safety for victims is the bottom line.

If you are starting a program to work with offenders, it is important to carefully think through your objectives to ensure that you are taking the necessary steps to ensure that victim safety is central to your work. If you are currently working in a program, it is equally important to periodically evaluate your practices. Are you adhering to your original goals?

The following framework will help you assess your principles and guidelines for ensuring program accountability. It is by no means an exhaustive list—you may choose to add or refine.[29]

Schedule a daylong retreat to evaluate and talk through the vision of your program and how you might connect or reconnect with the principles that will maintain your accountability and effectiveness. If you use the following outline, put these ten principles on flip chart paper or make an overhead. Facilitate a discussion on each point. Allow sufficient time for dialogue. Are you meeting your expectations? What needs improvement? What obstacles are getting in the way? What steps might you take to overcome the obstacles?

1. Program Goals

- To work to end domestic violence by creating a culture of deterrence.

- To ensure the program is collaborating with the justice system, human service providers, and battered women's programs.

- To ensure safety for the partners of group participants in the program.

- To teach offenders alternatives to coercive, controlling, and violent behavior in intimate relationships.

2. Program Philosophy

- Violence is intentional.

- Battering is a system of abusive behaviors that are used to maintain control.

- Most cultures have supported male dominance in families.

- Individual men can change.

- Except in cases of self-defense, there are always alternatives to violence.

3. Program Content

- Participants need to take full responsibility for their behavior.
- Facilitators will respectfully challenge sexist beliefs and attitudes.
- Groups will support men to change controlling and violent behavior.
- Facilitators will confront minimization, denial, and blame.
- The group process should be compassionate but not colluding.
- Facilitators will teach men to develop relationships with women based on equality.

4. Involvement with Battered Women and Shelters

- Programs will not compete with shelter programs for funding.
- Advocates should be involved in the development of program policies related to partner safety.
- Communication procedures on partner safety will be in place with the shelter.
- Partners will be notified and offered detailed information about the offender program.
- Programs should not elicit information from partners of participants until they have had an opportunity to explore safety planning and contact with a shelter.

5. Contract with Offenders

- Participants must follow all conditions of probation and orders from the court.
- Acts of violence and violation of court orders will be reported to the court.
- Participants must sign release-of-information and program contract agreement.

- Participants will pay all required fees.

- Participants must attend all required sessions and be on time.

- Participants must take part in group discussions.

- Participants must complete all required assignments.

- Participants will come to group free of the influence of alcohol and drugs.

- Participants will not use racist or sexist language.

6. Consequences for Breach of Contract

- Noncompliance with terms of the contract will result in suspension, and the participant will be reported to the court.

- Volunteers will not be treated differently than court-mandated offenders.

- Program staff may testify at revocation or review hearings regarding violations of a contract.

- After a violation, an offender may only be readmitted if there is a legal or program consequence, i.e., jail time, additional groups, community service, or other sanctions.

7. Assessment of Lethality

- All past and present threats will be explored by program staff.

- Threats of homicide or suicide will be thoroughly examined.

- The victim/shelter will be warned if the participant has been obsessed with or has stalked his partner.

- The victim/shelter will be warned if the offender appears to be reacting to a protection order or divorce in a dangerous way.

- The victim/shelter/law enforcement will be informed if the offender makes threats regarding the children.

- Program staff will discuss red-flag cases with facilitators and advocates.

8. Requirements for Group Facilitators

- Must be violence free in their own lives.

- Should be thoroughly trained in an effective model, and work for a period of time with an experienced facilitator.

- When possible, groups should be cofacilitated with male and female staff.

- Should not communicate or act in ways that perpetuate sexism or victim-blaming.

- Should be open to self-examination and feedback from monitors or supervisors on facilitation skills, inadvertent collusion, sexism, and control issues.

9. Evaluation of Programs

- Battered women's programs should be involved in designing evaluation tools.

- Before asking a partner of a participant to assess progress, the program will be certain of her safety.

- Evaluation should focus on safety to battered women, accountability, and changes the offender is making.

- Evaluation should examine the elimination or lessening of all forms of abuse.

- All practices and polices should be periodically evaluated.

10. Accountability to the Community

- Programs should work in concert with battered women's programs to reform the practices of the justice system, law enforcement, and other interveners.

- Policies and procedures should be reviewed by communities of color, neighborhood organizations, gay and lesbian groups, and other stakeholders.

- Programs should speak out and work with organizations working to reduce violence, bias, and racism.

The basic elements and recommendations for an offender program that follow are based on my experiences at the Duluth Domestic Abuse Intervention Project (DAIP) and other programs. They are provided only as an overview.

Intake, Orientation, and Screening

Some programs have the financial resources to conduct individual intakes for court-mandated offenders. For mental health agencies utilizing third-party payments, individual assessments may be a necessity. However, in our program in Duluth, we made the decision to conduct group intakes and group orientations. Initially, the reason was economics, but we soon realized there were other benefits to a group process. Having the men together at this stage provided an early familiarization with the program. Some men felt less resistance when they were able to hear other men's stories from the outset.

At intake, the men fill out forms that provide personal information, police and court involvement, history of violence, history of substance abuse, level and severity of violence against a partner, and disciplining practices with their children. All participants must sign a Contract for Participation and a Release of Information that allows program staff to contact other treatment providers and, most important the offender's partner.

Following the intake, program staff conducts an orientation during which expectations of the program are discussed. A handout packet is provided that describes the purpose and content of the classes, group rules, legal explanations regarding future acts of violence, a review of the protection order and other requirements that might be ordered by a judge (exclusion from the house or victim's place of work, parenting classes, etc.), and an introduction to techniques that a participant can immediately begin practicing if he wants to stop his use of violence. Sometimes a former offender will cofacilitate the group and talk about his experiences and his change process. These group intake and orientation sessions take about three hours.

The DAIP in Duluth is unique in that the court sends all offenders to this program rather than to multiple agencies that provide counseling. The DAIP conducts the intake and orientation, and also screens for substance abuse and mental health problems. Four mental health agencies have agreed to work with the project and consequently get most of the referrals; the project provides classes for the rest. This arrangement is important because offenders are not able to shop around for the "easiest" program—the mental health agencies and the project all use the same curriculum and follow the same policies. If an offender fails to attend, the mental health agency notifies the DAIP, which then reports the offender back to the court and tracks the case until disposition. The courts prefer this process because they only deal with one entity.

The courts in Minnesota have been commendable about ordering chemical dependency evaluations for offenders with drug or alcohol histories. If out- or inpatient treatment is ordered, the domestic abuse groups do not start until the participant completes the substance abuse program. If an evaluation has not been ordered, but staff members at the DAIP suspect a problem, they can refer the offender back to the court to complete an evaluation.

If an offender has psychological problems, or it is deemed he would be disruptive to the group, staff will refer him to one of the mental health agencies for individual treatment, or back to the court for noncompliance. This doesn't happen frequently, but group leaders should not be subjected to an abusive participant or someone who is constantly trying to sabotage the process.

Partner Orientation and Safety Procedures

A battered women's advocate from the Domestic Abuse Intervention Project calls the partner of every offender ordered into the program and obtains a history of the violence. During the course of the program, if a victim informs the advocate that her partner is still being abusive, the advocate will help her develop a safety plan and discuss options. Confronting an offender with information from the partner in the group or in private is usually counterproductive and often dangerous. However, program staff must make it clear to the offender that he has limited confidentiality. At the orientation session it is explained that staff will investigate and inform the courts if an offender self-reports an incident or makes threatening comments in group.

All partners of offenders in the program are invited to an orientation session. The purpose of this session is to provide:

- A safe place where women can relate to other women in similar situations.

- Information about the dynamics of an abusive relationship and the effects of the violence on children.

- An opportunity for battered women to increase their awareness of the institutional and cultural support for violence against women in our society.

- Information about community resources including counseling, programs the shelter offers including neighborhood support groups, and how to obtain a protection order.

- Information about the content of the classes that their partners will attend and how and who to contact if their partner uses violence.

- A process to evaluate whether their partners are actually making changes.

- Ongoing advocacy and to help women develop safety plans.

An often overlooked component of an offender program is the safety of staff. Once, while observing an offender group in Los Angeles, I watched as a group member began cleaning his fingernails with a switchblade knife. The group leaders never said a word! Over the years, I have been threatened by program participants, and someone even fired a gun through my office window. Most men who batter would never consider assaulting a staff person, but some offenders are unpredictable. To ensure the safety of the victim—and staff as well—group leaders should read the police reports and review the histories of violence of program participants.

Some ideas for staff safety include:

- Developing an overall staff safety plan.

- Encouraging group leaders to have unlisted phone numbers.

- Requiring two facilitators for every group.

- Establishing a means to communicate with other staff members or the police if there is a problem.

- Terminating participants who are exhibiting bizarre behavior or who are threatening in any way.

- Designing an evening group safety plan.

Rules, Fees, and Program Policies

Most programs charge a fee for their classes or groups. A sliding fee ensures that all offenders can participate regardless of income. Some programs receive money from the city or county to cover indigent men, although every participant should pay something.

Group rules usually cover attendance, tardiness, homework requirements, and general expectations of minimum participation. The rules also prohibit participants from using sexist or racist language, or being under the influence of any substance, including alcohol. Sometimes flexibility on attendance is needed for those men who have shift work or must be out of town because of their employment. Sessions can always be made up, especially if the group is open-ended.

Offenders who use violence or make threats while in the program must be reported back to court. Starting the program over, partial jail time, or revocation of probation—executing the entire jail sentence—should be expected as a consequence. If the offender is a volunteer participant, some kind of alternative sanction must be put into place.

The Role of the Group Leader

The growth of offender groups has resulted in serious questioning of the qualifications of group leaders and counselors. Having a degree in counseling or social work doesn't necessarily qualify someone to run a group for men who batter. Many extremely competent professionals in the mental health field have limited experience of domestic assault cases and fail to understand the complex dynamics of battering, yet they are frequently running these groups.

An analogy might be a human resource director who has not had the opportunity to explore, internalize, and reflect on personal and institutional racism. Imagine this person confronted with racial tension in an organization. He or she would be unprepared to handle a difficult situation appropriately in the workplace, not because of lack of qualification, but because he or she would have only a superficial understanding of racial problems and the processes needed to work through them. Similarly, men and women who work with domestic abuse offenders are at a distinct disadvantage if they have not been immersed in a gender analysis of violence against women. Group leaders may have good group process and therapy skills, but may lack the knowledge, tools and confidence to address the underlying sexism.

If you are starting a program, try to recruit people who have been working on violence-against-women issues in your community. In Duluth, we recruited individuals from a range of disciplines to run our groups—teachers, ministers, and activists in addition to mental health practitioners. The political analysis *is* important. Before facilitating a group, a recruit should attend a comprehensive training program and if possible work with a skilled group leader for a period of time.

Tips for the Group Leader

Never stop learning

The issue of gender violence reaches the inner core of any man or woman doing this work. It is impossible to divorce your own feelings, beliefs, and experiences from your work with men who batter. We've all been socialized by the cultures in which we live, and we've all had conflicts in our relationships. When you are facilitating a group, avoid the *us-and-them* attitude—the men in your group will sense it, and will shut down. In dialogue with men in my groups, I will often talk about my own experiences and struggles with sexist beliefs and how I worked and continue to work on my issues.

Believe in the capacity of men to change

Try to be affirming in your group. Let men in the groups know when you think they're working hard on an issue, and acknowledge their successes. Don't give up on resistant men—some men who batter keep the rough facade to cover the pain and fear they often feel but will usually never articulate. I remember one man who rarely said anything in the group, and when he did, it was usually negative. I thought he was just putting in his time and doubted he would ever change. Sometime later, his partner called to report how much things had changed in their marriage and how they both attributed the altered behavior to the group.

Stay connected with battered women's programs

Practitioners are often isolated from battered women and their advocates. Sometimes I'm invited to sit in on a women's group or listen to a group of battered women tell their stories at a training, and I always take advantage of this opportunity. I do so in part because all you hear are men's stories when you facilitate offender groups. Talking to battered women is a reality check for me.

In one group I led, a man named Darrell told me how great things were going in his relationship, and how he was using the tools we were teaching to better communicate in a noncontrolling manner with his wife Carole. Later that week, I was sitting in on a woman's support group when a woman named Carole began telling a story very similar to what Darrell had told earlier in the week. The good communication Darrell was so proud of turned out to be some very serious threats to take the children and leave the state unless Carole gave up the idea of going back to school.

Ensure that victim safety is central

Be on the alert for threatening actions, comments, and behaviors in the groups you lead. If you have concerns, another staff person or a shelter advocate can check on a victim while the participant is in a meeting. Craft policies and procedures that always keep victim safety at the core of your work. Sometimes an innocuous or well-meaning idea can be counterproductive. For instance, I remember one handout we had for conflict resolution. The idea was for the couple to find a time and place where they could discuss a problem. The instructions stated that each person should have a period of time to give his or her side of the problem or issue. After one person finished, he or she then had to listen while the other gave his or her perspective, without interruption. On the surface this seemed like a good exercise. But as one woman stated in an earlier chapter, telling her husband how she felt or what she thought about a problem was essentially a recipe for getting beaten up.

Be compassionate without colluding

Part of your role is to facilitate an environment and group process in which men can think critically and reflect on who they are as men and how they got to the point that they started battering. In dialogue you can ask pointed questions, challenge ideas that are presented, and speak your own truth without being dogmatic or shaming. Dialogue is successful when you are genuinely curious about what a man thinks, despite your level of disapproval. Be careful not to validate sexist thinking during this process. You don't need to confront all the time, but make sure you are checking things out with the men and analyzing a compilation of comments before you adjourn the group.

Remember the group members are watching

Ideally, groups should be cofacilitated with a man and woman. Spend some time together prior to the group reviewing the material you will be presenting, and be clear about your respective roles. For instance, in our groups we try to alternate every other week who has the role of writing feedback and comments on the blackboard. The other group leader pays more attention to how the men are responding, asking questions of individual men and keeping the group process focused.

Be open to critical feedback from your cofacilitator or staff members monitoring the group. Male and female group leaders should model respectful interaction. I've observed some groups in which the male group leader has failed to confront and other groups in which the male group leader feels compelled to confront all the time. Similarly, in other groups I've seen female group leaders being overly angry at the men or put in the awkward position of always defending women. Balance and support are key ingredients to successful cofacilitation. When the group is completed, process together what worked and what didn't.

Keep the group focused

It is very easy to get sidetracked when you're facilitating a group. Often a group member will go off on a tangent in an attempt to defend his position, especially when it comes to rationalizing his behavior. When dialogue breaks down and the group gets diverted, bring it back into focus by punctuating that men who batter are making clear choices when they are violent and controlling. Emphasize that there are always alternatives. Challenge the group members to think more critically about their beliefs. If you have someone who is dominating the discussion, respectfully interrupt and bring others into the dialogue by asking another group member what he thinks about the issue being discussed.

Start your sessions effectively

Most groups have what is commonly called a check-in during which group members explain why they were ordered into the program. Some check-ins require the men to report what happened to them during the past week and to talk about issues affecting their lives. Some groups have the men talk about the violent incident that got them ordered into the program, or their most violent incident. We decided to abandon these check-ins because they were time consuming, group members were using the check-in to avoid the material to be covered, and some of our groups sounded like AA meetings. I observed one group in which the check-in took an hour and fifteen minutes; consequently, the group leaders had only a half-hour to cover the material. Three possible alternatives might be considered.

1. Eliminate the check-in altogether. Just begin the group with the material you are going to cover.

2. Observe a three- or four-minute time of silence or meditation before beginning. It is helpful to know the process of meditative breathing if you plan to use this approach. Some group leaders in Duluth have found that this time allows the men to relax, reduce their apprehension, and get rid of their negative self-talk. After the meditation, the group leaders immediately get into their material for the day.

3. Allow a brief report on Action Plans. In the Duluth curriculum, Action Plans are weekly life plans that individual men may be working on to ensure they are practicing ways of being nonviolent and noncontrolling. In lieu of the check-in, men can report on progress they are making on their commitment to change their behavior. This process is limited to fifteen minutes.

Related Groups and Programs

A support group can be an important component of your program. Men who are serious about making changes need a place where they can continue to talk about gender and violence issues and get support from other men. Unfortunately, offering a support group may be difficult due to limited resources, and few court-ordered offenders take advantage of this service when it exists.

In Duluth, parenting classes have been required by the court if there is evidence a man is inappropriately disciplining his children. In addition, the State of Minnesota funds a number of child safety centers. One of the goals of the Duluth child safety center—the Visitation Center—is to reduce the trauma to children when a judge has ordered an offender excluded from the household or has set a visitation schedule. The Visitation Center is a place where children can be safely picked up and dropped off without the couple having contact. It also provides a neutral location where supervised visitations can take place in a fun and safe environment for the children. The shelter in Duluth also provides groups for children who have been exposed to domestic violence.

Culturally Specific Groups

It is always a good idea to discuss implementation of an offender program with diverse groups in your community. For instance, the Native American community in Duluth is the largest minority group in the city. At the Domestic Abuse Intervention Program, we have made every effort to offer parallel programs for Native American and non-Native families. Court-mandated Native American men usually attend an Indian men's offender group. The Duluth curriculum was adapted for these groups to incorporate traditional Native American values about healing and living in balance. In other cities with large Latino, African American, and Asian populations culturally specific groups should be offered.

Gay Men's Groups

It is estimated that of the 9.5 million gay men in the United States, about 500,000 are victims of domestic assault. Services for gay offenders and victims exist predominantly in larger cities, but increased awareness of the extent of the problem has resulted in program development in the gay and lesbian communities around the country.[30] While most state statutes don't differentiate between same-sex violence and heterosexual domestic violence, mental health agencies have been slow to offer groups for gay perpetrators and victims. It is inadvisable to order a gay man into a traditional (straight) offender group in which he would in all probability have to be "closeted" due to the reaction of other men. Consult members of the gay community about how to start a group and how to get the word out to various interveners in the community.

Standards and Monitoring

How do we assess group leaders or counselors who are running offender groups? How do we pinpoint areas that can be improved so we reach our mutual goals? As more and more states develop standards for programs doing this work, the question of who should certify and monitor compliance has become an issue. Certifying organizations include the Department of Corrections, the Department of Probation and Parole, a coalition of domestic abuse programs and state coalitions, and state agencies. Some states have resisted standards because they professionalize the job description to the point where only group leaders with advanced degrees can do the work. Even some battered women's shelters require advanced degrees due to state laws and standards. This is unfortunate. The battered women's movement and many domestic abuse programs have grassroots origins. Some of the best advocates and men's group leaders that I have seen have not held advanced degrees, but have personal life experiences that make them uniquely effective.

Whether your state has standards or not, evaluating programs and the groups they offer is important. The Group Observation Guide (see page 256)—which I originally designed for the Department of Correction in Los Angeles County—is a tool to evaluate whether group leaders and the offender program are adhering to standards or principles to ensure accountability. It is designed to provide critical feedback for the group leader and also to assess overall program goals. Some programs will have a supervisor, veteran group leader, or victim advocate sit in on the group for several sessions. The Guide allows an assessor an objective means to evaluate several key areas. Evaluations can be very specific or general. Please feel free to use the Group Observation Guide in your program.

Another way to monitor groups is to periodically bring in an outside observer. In Duluth, we contracted with a person who had considerable experience running offender groups. This person observed on several occasions and provided feedback to the group leaders. A key to the observation was determining whether what was happening in the group was endangering women. The observation also assessed the group process and provided ideas for group leaders to better use the Duluth curriculum. Group leaders overwhelmingly appreciated the feedback.

The following is an example of how the Group Observation Guide can be used:

Group Observation Guide

Date: _____

Group Observed: _____

Observed by: _____

1. Group Leaders Presented a Clear Analysis of Battering

The group leader(s) exemplified a clear understanding of battering. They facilitated a challenging process that helped participants make the connection between sexist beliefs and their violent or controlling behavior.

Yes   **No**   Document examples and provide suggestions.
X

Interesting dialogue at various stages of the group on men's attitudes about marriage. Group leaders did a good job of asking questions about beliefs when the group was analyzing the video—good dialogue.

The group leaders could have challenged some statements participants made about women. The comment "Men historically have protected women" was made. Other participants agreed and gave examples, but these were not really challenged. For instance, a group leader could have asked, "Protected from whom?" A discussion could have emerged about men's physical and sexual violence as a basis for women needing protection.

2. Focused the Group on the Purpose of the Abusive Behavior

The group leader(s) were clear with group members that the uses of violence and other abusive behaviors are intentional acts designed to control their partners.

Yes   **No**   Document examples and provide suggestions.
X

Group leaders asked good questions about the intent of certain behaviors. They discussed and did a good job of asking for comparable examples from other men.

3. Stressed That There Are Always Alternatives to Violence

The group leader(s) consistently pointed out that, except for true cases of self-defense, there are always alternatives to using violence and other abusive behavior.

Yes   **No**   Document examples and provide suggestions.
      X

Group leaders failed to challenge group participants when they made the following comments: "She was blocking the door, so I didn't have a lot of options." "She was drunk, so I had to restrain her because she was going to take the car."

Group leaders could have asked other group participants if they thought the men who made these comments had any alternatives. Group leaders could have done an exercise on alternatives.

4. Confronted Minimizing and Denying Statements

The group leader(s) confronted minimizing and denying statements made by group participants at some time during the group.

Yes   **No**   Document examples and provide suggestions.
X

Group leaders challenged minimizing and denying statements like "I didn't really hurt her" and "I sort of grabbed her." They did this in a helpful way that didn't shut down the men making the comments.

5. Confronted Blaming Statements

The group leader(s) challenged blaming statements or rationalizations for the abusive behavior.

Yes   **No**   Document examples and provide suggestions.
X

Group leaders challenged the following blaming statement: "She kept pushing my buttons so I hit her." They brought others into the discussion and consequently the other participants did most of the challenging.

6. Confronted Sexist Comments and Language

The group leader(s) confronted sexist comments or inappropriate joking at some time during the group.

Yes   **No**   Document examples and provide suggestions.
X

Group leaders wrote the following comments made by several group members on the board and addressed them all together at an appropriate time: "Women just manipulate men for money." "It must have been that time of the month." "The wife knows how far to push me."

This was good, because the comments didn't get lost, but the process didn't stop.

7. Avoided Making Colluding Comments

The group leaders(s) avoided making colluding comments or statements that group members could interpret as supporting their use of violence or other abusive behavior.

<u>Yes</u>   **<u>No</u>**   Document examples and provide suggestions.
          X

One group leader said, "I can understand how that would set you off." "You shouldn't let her hook you into an argument."

These comments gave the impression that you believed his abusive behavior was in some way justified.

8. Encouraged Group Members to Participate

The group leader(s) used techniques and approaches that encouraged group members to participate.

<u>Yes</u>   **No**   Document examples and provide suggestions.
X

Group leaders got other participants involved by asking questions. "Bill, have you ever had a similar experience?" "We haven't heard from you tonight, Anthony."

Group leaders engaged the group by having each group member respond to questions in an exercise on trust.

9. Promoted Critical Thinking and Dialogue

The group leader(s) were able to facilitate dialogue.

<u>Yes</u>   **No**   Document examples and provide suggestions.
X

Good job here. The group leader posed questions that moved the dialogue into a deeper level. One example was when the group leader questioned in the following manner. "Dale said that boys are groomed to be leaders, so it's only natural that they should have more authority in the family. I know a lot of men believe this—I grew up with this notion, too. What do others think about this?"

10. Provided Ample Opportunity to Present Material

The group leaders used a lesson plan, were well organized, and had sufficient time to present the material.

<u>Yes</u>   **No**   Document examples and provide suggestions.
X

The "check-in" did not take the bulk of the group time. Group leaders had a lesson plan that allowed for optimum group participation—used the video in a constructive manner. Good job of moving the group forward when the dialogue got stuck.

11. The Safety of Victims Was Evident

The facility, policies, group rules, and process observed in the groups had victim safety as a priority.

   <u>Yes</u>   **<u>No</u>**   Document examples and provide suggestions.
   X

Was only able to observe that the group leader did not divulge information from a partner that would put her at risk when asked by a group member.

Group leaders indicated that they had read the police reports. This program did have a policy of making partner contacts and had good written policies on victim safety.

12. Adhered to Group Rules

The group rules were clearly understood by all group members and group leaders maintained order and a safe environment by having clear expectations.

   <u>Yes</u>   **No**   Document examples and provide suggestions.
   X

Group members were on time, the group started on time, and participation was good. Most group members had completed their assignments.

13. Modeled Positive Nonsexist Attitudes and Actions

The group leader(s) modeled an equal and respectful relationship in their group.

   <u>Yes</u>   **No**   Document examples and provide suggestions.
   X

The male and female group leaders worked together in a respectful manner. The responsibility for confronting sexist comments wasn't left solely to the female group leader.

The male group leader seemed a bit overprotective by making sure he challenged the sexism in the group. Might be something to discuss.

14. Facilitated a Respectful Group Process

The group leader(s) exhibited leadership that provided an open and respectful group process for all participants.

<u>Yes</u>   <u>No</u>   Document examples and provide suggestions.
X

The group leaders provided positive feedback, affirmed changes group partici-
pants had made, were aware of nonverbal cues, didn't let one group member
dominate, and were respectful of the diversity of the group.

15. Program Had Written Policies and Procedures

The program has a written policy on reporting acts of violence and
violations of court orders to the court. The program has a duty-to-
warn policy and procedures for ensuring that partners' safety is a part
of all administrative and group functions. The program complies with
all requirements set forth in the statutes.

<u>Yes</u>   <u>No</u>   Document examples and provide suggestions.
X

We reviewed polices and procedures and they are in compliance with the stan-
dards required by law.

Comments

Suggestions for Improvement

Other recommendations

Appendix B

Useful Handouts

The following text and forms may be useful as handouts for counselors and group leaders, and may be reproduced. The page numbers on which they appear in the book are in parentheses below.

Power and Control Wheel

Using Coercion and Threats
Making and/or carrying out threats to do something to hurt her • threatening to leave her, to commit suicide, to report her to welfare • making her drop charges • making her do illegal things

Using Intimidation
Making her afraid by using looks, actions, gestures • smashing things • destroying her property • abusing pets • displaying weapons

Using Emotional Abuse
Putting her down • making her feel bad about herself • calling her names • making her think she's crazy • playing mind games • humiliating her • making her feel guilty

Using Isolation
Controlling what she does, who she sees and talks to, what she reads, where she goes • limiting her outside involvement • using jealousy to justify actions

Denying, Minimizing, and Blaming
Making light of the abuse and not taking her concerns about it seriously • saying the abuse didn't happen • shifting responsibility for abusive behavior • saying she caused it

Using Children
Making her feel guilty about the children • using the children to relay messages • using visitation to harass her • threatening to take the children away

Using Male Privilege
Treating her like a servant • making all the big decisions • acting like the "master of the castle" • being the one to define men's and women's roles

Using Economic Abuse
Preventing her from getting or keeping a job • making her ask for money • giving her an allowance • taking her money • not letting her know about or have access to family income

Equality Wheel

Negotiation and Fairness
Seeking mutually satisfying resolutions to conflict • accepting change • being willing to compromise

Nonthreatening Behavior
Talking and acting so that she feels safe and comfortable expressing herself and doing things

Respect
Listening to her nonjudgmentally • being emotionally affirming and understanding • valuing opinions

Trust and Support
Supporting her goals in life • respecting her right to her own feelings, friends, activities, and opinions

Honesty and Accountability
Accepting responsibility for self • acknowledging past use of violence • admitting being wrong • communicating openly and truthfully

Responsible Parenting
Sharing parental responsibilities • being a positive nonviolent role model for the children

Shared Responsibilities
Mutually agreeing on a fair distribution of work • making family decisions together

Economic Partnership
Making money decisions together • making sure both partners benefit from financial arrangements

Guidelines for Remaining Nonviolent

I, _____ , accept and commit to the following
principles:

1. Violence is not okay unless I am truly in fear of being hurt,
   and then I should only use as much force as I need to defend
   myself.

2. In the future, I will be aware of flash points—issues or situations where I become agitated or very angry—that in the past
   have prompted violence by me or my partner.

3. I will leave situations—take a time-out—rather than use violence.

4. I will accept the fact that my use of violence is based on my
   desire to control a situation. I do not always need to be in control, to be proven right, or to win.

5. I will strive toward respectful resolutions of conflicts without
   being abusive.

_____   _____
(Name)   (Counselor)

Time-out Rules

1. Take a time-out when you recognize your cues and before your anger level escalates.

2. Take a time-out when you feel like you want to become abusive; do not take a time-out to avoid conflict.

3. Tell your partner you are taking a time-out.

4. Tell your partner how long you'll be gone.

5. Do not drink, use drugs, or drive.

6. Call a friend or group member for support.

7. Do calming exercises like walking, shooting free throws at a basketball court, or meditating.

8. Think positive thoughts. Do not dwell on the problem that caused you to become angry.

9. If you are still agitated and need more time than you agreed to, call your partner and let her know.

10. Your partner is not obliged to take a time-out; you take a time-out for *yourself*.

11. If your partner indicates that she is afraid of you, stay away. Find an alternative place to stay until things have calmed down.

12. When you return, do not insist that you and your partner should solve or resolve the conflict you were having.

13. If you notice your cues again, take another time-out.

14. Whenever you follow the time-out rules, make a note of the positive way you handled the situation and its results.

An important note

You may want to practice a time-out when you are not angry so that you and your partner understand the process and each other's expectations. Your partner needs to know the rules of the time-out so she knows what to expect.

Negotiation Guide

1. Regardless of how angry or hurt I feel I will remain non-violent.

2. If I disagree with my partner's position I will still be respectful toward her.

3. I will remain seated during the discussion.

4. I will not yell, scream, or use my voice in an intimidating manner.

5. I will not threaten my partner in any way.

6. I will not use put-downs, call my partner names, or be sarcastic or belittling.

7. I will not bring up past incidents to prove a point.

8. I will avoid blaming or shaming statements.

9. I will strive not to get defensive.

10. I will listen to my partner's position and refrain from interrupting.

11. I will commit to work toward a compromise.

12. I will be willing to explore my own issues and take responsibility for mistakes I have made.

13. I will respect my partner's wishes to end the discussion.

14. I will be honest.

15. I will talk about my feelings but will not use them as a way to manipulate my partner.

Fair Discussion Guide

1. A good discussion needs two people ready to talk. Don't force a discussion.

2. You know each other's weak spots. Don't use them to hurt your partner.

3. Before you begin the process of negotiation, you must first be committed to a fair process. You must be ready to:

- Listen—try to understand what the other person is saying.

- Work toward a mutually satisfying solution.

- Hear things you disagree with or find painful without reacting abusively.

- Accept that some things may need to change.

- Find a neutral person you both trust to help with the discussion.

4. Review these rules together and add any that you both decide are important:

- Talk quietly and calmly.

- Keep the discussion free of manipulation or mind games.

- Stick to the issues at hand.

- Set time limits for discussion.

5. Define the problem—it may be different for each person. What is negotiable? How does each person perceive and define the problem? Who else will be affected and how?

6. Identify goals, both short-term and long-term. What needs to be part of an immediate and then a final solution? If a compromise is needed, list several long-term solutions you both think are fair.

Notes

1. Melanie Shepard, "Predicting Batterer Recidivism Five Years After Intervention," *Journal of Family Violence* (1992).

2. Rebecca Emerson Dobash and Russell P. Dobash, *Violence Against Wives* (New York: The Free Press, 1983).

3. U.S. Department of Justice, Uniform Crime Reports, 1989; *Crime in the United States* (Washington, DC).

4. Paulo Freire, *Pedagogy of the Oppressed* (New York: Continuum, 1992).

5. bell hooks, *Ain't I A Woman* (Boston: South End Press, 1981).

6. Marie M. Fortune, *Keeping The Faith* (San Francisco: HarperCollins, 1987).

7. Dobash and Dobash, *Violence Against Wives.*

8. A. Rosenblum and K. O. O'Leary, "Children: The Unintended Victims of Marital Violence," *The American Journal of Orthopsychiatry,* vol. 51 (1981).

9. Anne Ganley, *Treating Men Who Batter: Theory, Practice, and Programs,* ed. P. Lynn Caesar and L. Kevin Hamberger (New York: Springer Publishing Company, 1989).

10. Barbara Hart, *Safety for Women: Monitoring Batterers' Programs* (Harrisburg, PA: Pennsylvania Coalition Against Domestic Violence, 1988).

11. Joe Morse, "How We Learn About Violence Exercise" (Boston: EMERGE).

12. Michael Paymar and Ellen Pence, *Power and Control: The Tactics of Men Who Batter* (Minnesota Program Development, Inc. 1985).

13. Iris Chang, *The Rape of Nanking* (New York: Penguin Books, 1997).

14. James Gilligan, *Violence: Our Deadly Epidemic and Its Causes* (New York: Grosset/Putnam, 1996).

15. Stephen Sparccarelli, J. Douglas Coatsworth, and Blake Sperry Bowden, "Exposure to Serious Family Violence Among Incarcerated Boys: Its Association With Violent Offending and Potentially Mediating Variables," *Violence and Victims,* vol. 10, no. 3 (New York: Springer Publishing Co., 1995).

16. Peter G. Jaffe and David A. Wolfe, *Children of Battered Women,* ed. Susan K. Wilson (Newbury Park, CA: Sage Publications, 1990).

17. Freire, *Pedagogy of the Oppressed.*

18. Jennifer Katz, Ileana Arias, Seven R.H. Beach, Gene Brody, and Paul Roman, "Excuses, Excuses: Accounting for the Effects of Partner Violence on Marital Satisfaction and Stability," *Violence and Victims* (New York: Springer Publishing Co., 1995).

19. M'Liss Switzer and Katherine Hale, *Called to Account* (Seattle: Seal Publishing, 1984).

20. Dave Grossman, *On Killing: The Psychological Cost of Learning to Kill in War and Society* (Boston: Little, Brown and Co., 1995).

21. James Garbarino, *Lost Boys: Why Our Sons Turn Violent and How We Can Save Them* (New York: The Free Press, 1999).

22. Marlin Mousseau, "Project Medicine Wheel" (Pine Ridge Indian Reservation).

23. Angela Browne, *When Battered Women Kill* (New York: The Free Press, 1984).

24. Lenore Walker, *The Battered Woman* (New York: The Free Press, 1984).

25. Michael Paymar and Ellen Pence, *Education Groups for Men Who Batter: The Duluth Model* (New York: Springer Publishing Co., 1993).

26. Shepard, "Batterer Recidivism."

27. Jeffery L. Edleson and Richard M. Tolman, *Intervention for Men Who Batter* (Newbury Park, CA: Sage Publications, 1992).

28. Edward W. Gondolf, *Do Batterer Programs Work?: A 15-Month Follow-up of Multi-Site Evaluation,* (Kingston, NJ Domestic Violence Report, 1998).

29. Barbara Hart, with adaptations from the author. *Principles for Offender Programs.*

30. David Island and Patrick Letellier, *Men Who Beat the Men Who Love Them* (Binghamton, NY: Harrington Park Press, 1991).

Resources

The following resources may be useful for men, women, and practitioners reading this book. Most states in the U.S. and many provinces in Canada have organizations that provide referral information for victims of domestic violence. The state coalitions and other organizations listed below should also have information about counseling programs for men who batter. Included in this list are national organizations that provide training, technical assistance, and resources in specific areas of domestic abuse prevention and intervention.

State Coalitions on Domestic Violence

Alabama Coalition against Domestic Violence
P.O. Box 4762
Montgomery AL 36103-4762   (334) 832-4842

Alaska Network on Domestic Violence and Sexual Assault
130 Seward St., Room 501
Juneau AK 99801   (907) 586-3650

Arizona Coalition against Domestic Violence
100 W. Camelback St., Suite 109
Phoenix AZ 85013   (602) 279-2900

Arkansas Coalition against Domestic Violence
#1 Sheriff Lane, Suite C
Little Rock AR 72114   (501) 812-0571

California Alliance against Domestic Violence
619 Thirteenth St., Suite 1
Modesto CA 95354   (209) 524-1888

Colorado Domestic Violence Coalition
P.O. Box 18902
Denver CO 80218   (303) 831-9632

Connecticut Coalition against Domestic Violence
135 Broad St.
Hartford CT 06105   (860) 524-5890

D.C. Coalition against Domestic Violence
P.O. Box 76069
Washington DC 20013   (202) 783-5332

Delaware Coalition against Domestic Violence
P.O. Box 847
Wilmington DE 19899 (302) 658-2958

Florida Coalition against Domestic Violence
308 E. Park Ave. (800) 500-1119
Tallahassee FL 32301 (850) 425-2749

Georgia Advocates for Battered Women and Children
250 Georgia Ave. SE, Suite 308 (800) 643-1212
Atlanta GA 30312 (404) 524-3847

Hawaii State Coalition against Domestic Violence
98-939 Moanalua Rd.
Aiea HI 96701-5012 (808) 486-5072

Iowa Coalition against Domestic Violence
1540 High St., Suite 100 (800) 942-0333
Des Moines IA 50309-3123 (515) 244-8028

Idaho Coalition against Sexual and Domestic Violence
200 N. Fourth St., Suite 10-K
Boise ID 83702 (208) 384-0419

Illinois Coalition against Domestic Violence
730 E. Vine St., Suite 109
Springfield IL 62703 (217) 789-2830

Indiana Coalition against Domestic Violence
2511 E. 46th St., Suite N-3 (800) 332-7385
Indianapolis IN 46205 (317) 543-3908

Kansas Coalition against Sexual and Domestic Violence
820 S.E. Quincy, Suite 600
Topeka KS 66612 (785) 232-9784

Kentucky Domestic Violence Association
P.O. Box 356
Frankfort KY 40602 (502) 875-4132

Louisiana Coalition against Domestic Violence
P.O. Box 3053
Hammond LA 70404-3053 (504) 542-4446

Maine Coalition for Family Crisis Services
128 Main St.
Bangor ME 04401 (207) 941-1194

Maryland Network against Domestic Violence
11501 Georgia Ave., Suite 403 (800) MD-HELPS
Silver Springs MD 20902-1955 (301) 942-0900

Massachusetts Coalition of Battered Women's Services
14 Beacon St., Suite 507
Boston MA 02108 (617) 248-0922

Michigan Coalition against Domestic Violence
P.O. Box 16009
Lansing MI 48901 (517) 484-2924

Minnesota Coalition for Battered Women
450 Syndicate St., Suite 122 (800) 646-0994 (in metro area)
St. Paul MN 55104 (573) 646-6177

Missouri Coalition against Domestic Violence
331 Madison St.
Jefferson City MO 65101 (314) 634-4161

Mississippi State Coalition against Domestic Violence
P.O. Box 4703 (800) 898-3234
Jackson MS 39296-4703 (601) 981-9196

Montana Coalition against Domestic Violence
P.O. Box 633
Helena MT 59624 (406) 443-7794

Nebraska Domestic Violence and Sexual Assault Coalition
315 South Ninth #18 (800) 876-6238
Lincoln NE 68508-2253 (402) 476-6256

Nevada Network against Domestic Violence
2100 Capurro Way, Suite E (800) 500-1556
Sparks NV 89431 (702) 358-1171

New Hampshire Coalition against Domestic and Sexual Violence
P.O. Box 353 (800) 852-3388
Concord NH 03302-0353 (603) 224-8893

New Jersey Coalition for Battered Women
2620 Whitehorse/Hamilton Square Road (609) 584-8107
Trenton NJ 08690 (800) 224-0211 (for battered lesbians in NJ only)

New Mexico State Coalition against Domestic Violence
P.O. Box 25363 (800) 773-3645 (in NM only)
Albuquerque NM 87125 (505) 246-9240

New York State Coalition against Domestic Violence
79 Central Ave. (800) 942-6906
Albany NY 12206 (518) 432-4864

North Carolina Coalition against Domestic Violence
P.O. Box 51875
Durham NC 27717 (919) 956-9124

North Dakota Council on Abused Women's Services
State Networking Office
418 E. Rosser Ave., Suite 320   (800) 472-2911 (in ND only)
Bismark ND 58501   (701) 255-6240

Ohio Domestic Violence Network
4041 N. High St., Suite 101   (800) 934-9840
Columbus OH 43214   (614) 784-0023

Oklahoma Coalition against Domestic Violence and Sexual Assault
2200 N. Classen Blvd., Suite 610   (800) 522-9054
Oklahoma City OK 73801   (405) 557-1210

Oregon Coalition against Domestic and Sexual Violence
520 Northwest Davis St., Suite 310
Portland OR 97204   (503) 223-7411

Pennsylvania Coalition against Domestic Violence
6440 Flank Dr., Suite 1300   (800) 932-4632
Harrisburg PA 17112-2778   (717) 545-6400

Rhode Island Coalition against Domestic Violence
422 Post Road, Suite 104   (800) 494-8100
Warwick RI 02888   (401) 467-9940

**South Carolina Coalition against Domestic Violence
and Sexual Assault**
P.O. Box 7776   (800) 260-9293
Columbia SC 29202-7776   (803) 750-1222

**South Dakota Coalition against Domestic Violence
and Sexual Assault**
P.O. Box 141   (800) 572-9196
Pierre SD 57401   (605) 945-0869

Tennessee Task Force against Domestic Violence
P.O. Box 120972   (800) 356-6767
Nashville TN 37212   (615) 386-9406

Texas Council on Family Violence
8701 N. Mopac Expressway, Suite 450
Austin TX 78759   (512) 794-1133

Utah Domestic Violence Advisory Council
120 N. 200 W.   (800) 897-LINK
Salt Lake City UT 84145   (801) 538-4100

**Vermont Network against Domestic Violence
and Sexual Assault**
P.O. Box 405
Montpelier VT 05601   (802) 223-1302

Virginians against Domestic Violence
2850 Sandy Bay Road, Suite 101 (800) 838-VADA
Williamsburg VA 23185 (804) 221-0990

Washington State Coalition against Domestic Violence
2101 Fourth Ave. E., Suite 103 (800) 562-6025
Olympia WA 98506 (360) 352-4029

West Virginia Coalition against Domestic Violence
4710 Chimney Drive, Suite A
Charleston WV 25302 (304) 965-3552

Wisconsin Coalition against Domestic Violence
1400 E. Washington Ave., Suite 232
Madison WI 53703 (608) 255-0539

**Wyoming Coalition against Domestic Violence
and Sexual Assault**
341 East E. St., Suite 135A (800) 990-3877
Pinedale WY 82601 (307) 367-4296

Child Abuse Resources

Military Family Resource Center (800) 336-4592
(703) 696-5806

Publishes the *Military Family* newspaper and operates the Military Family Clearinghouse, which provides information and services to military families.

National Child Abuse Hotline (800) 422-4453

Parents Anonymous (800) 421-0353

National and Local Organizations

Battered Women's Justice Project
4032 Chicago Ave.
Minneapolis MN (800) 903-0111

Provides training, technical assistance and resources. This project will connect you to various organizations nationally for up-to-date research and assistance on domestic abuse issues. After dialing the central 800 number, you may choose from three extensions:

Extension #1 — Duluth Domestic Abuse Intervention Project (National Training Project). This project addresses the criminal justice system's response to domestic violence, including the development of batterer programs and law enforcement training.

Extension #2 — Pennsylvania Coalition against Domestic Violence. The project addresses civil court access and legal representation for battered women.

Extension #3 — National Clearinghouse for the Defense of Battered Women. This project addresses battered women's self-defense issues.

Center for the Prevention of Sexual and Domestic Violence
936 N 34th St., Suite 200
Seattle WA 98103 (206) 634-1903
Provides training and materials on domestic violence to the religious community.

Department of Justice Response Center (800) 421-6770
Provides a manual (free of charge) on various batterer intervention models and criminal justice strategies.

The Family Violence Project
Hall of Justice
850 Bryant St. (415) 553-9044
San Francisco CA 94103 Crisis Line (415) 552-7550
Provides extensive legal and court advocacy to victims of felony domestic assault, including crisis intervention, case assessment, monitoring cases, and preparing court orders.

Health Resource Center on Domestic Violence
Family Violence Prevention Fund
383 Rhode Island St., Suite 304
San Francisco CA 94103-5133 (888) 792-2873
Provides information and technical assistance on health care issues related to domestic violence.

National Clearinghouse for the Defense of Battered Women
125 South 9th St., Suite 302
Philadelphia PA 19107 (215) 351-0010
Provides information on battered women's self-defense issues.

National Clearinghouse on Marital and Date Rape
2325 Oak St.
Berkeley CA 94708 (510) 524-1582

National Coalition against Domestic Violence
P.O. Box 18749
Denver CO 80218-074 (303) 839-1852
Provides information to battered women on programs and services throughout the country on domestic violence issues.

National Gay and Lesbian Task Force
1734 14th St. NW   (202) 332-6483
Washington DC 20009-4309   (202) 332-0207
                                        24-hour hotline: (415) 333-HELP

National Network to End Domestic Violence
666 Pennsylvania Ave. SE, Suite 310
Washington DC 2003   (202) 543-5666
Produces NEXUS, a publication for battered women's advocates and related
materials. Provides direct support to local programs and state coalitions.

National Organization for Changing Men/BrotherPeace
P.O. Box 451
Watseka IL 60970
Promotes social change activities for men working to end violence against
women.

National Organization for Men against Sexism (NOMAS)
PO Box 509   (607) 697-6179
Owego NY 13827   www.nomas.org
Organizes the National Men and Masculinity Conference and coordinates the
Ending Men's Violence Network, linking programs nationally that work with
men against domestic violence, rape, sexual harassment, and related issues of
male violence.

N.Y. City Gay and Lesbian Anti-Violence Project
1208 West 13th Street
New York NY 10011   24-hour hotline: (212) 807-0197

The Oakland Men's Project/TODOS
1203 Preservation Park Way, Suite 200
Oakland CA 94612   (510) 444-6448
Conducts educational workshops and community organizing and training
activities to empower adults and young people to stop violence.

Pennsylvania Coalition against Domestic Violence
524 McKight Street
Reading PA 19601   (717) 671-4767
Provides legal and policy assistance on issues related to domestic violence.

Seattle Counseling Service for Sexual Minorities
1820 East Pine St.
Seattle WA 98122   (206) 323-1768

Training and Technical Assistance

Cangleska, Inc.
Sacred Circle   (877) 733-7623 (toll free)
Offers technical assistance, information packets, and model tribal codes, and
will identify model training in Indian country.

Common Purpose Inc.
P.O. Box 88
Jamaica Plain MA 02174
Provides training for practitioners working with men who batter, in English
and Spanish.

EMERGE
2380 Massachusetts Ave., Suite 101
Cambridge MA 02140   (617) 547-9879
Provides training for practitioners working with men who batter, some in
Spanish.

Mending the Sacred Hoop (Technical Assistance Project)
202 East Superior Street
Duluth MN 55802   (218) 722-2781
Provides on-site training and technical assistance to Native American tribal
programs and governments.

National Training Institute
Batterers Intervention Project
South Main St.
New City NY 19506   (914) 634-5729
Provides training for practitioners working with men who batter.

National Training Project
202 East Superior Street   (218) 722-2781
Duluth MN 55802   www.duluth-model.org
Provides on-site training and technical assistance for the criminal justice system, law enforcement, and advocates. Provides trainings in Duluth and
regionally on the Duluth curriculum for working with men who batter.

VCS Community Change Project
77 S. St.
New York NY 10956   (914) 634-5729
Provides trainings on domestic abuse offender programs in New York and
nationally.

Recommended Books, Manuals, & Films

Books

Ain't I A Woman: Black Women and Feminism by bell hooks (Boston: South End Press, 1981).

Assessing Dangerousness: Violence by Sexual Offenders, Batterers, and Child Abusers, ed. Jacquelyn C. Campbell (Thousand Oaks, CA: Sage Publications, 1995).

Backlash: The Undeclared War Against American Women by Susan Faludi (New York: Crown Publishers, 1991).

Battered Wives by Del Martin, revised edition (Volcano, CA: Volcano Press, 1981).

Coordinated Community Response to Domestic Violence: Lessons From Duluth and Beyond by Ellen Pence and Melanie Shepard (Newbury Park, CA: Sage Publications, 1999).

Education Groups For Men Who Batter: The Duluth Model by Michael Paymar and Ellen Pence (New York: Springer Publishing Company, 1993). Order from: (218) 722-2781.

Free Yourself from an Abusive Relationship: Seven Steps to Taking Back Your Life by Andrea Lissette and Richard Kraus (Alameda, CA: Hunter House, 2000).

Intervention for Men Who Batter by Jeffery L. Edleson and Richard M. Tolman (Newbury Park, CA: Sage Publications 1992).

Living With the Enemy by Donna Ferrato (New York: Aperture Books, 1991).

Lost Boys: Why Our Sons Turn Violent and How We Can Save Them by James Garbarino (New York: The Free Press, 1999).

Men's Work: How to Stop the Violence That Tears Our Lives Apart by Paul Kivel (New York: Hazelden/Ballantine, 1992).

Men Who Batter: An Integrated Approach for Stopping Wife Abuse by Edward Gondolf (Holmes Beach, FL: Learning Publications, 1985).

Pedagogy of the Oppressed by Paulo Freire (New York: Continuum, 1992).

Safety Planning With Battered Women: Complex Lives/Difficult Choices by Jill Davies (Thousand Oaks, CA: Sage Publications, 1997).

Violence Against Wives by R. Emerson Dobash and Russell P. Dobash (New York: The Free Press, 1983). An historical analysis of wife assault.

Violence: Our Deadly Epidemic and Its Causes by James Gilligan (New York: Grosset/Putnam, 1996).

When Battered Women Kill by Angela Browne (New York: The Free Press, 1984).

When Love Goes Wrong: What to Do When You Can't Do Anything Right—Strategies for Women with Controlling Partners by Susan Schechter and Ann Jones (New York: HarperCollins, 1992). Order from: (800) 331-3761. An important book for battered women.

When Violence Begins at Home: A Comprehensive Guide to Understanding and Ending Domestic Abuse by K.J. Wilson (Alameda, CA: Hunter House, 1997).

Women and Male Violence: The Visions and Struggles of the Battered Women's Movement by Susan Schechter (Boston: South End Press, 1982).

Manuals and Curriculums

Accountability: Program Standards for Batterer Intervention Services by Barbara Hart (Reading, PA: Pennsylvania Coalition Against Domestic Violence, 1992).

Batterer Intervention: Program Approaches and Criminal Justice Strategies by Kerry Healey and Christine Smith (National Institute of Justice).

Coordinated Community Response to Domestic Assault Cases: A Guide for Policy Development by Ellen Pence (Duluth: Minnesota Program Development Inc., 1985, updated 1996).

Days of Respect: Organizing a School-Wide Violence Prevention Program by Ralph Cantor with Paul Kivel, Allan Creighton, and the Oakland Men's Project (Alameda, CA: Hunter House, 1997).

The Duluth Safety and Accountability Audit: A Guide to Assessing Institutional Responses to Domestic Violence by Ellen Pence and Kristine Lizdas (Duluth: Minnesota Program Development Inc., 1998).

Helping Teens Stop Violence by Allan Creighton and Paul Kivel (Alameda, CA: Hunter House, 1990).

The Justice System Response to Domestic Assault Cases: A Guide for Policy Development by Ellen Pence with Michael Paymar, Coral McDonnell, and Madeline Duprey. Order from: National Training Project, 206 West Fourth St., Duluth MN 55806; (218) 722-2781.

Learning To Live Without Violence: A Handbook for Men by Daniel J. Sonkin and Michael Durphy, updated edition (Volcano, CA: Volcano Press, 1989). Order from: (209) 296-3445.

Living With My Family: A Child's Workbook About Violence in the Home by Wendy Deaton and Kendall Johnson (Alameda, CA: Hunter House, 1991).

Making the Peace: A 15-Session Violence Prevention Curriculum for Young People by Paul Kivel, Allan Creighton, and the Oakland Men's Project (Alameda, CA: Hunter House, 1997).

No More Hurt: A Child's Workbook About Recovering from Abuse by Wendy Deaton and Kendall Johnson (Alameda, CA: Hunter House, 1991).

Learning To Live Without Violence: A Worktape for Men by Daniel J. Sonkin and Michael Durphy (Volcano, CA: Volcano Press, 1989). An audio cassette adaptation, 115 minutes. Order from: (209) 296-3445.

Power and Control: The Tactics of Men Who Batter by Michael Paymar and Ellen Pence. Order from: National Training Project, 206 West Fourth St., Duluth MN 55806; (218) 722-2781.

Safety for Women: Monitoring Batterers' Programs by Barbara Hart. Order from: Pennsylvania Coalition Against Domestic Violence, 6400 Flank Dr., Gateway Corporate Center, Suite 1300, Harrisburg PA; (800) 537-2238.

Understanding Domestic Violence: Improving the Health Care Response to Domestic Violence: A Resource Manual for Health Care Providers by Anne Ganley (Harrisburg, PA: Family Violence Prevention Fund).

Wife Abuse in the Armed Forces by Lois West, W. Turner, and Ellen Dunwoody. Order from: Center for Women's Studies, 2000 P St. NW, Suite 508, Washington DC 20036.

Wife Assault: A Training Manual for Counselors and Advocates by Debra Sinclair (Toronto: Ontario Publications, 1985). Order from: (800) 268-7540.

Films

Battered, directed by Lee Grant. Order from: Joseph Feury Productions, Inc., 120 Riverside Dr., New York NY 10024. A dramatic look at the experiences and feelings of women who have been battered.

Men's Lives. Order from: New Day Films, P.O. Box 315, Franklin Lakes NJ 07417. Examines male socialization.

Profile of an Assailant. Order from: National Training Project, 206 West 4th St., Duluth MN 55806; (218) 722-2781. A candid discussion with a man who battered and the experiences of battered women are highlighted in this film. This film is useful for training and programs for men who batter.

Time Out Series: Deck The Halls, Up The Creek, Shifting Gears. Order from: ODN Productions, 74 Varick St., New York NY 10013. Short films designed for programs for men who batter.

To Have and To Hold. Order from: New Day Films, P.O. Box 315, Franklin Lake NJ 07417. Useful for support groups for battered women and programs for men who batter.

Index

WHEN VIOLENCE BEGINS AT HOME:
A Comprehensive Guide to Understanding and Ending Domestic Abuse by K.J. Wilson, Ed.D.

This definitive guide addresses the needs of multiple audiences, including battered women from various backgrounds, teenaged victims of dating violence, educators, community leaders, and even batterers themselves. Special chapters clarify the responsibilities—and limitations—of friends and family, shelter employees, health care providers, law enforcement officers, employers, and clergy. A comprehensive listing of local and national resources directs anyone interested in this issue to information and a network of people who can help.

416 pages ... Paperback $19.95 ... Hard cover $29.95

FREE YOURSELF FROM AN ABUSIVE RELATIONSHIP:
Seven Steps to Taking Back Your Life by Andrea Lissette, M.A., CDVC, and Richard Kraus, Ph.D.

This is a lifesaving guide for women who are victims of violence and abuse. *Step One* describes different kinds of abuse: emotional, physical, sexual, financial, social, and spiritual. *Step Two* is about abusers and who they abuse, with sections on children and senior citizens. *Step Three* deals with violent crises and stalking, rape, and assault. It includes an in-depth look at legal help and court proceedings. *Step Four* shows women how to live as survivors, with practical advice on money matters and work issues. *Step Five* discusses the decision to stay or leave, and the last two steps move from healing and rebuilding to *Becoming and Remaining Abuse Free.*

304 pages ... Paperback $16.95 ... Hardcover $25.95

CAPTIVE HEARTS, CAPTIVE MINDS: Freedom and Recovery from Cults and Abusive Relationships
by Madeleine Tobias and Janja Lalich

More than 15 million people around the world are involved with cults or in abusive relationships. Whether the focus is religion, politics, therapy, or self-improvement, cults exact an inestimable cost. Survivors typically suffer from emotional problems such as fear, depression, low self-esteem, and post-traumatic stress. This book helps them understand their experience, heal psychological scars, and re-establish healthy lives. Written by former cult members, this book offers renewed hope for a better life.

320 pages ... Paperback $14.95 ... Hard cover $24.95

To order books see last page or call (800) 266-5592

MAKING THE PEACE: A 15-Session Violence Prevention Curriculum for Young People by Paul Kivel and Allan Creighton, with the Oakland Men's Project

This is a highly respected violence prevention curriculum for youth group leaders and educators. The ready-to-use exercises, roleplays, and discussion guidelines show students how to explore the roots of violence in the community and their lives; deal with dating violence, fights, suicide, guns, and sexual harassment; and develop practical techniques for stopping violence. The Oakland Men's Project is a multicultural non-profit organization dedicated to violence prevention and to building alliances across lines of gender, race, sexual orientation, and age.

192 pages ... 35 reproducible handouts ... Paperback ... $24.95

DAYS OF RESPECT: Organizing a School-Wide Violence Prevention Program by Ralph Cantor, with Paul Kivel, Allan Creighton, and the Oakland Men's Project

A unique, collaborative program that empowers students to create a climate of respect and tolerance in their school. The Days of Respect program, developed by an experienced teacher and the Oakland Men's project, speaks directly to young people's immediate need for participation and respect. It brings students, teachers, administrators, parents, and members of the community together to create a school-wide event on the theme of violence prevention.

64 pages ... 21 reproducible handouts ... Paperback ... $14.95

HELPING TEENS STOP VIOLENCE: A Practical Guide for Counselors, Educators, and Parents by Allan Creighton with Paul Kivel

Today's teenagers live in a violent world. They can be subjected to violence at home, at school, and in society. For the past several years, the Oakland Men's Project (OMP) and Battered Women's Alternatives (BWA) have conducted seminars and workshops with teens and adults around the country, weaving issues of gender, race, age, and sexual orientation into frank discussions about male violence and its roots. This book by the founders of OMP and BWA provides guidelines on how to help teenagers help themselves out of the cycle of abuse and reduce the violence in the world around them.

168 pp.... 16 b&w photos ... Paper $14.95 ... Spiral bound $17.95

To order books see last page or call (800) 266-5592

TRAUMA IN THE LIVES OF CHILDREN: Crisis and Stress Management Techniques for Counselors, EMTs, and Other Professionals by Kendall Johnson, Ph.D. New 2nd Edition

Written by one of the foremost trauma experts in the country, this book explains how schools, therapists, and families can and must work together to help children traumatized by natural disasters, parental separation, violence, suicide, death of a loved one, or any other trauma a child may face.

352 pages ... Paperback $19.95 ... 2nd Edition

GROWTH AND RECOVERY WORKBOOKS FOR CHILDREN by Wendy Deaton, MFCC, and Ken Johnson, Ph.D.

A creative, child-friendly program for children ages 6–12, these popular workbooks are filled with original exercises to foster healing, self-understanding, and optimal growth. They are written by a winning author team for professionals to use with children. The Workbooks are designed for one-on-one use between child and professional. Tasks are balanced between writing and drawing, thinking and feeling, and are keyed to the phases and goals of therapy: creating a therapeutic alliance—exploring delayed reactions—integrating and strength-building.

Each Workbook is formatted to become the child's very own, with plenty of space to write and draw, friendly line drawings, and a place for the child's name right on the colorful cover. Each also comes with a "Therapist's Guide" which includes helpful references to Dr. Johnson's book *Trauma in the Lives of Children*.

Some of the titles in the series:

LIVING WITH MY FAMILY helps children traumatized by domestic violence and family quarrels identify and express their fears. NO MORE HURT provides children who have been physically or sexually abused a "safe place" to explore their feelings. A SEPARATION IN MY FAMILY is for children whose parents are separating or have already separated or divorced.

Call for more details, and a complete list of workbooks.

A selection of Behavioral Science Book Service

Workbooks $9.95 each ... Practitioner Packs $19.95 each
Workbook Library (all 10 in the series) $75.00

To order books see last page or call (800) 266-5592

ORDER FORM

10% DISCOUNT on orders of $50 or more —
20% DISCOUNT on orders of $150 or more —
30% DISCOUNT on orders of $500 or more —
On cost of books for fully prepaid orders

NAME

ADDRESS

CITY/STATE   ZIP/POSTCODE

PHONE   COUNTRY (outside of U.S.)

TITLE	QTY	PRICE	TOTAL
Violent No More, 2nd Edition (paperback)	@	$16.95	
Violent No More, 2nd Edition (hard cover)	@	$26.95	

Prices subject to change without notice

Please list other titles below:

	@	$	
	@	$	
	@	$	
	@	$	
	@	$	
	@	$	
	@	$	

Check here to receive our book catalog ❑   FREE

Shipping Costs:
First book: $3.00 by book post ($4.50 by UPS, Priority Mail, or to ship outside the U.S.)
Each additional book: $1.00
For rush orders and bulk shipments call us at (800) 266-5592

TOTAL
Less discount @____%   (   )
TOTAL COST OF BOOKS
Calif. residents add sales tax
Shipping & handling
TOTAL ENCLOSED
Please pay in U.S. funds only

❑ Check ❑ Money Order ❑ Visa ❑ Mastercard ❑ Discover

Card # _____ Exp. date _____

Signature _____

Complete and mail to:
Hunter House Inc., Publishers
PO Box 2914, Alameda CA 94501-0914
Orders: (800) 266-5592   email: ordering@hunterhouse.com
Phone (510) 865-5282 Fax (510) 865-4295
❑ Check here to receive our book catalog

VNM2 2/00